ERRANT INTELLIGENCE

Artificial intelligence is often framed as a quest to replicate the human brain, promising frictionless cognition and a future of seamless automation. But what if this pervasive narrative obscures a deeper, more "errant" truth?

Errant Intelligence challenges the prevailing biological and individualistic interpretations of machine learning, arguing instead for a radical understanding of machine intelligence. The book embraces the deviations, inconsistencies, and "errant behaviour" as fundamental to the discovery of new knowledge, moving beyond the illusion of mere optimisation. Drawing on media theory, cybernetics, and a unique psychoanalytic lens, it explores the "technological unconscious" of machine learning. It traces the historical roots of AI, from early automatons and the Turing machine to natural language processing and contemporary machine learning systems. Challenging the idea of an autonomous, self-generating AI, the book exposes the hidden labour, assumed logics, and inherent biases that animate its operation. It re-evaluates computational thinking, insisting on its inherently social, collective, and symbolic character, and revealing how language and logical paradoxes are not obstacles but constitutive forces that shape intelligent machines.

Errant Intelligence offers a vital new framework for understanding the profound co-evolution of human and machine learning. It's time to "unlearn" our assumptions and embrace the productive ambiguity and fallibility at the core of machine intelligence.

Clemens Apprich is Professor of Media Theory and History at the University of Applied Arts Vienna, Austria. His current research focuses on computational cultures, particularly machine learning. He is the author of *Technotopia: A Media Genealogy of Net Cultures* (2017) and co-author of *Pattern Discrimination* (2019).

ERRANT INTELLIGENCE

A Media Theory of Machine Learning

Clemens Apprich

Routledge
Taylor & Francis Group
LONDON AND NEW YORK

Designed cover image: Andreas Garber-Pawlik, Bernhard Poppe / dform, Vienna
Font (Cover): Domino Mono, Bold C / TYPE01

First published 2026
by Routledge
4 Park Square, Milton Park, Abingdon, Oxon OX14 4RN

and by Routledge
605 Third Avenue, New York, NY 10158

Routledge is an imprint of the Taylor & Francis Group, an informa business

"Open access publication made possible by the University of Applied Arts Vienna"

British Library Cataloguing-in-Publication Data
A catalogue record for this book is available from the British Library

ISBN: 978-94-6372-307-7 (hbk)
ISBN: 978-1-041-17503-2 (pbk)
ISBN: 978-1-003-69014-6 (ebk)

DOI: 10.4324/9781003690146

Typeset in Times New Roman
by Deanta Global Publishing Services, Chennai, India

To my father, an errant soul.

CONTENTS

PREFACE

It was at a podium discussion with students at Leuphana University in Lüneburg when Wolfgang Hagen said the crucial sentence: "There is no such thing as artificial intelligence." This must have been in 2018 at a time when broader discussions about AI and machine learning – at least in Germany – were still in their infancy. The students in the room were craving some answers. Looking into irritated faces, Wolfgang added, "Of course, there is such a thing as an artificial hip, because we have a natural one. But what should be replaced by artificial intelligence?" Posing more questions, instead of providing hasty answers, is typical of a critical mind like Wolfgang. Together with a whole generation of media theorists, he developed a critical understanding of media technologies that is now known as "German Media Theory," and that runs through this book.

Back then, sitting on the podium with him, I felt the urge to contradict him. And did so under the rather poorly disguised pretext that students deserved some direct answers. But the question stayed with me: what is the equivalent of artificial intelligence? What does it replace? Natural intelligence? Already in the mid-90s, Stephen Jay Gould's *The Mismeasure of Man* revealed the scientific weaknesses, but also political dangers of searching for a biologically based intelligence. In his historical study, Gould shows how skull and body measurements, as well as the still omnipresent IQ test, perpetuate the notion of a racist scientism based on biology. Therefore, aligning artificial intelligence with the brain, as occurs in current debates, has been and still is deeply problematic.

Given the inflationary use of the term today, understanding the problematic entanglements of artificial intelligence is all the more important. Firstly, we must ask, what type of AI are we dealing with? What is the broader epistemic setting in which it operates? What does it tell us about the time we are living in? The logic behind today's algorithmic cultures (i.e. most AI systems) is haunted by our past, resulting in widely discussed issues such as algorithmic bias and data-based discrimination. Secondly, we need to ask whether AI and machine learning technologies are even necessary for solving these issues, or if they are perhaps part of the problem. Against this background, and despite the temptation to seek simple answers, this book explores the rather errant history of machine learning and its implications for our understanding of AI today.

The book introduces "errancy" as a core concept for understanding the unpredictable dynamics of learning. It argues that errors, deviations, and unpredictability are not merely obstacles to be overcome, but rather fundamental aspects that facilitate the discovery of new knowledge. "Errant intelligence" is defined as the ability to learn from uncertainties and deviations by breaking with preprogrammed (i.e. habitual) routines. The book essentially advocates "unlearning" the prevalent history of machine learning, which is deeply rooted in a biologically reductionist perspective. Rather than reducing intelligence to individual brains, it proposes that learning – and thus intelligence – should be understood as an inherently social, symbolic, and often errant process. From this perspective, humans and machines produce intelligence collectively through their ambiguous and often also conflictual interactions.

Artificial intelligence is conventionally understood in terms of what it does pattern recognition, language generation, game-playing, image classification – rather than in terms of what it needs. However, this functional definition obscures the material and epistemic conditions that make AI possible. While machine intelligence relies on computational infrastructure, datasets, and design principles, it is also deeply entangled in our epistemic frameworks. Training algorithms, loss functions, inference rules, and data annotation are not neutral containers but theoretical choices that are realised each time we deploy an AI system. Every query to ChatGPT, Claude or Gemini reactivates hidden assumptions about language, meaning, and knowledge that are embedded in machine learning processes. Understanding intelligence, whether machine-based or not, as something errant means attending to these material, logical, and socio-technical conditions – and all the paradoxical outcomes they cause.

Not only is errancy the central concept of this book, but its creation has also been an errant journey. It began in Lüneburg, took me to Montréal and Groningen, and then back to Vienna, where I had studied philosophy and first encountered the weird and fascinating history of the mind. While my studies in Vienna sparked my interest, it was the vibrant intellectual environment in Lüneburg that allowed it to flourish. It was here that I learned more about the "deep history" of the digital age and how it emerged through the interplay between humans and machines. Much of this, of course, would not have been possible without the generous support of my colleagues at the Centre for Digital Cultures, an international hub for current debates in media theory. It was also in Lüneburg that I first met Wendy Hui Kyong

Chun. She not only gave invaluable insights into the book, but also the necessary direction for my academic journey. Since then, everything has fallen into place.

My time in Montréal had a profound influence on this book. I initially discussed the concept with Yuriko Furuhata and Marc Steinberg, followed by further exchanges with Orit Halpern and Thomas Lamarre. The latter two have also read and commented on sections of the book, for which I am very grateful. It was also back then that I formed a great camaraderie with Joshua Neves. He became a dear travel companion on this journey, always listening to my concerns, whether theoretical or not. The intensive, albeit brief, time spent in Groningen was crucial as well. The Research Centre for Journalism and Media Studies, with all its wonderful colleagues, and our small study group on critical data studies provided a great environment in which I was able to continue and flesh out the work.

After a brief detour, the book finally found a home with Amsterdam University Press, a publisher that has recently undergone significant changes itself. I would like to thank Maryse Elliott for taking on the book project and Paige Loughlin for ensuring a smooth transition. I am also grateful for Louisa Nyman's and Senthil Duraipandian's support with copyediting, and for Andreas Pawlik and his team's support with the cover design. Many more people were involved in producing the book. Although I don't know you personally, I appreciate your efforts in making this happen.

Some parts of the book have appeared in other publications in one form or another. Chapter 1 is based on a book chapter entitled "Dancing with Machines: On the Relationship of Aesthetics and the Uncanny," which was published as part of the INTRA-project run by Christina Jauernik and Wolfgang Tschapeller. Chapter 2 draws on the article "Die Maschine auf der Couch, oder: Was ist schon künstlich an Künstlicher Intelligenz?" which was published in the journal *Zeitschrift für Medienwissenschaft*. Parts of Chapter 3 have been published as a book chapter entitled "As We May Have Thought: How Memory Gets Exteriorised Through Media Technologies and What That Means for Critique in Digital Cultures" in an anthology edited by Erich Hörl, Nelly Yaa Pinkrah, and Lotte Warnecke. A first examination of the psychic apparatus was given in the article "Secret Agents: A Psychoanalytic Critique of Artificial Intelligence and Machine Learning," published in *Digital Culture & Society*. Chapter 4 includes parts of two pieces: "Learning How to Learn. Abduction as the 'Missing Link' in Machine Learning," published as an article in *Computational Culture*, and "TensorFlow: A Playground for Neural Networks," published as a chapter in an anthology edited by Simon Denny, Timon Beyes, Robin Holt, Claus Pias, and Bettina Steinbrügge. Thank you for giving me the opportunity to develop my ideas here first.

Finally, I would like to thank my new academic home, the University of Applied Arts Vienna, and in particular the Department of Media Theory and the Weibel Institute for Digital Cultures. Not only does it give me great joy to lead these two units, but the institutional support I have received has helped me to finalise the book. Discussions with my colleagues were central to bringing this project to a conclusion, particularly those with Kristina Pia Hofer, Valerie Messini, Sophie Publig, Denise Sumi, Mikkel Rørbo, Naoki Matsuyama, Amanda Holmes, and Antonia Birnbaum. Alex Quicho, one of our first Weibel Fellows, also provided valuable insights and feedback on the concluding chapter. My time at the university has certainly been eventful so far. I would like to thank Silvia Stocker for her support throughout.

I would also like to express my deepest gratitude to Nelly Yaa Pinkrah for her intellectual encouragement and so much more. While writing this book, our own little project, Moja, has grown into the most beautiful thing I could ever have imagined. She shows me every day that making plans is merely the beginning of the journey; the rest is up to sheer luck.

INTRODUCTION

From the Digesting Duck to the Mechanical Turk to Sophia the Robot, modern thought has long been fascinated by the idea of giving life to inanimate things. In particular, the Jewish folk story of the Golem takes a central role in the development of this imaginary. With the advent of modernity, various golem-making techniques began to appear in Kabbalistic records.[1] In order to animate the inanimate, the Kabbalists used certain combinations of the Hebrew alphabet. The most famous version of this is attributed to Judah Loew ben Bezalel (1513–1609), better known as the Maharal of Prague. The story goes that after creating a golem from the cold clay of the Vltava riverbank, he wrote the word *Emet* (Hebrew for "truth") on its forehead.[2] As a result of this, the clay giant came to life, determined to protect the rabbi's community against anti-Semitic attacks. Once the danger had passed, a variation of the same code was re-inscribed onto its forehead. By removing the letter "e" from the mark – leaving only the word *Met* (Hebrew for "death") – the rabbi turned the creature back into a shapeless clod, which is believed to still lie in the attic of the Old New Synagogue.[3] It was this story that Gershom Scholem, another scholar of the Kabbalah, had in mind when, four hundred years later, he named one of the first Israeli computers "Golem Aleph" (aleph being the first letter in *Emet*). In his dedicatory remarks to the Golem, he concluded by saying, "So I resign myself and say to the Golem and its creator: 'Develop peacefully and don't destroy the world.'"[4] Both the golem from mud and the golem from silicon were brought to life by code; and in both cases, the symbolic bears the imprint of destruction. This ambiguity, expressed through the mythological figure of the Golem, a being that wanders between life and death, between consciousness and

DOI: 10.4324/9781003690146-1

unconsciousness, between what we consider to be intelligent and what we consider not to be, lies at the heart of this book. Often used as a metaphor for artificial intelligence, it is the errant character of the Golem that helps to illuminate the long and vagrant history of "intelligent machinery."[5]

Norbert Wiener, considered the "father of cybernetics," knew about the powerful implications of the Golem myth when he wrote his final book, *God & Golem, Inc.*[6] In it, he addresses the often-overlooked relationship between science and religion, particularly with regard to "problems of communication and control, whether in machines or in living organisms."[7] By comparing cybernetics with religion, he sheds light on the conflictual relationship between humans and machines. Wiener concludes that digital computers are, in fact, today's incarnation of the Golem. With their ability to self-learn and self-improve, they can grow beyond their initial purpose, turning into an errant figure that escapes its master's control. Much like Goethe's *Zauberlehrling* or Mary W. Shelley's *Frankenstein*, two characters deviating from the path intended for them, the legend of Prague expresses "the 'horrors' that science and technology can wreak. Yet it is the Golem that underscores the ambivalent relationship we have with scientific and technological progress."[8] With the creation of digital computers, the ambivalence has increased as they confront us with our own limitations. Not merely in the sense that the computer becomes an autonomous, human-replacing system, but also in that it reveals the limits of our intellectual capacities. In this sense, any creative act possesses the potential danger of falling into disarray.[9] God introduced the possibility of sinning as a transgression of divine law by creating man in its own image. And by creating machines in man's image, humans pass on the ability to learn, thus far only reserved for (self-)conscious, living beings. What fascinates us about these new machines, then, is "the broader question of the agency of the immaterial and the inanimate."[10] As cultural theorist Mark Fisher suggests, this question touches upon a psychoanalytic understanding of the world. What he calls "weird psychoanalysis" deals with the alienating feeling of not being the master in our own house, a feeling that can be encountered in related phenomena such as the death drive or the appearance of a *doppelgänger*.[11]

The encounter with this ambiguity and the attempt to theorise it is what cybernetics and psychoanalysis have in common. Both can be seen as materialist theories of unconscious processes that question the mastery of modern subjectivity and thought. The unconscious, in this regard, is the material condition of the modern subject, which cannot be experienced and yet constitutes the possibility of all experience. It is this self-contradictory process that lies at the very core of psychoanalytic thinking. It tries to come to terms with the split between the inner and the outer, the unconscious and the conscious. What Sigmund Freud depicts as a psychic apparatus begins as an attempt to define neurologically its ability to sift through external stimuli.[12] The theory of this material underpinning, which he later revised but never entirely abandoned, shows the close relationship between psychoanalytic thinking and a certain understanding of technicity.[13] As an analytical method, psychoanalysis is anti-hermeneutic because it does not attempt to decipher a deeper – that is, synthetic – meaning, but instead tries to de- and re-construct cognitive agency piece by piece.[14] Extending psychoanalysis into the cybernetic realm of computation, media theorist Friedrich Kittler notes that with the advent of the digital computer as a universal machine, which integrates all former media technologies, a fully automated (i.e. unconscious) writing system has emerged that makes it possible to think of cognition in purely computational (i.e. algorithmic) terms.[15] As a result, humans as the (until then) only agents of cognitive processes are no longer integral to the production of intelligent behaviour, an idea that resonates with today's debates about artificial intelligence and the associated fear of humans being replaced by machines.[16]

Machine learning algorithms are indeed the modern incarnation of the golem, understood as the materialisation of a collective, that is symbolic, mind. In the words of Gustav Meyrink in his 1915 novel, *Der Golem*, the animated being represents "spiritual growth without any inherent consciousness."[17] With algorithms automatically running on digital machines, the unconscious has migrated into computer networks, where it is calculated on a continuous basis and provides the means to produce intelligent systems.[18] This is why we should depict this new form of intelligent life in machinic rather than organic terms. Following Gilles Deleuze and Félix Guattari's attempt to update psychoanalytic thinking for our networked sociality, John Johnston notes that the idea of a becoming-machinic "involves changes in our understanding of the nature and scope of computation in relation to dynamical systems and evolutionary processes."[19] It is here that we can begin to grasp the possibilities, but also the limits, of a machinic intelligence that is neither exclusively biological nor artificial, but errant. Just as the golem depends on language and code as its source of life, the digital machine runs on symbolic processes that it cannot fully control. Rather than being a simple mechanism, the digital machine is not self-sufficient in itself but becomes machinic through its embeddedness in a larger network of signs and symbols. For this reason, algorithms are not confined to specific domains of knowledge: as abstract machines, they affect the social field as a whole. Because they constantly process, categorise, and abstract the world around them, they refer to the symbolic (i.e. collective) realm as the precondition for the creation of any socio-technical being, artificial or not.[20]

1. Animating Intelligence

Current debates about artificial intelligence usually tend to think of it in terms of simulation: simulation of the brain, simulation of life, simulation of the universe.[21] This line of thinking perpetuates the idea of an intelligence that is merely a reproduction of something pre-given. Instead of adhering to the idea that intelligence is something that can or, depending on your beliefs, cannot be simulated, I will focus in this book on the symbolic processes needed to animate intelligent behaviour. The animation of intelligence by means of computational technologies ultimately requires a "digital basis" to allow for abstraction.[22] Yet, within this abstract space, humans and machines are actually part of the same symbolic realm because they are subject to the same processes according to the same discrete logic. Therefore, instead of an artificial intelligence, which invokes the idea of a fixed, pre-given entity, I propose an intelligence that emerges from our engagement with machines. Focusing on animation rather than simulation helps to shift the perspective from what intelligent machines *are* to how they *work*. It is this performative character that has been associated with cybernetic epistemology, which acknowledges the ambiguous relationship we entertain with machines.[23] Moreover, with this shift in perspective, away from an autonomous and towards an errant, that is protean understanding of intelligence, the simple automaton becomes an open structure that allows for interdependence and therefore a certain amount of indeterminacy.[24] Whereas the mechanistic automaton is defined by repetition alone, an animated machine emphasises the errancy inherent in any learning activity, which is open to new insights and unexpected outcomes.[25]

The idea of a learning and therefore intelligent machinery can be traced back to the theoretical work of Alan M. Turing at the end of World War II.[26] By establishing the possibility of a universal computer, he introduced the concept of a discrete, symbol-processing machine that could emulate any other programmable machine.[27] It was this idea that constituted the basis for a digital machine able to learn. This concept was shared by his colleagues Warren McCulloch and Walter Pitts, who in 1943 conceptualised the nerve cell activity of the brain by using the mathematical language of logic gates.[28] They proposed that networks of simple binary units, modelled after the neurons in the brain, could simulate complex patterns of thought and behaviour through their connections and interactions. Such biologically inspired computation, known as connectionism, laid the foundation for artificial neural networks, which later gave rise to the argument that computers are indeed capable of simulating the human brain.[29] However, despite their intention to clarify the computational capacity of the brain through the logical necessities laid out by Turing, the implementation of neural nets in the physical world was hampered by the "trans-continuous alteration between digital and analog."[30] The nerve cell, just like any other computing device, never operates on an analogue basis alone, but must be made discrete in order to be computable.[31] Artificial neural networks are therefore always already mediated by symbolic processes, regardless of their material foundation.

In contrast to the connectionist, that is biological conception of intelligence as something inside our brains that can be artificially reproduced, I argue in this book for the errant character of AI, understood as a constant process of (re-)mediation.[32] I do so by drawing on the long and diverse tradition of psychoanalytically inspired media theory, which is well known for its focus on the unconscious and deviant dimensions of media and technologies. Drawing on concepts from psychoanalysis, particularly the writings of Sigmund Freud and Jacques Lacan, this theory seeks to understand how technology and media define the conditions under which individuals experience reality, just as unconscious forces in psychoanalysis shape human existence.[33] It can thus help us to move beyond today's understanding of AI as merely the technological reproduction of an otherwise natural phenomenon. This is necessary because a critique of AI's historical connection to brain physiology is almost entirely missing in today's AI discourse and its application in current machine learning methods; despite the fact that the principles of connectionism can be traced back to the early days of scientific psychology, and have been subjected to profound criticism ever since.[34] In particular, psychoanalysis sought to distance itself from a biological reductionism that was dominant in the late nineteenth century. Reducing intelligence to a biological level and explaining it through essentialist assumptions runs counter to a theory that links the human mind to unconscious processes.[35]

The errancy of AI is not limited to its history, though. As important as it is to critique a linear understanding of technological development, it is equally important to look at the inner workings. Hence, in digital computing, there is always something that resists symbolic abstraction and, by introducing contingency, disrupts a pre-written order. The computer, with its electronic switches – first in the form of vacuum tubes, then in the form of transistors – represents an attempt to mitigate the conflict between the continuous and the discrete, the analogue and the digital, the material and the symbolic. Of course, it can be argued that cognition has always been characterised by this conflict. To extract signals from noise, to sift through sensory input, some form of discretised filtering is needed.[36] Yet the conditions for doing so have become digital ones, as Kittler has shown.[37] The mathematical basis for generating information from an endless stream of data is provided by information theory, which introduces contingency into the otherwise rather rigid organisation of the Turing machine.[38] This contingent aspect distinguishes complex machines from simple automata. Thus, many functions we want computers to perform, especially tasks that require generalisation, are actually based on deviations, unpredictability, and even failure in ways that often surprise or confound expectations.[39] Nowhere is this more evident than in machine learning, where the computational output, paradoxically, always exceeds the input.[40] Because of its abstract nature, machine learning is ampliative: with each iteration, the machine produces a slightly different result. When a computer emulates intelligence, it is not simply imitating what we think of as intelligent behaviour, but actually challenges the very notion of it.[41]

While in early AI research the focus was on how "to make machines use language, form abstractions and concepts, solve kinds of problems now reserved for humans, and improve themselves,"[42] today's machine learning algorithms use statistical knowledge to train a model on a large dataset. The approach is based on the idea that computers can individually learn from experience, identify patterns, and make decisions without being explicitly programmed.[43] Hence, while in classic computation the data comes in and the algorithm calculates the output (deduction), statistical learning turns this process around: input and output generate the model to make self-guided predictions (induction). The idea of autonomous learning is further fuelled by the notion that we simply need to simulate the human brain, notably as neural networks, in order to make the machine learn.[44] What is overlooked, though, is the fact that learning always takes place in the form of symbolic (i.e. collective) processes. Hence, the question remains whether intelligence can be reduced to its biological basis or whether it is ultimately dependent on language as a collective practice – a question that will be discussed in the course of this book, looking at both current and historical machine learning applications (e.g. in the areas of natural language processing, recommendation systems, and predictive analytics) and considering alternative, in particular abductive machine learning methods.

Looking beyond established debates on artificial intelligence, which tend to flatten human-machine relations, my aim with this book is to push current discussions of machine learning to integrate and come to terms with its often-ambiguous reality. It thus does not seek to contribute to the so-called *new materialist turn*, which tries to reconcile artificial intelligence with a post-human notion of distributed cognitive agency, but insists on the *artifice* as a result of learning and practice. Drawing on Freud's psychic apparatus and a psychoanalytic understanding of computation, I will emphasise the need to understand intelligence in its errant and therefore deviating form. The errancy of AI allows for a different way of thinking, one that focuses on the ever-shifting basis of intelligence and its reliance on language-based (i.e. unconscious) processes. Rather than simulating a supposedly "natural" phenomenon like the brain, machine intelligence involves what cultural anthropologist Dietmar Kamper has called acts of "premitation" (*Vorahmung*), following the Old Greek term *mimesis.* Instead of a mere "simulation" (*Nachahmung*), mimetic practices, which are in fact based on learning activities, influence the course of things and leave the possible outcome open.[45] While simulation seeks to create an "artificial doublet" of the world, thereby putting forth the idea of an intelligence as an autonomous reproduction of the same, premitation promotes intelligence as a repetition of difference.[46] It can thus be seen as going beyond today's understanding of artificial intelligence with its focus on connectionism and neural networks.

2. Machine Learning

All models simplify. In machine learning, they do so by abstracting data, and consequently, "the transformation from input to output implies a perspective or evaluation that, the coordination between data and what they stand for, is projected back into spheres of human life."[47] It is here that intelligent behaviour emerges through errancy, as it evolves through the interaction between the human and the machine. This interplay makes it crucial to gain knowledge of the inner workings and assumptions of these models, without bypassing the contradictions they cause. This is the lesson psychoanalysis can teach us: it does not seek to resolve an inner conflict, but to work through it.[48] From this perspective, the issue with artificial intelligence is not so much to generate better data or models, but to confront the paradoxes that arise from them. Rather than turning the errancy of machine learning into an error that needs to be solved, the goal is to acknowledge the inconsistencies of computation. Drawing on psychoanalysis and the media theory it has inspired, this book therefore seeks to foster critical thinking about machine learning algorithms.[49] Instead of focusing solely on their current implementation as artificial neural networks, I will ask where these algorithms come from, how they work epistemologically, and where they might lead us collectively.

The real-world implications of today's machine learning have sparked a lively discussion about algorithmic bias and its discriminatory effects.[50] What becomes apparent from these debates is that artificially intelligent systems are not as "artificial" as we used to think.[51] As can be seen from current machine learning techniques, it still takes a lot of human knowledge in the form of social categories, epistemological patterns, but also discriminatory bias to animate their intelligence. What is more is that for artificial intelligence to be conceived as such, this knowledge has to be concealed.[52] The aim of this book, therefore, is to shed light on practices and epistemes related to machine learning by highlighting the sociotechnical production of it. Emphasising this aspect is crucial because the idea of automated intelligence plays right into the hands of an ideology that tends to omit its social character in order to maintain a fetish for autonomous machines and objective decision-making.[53] Contrary to the desire for a fully automated intelligence, I will take a look into the technological unconscious in order to grapple with and discuss the complex and often ambiguous relationship we entertain with our machines. In line with the psychoanalytical idea of the unconscious, machine-based intelligence provides a collective source of stored memories, intuitions, fantasies, and even dreams. It mediates between the psychic and the social, and can thus be seen as the latest manifestation of a general intellect.[54] In this book, then, I develop a media materialist critique of artificial intelligence and machine learning in order to bring forth its social dimension.[55]

In its most recent manifestation as neural networks, machine learning is often associated with the human brain. Not only do some of the most prominent research units in artificial intelligence adopt a neuroscientific imaginary (e.g. Brain AI Lab, Google Brain, Neuralink, OpenAI, DeepMind), but the connectionist premise, that is, the idea that intelligence can be reduced to the physiological wiring of the brain, has also fuelled the unabated belief that intelligent behaviour can be simulated by mimicking the brain. Yet, as noted above, mimetic practices are based on premitation, which does not correspond to reproduction, but to alteration and reinterpretation.[56] As a collective endeavour, machine learning is contingent on "practical knowledge that we fabricate by dealing with machines."[57] Hence, the "artificial" in artificial intelligence refers to the co-creation of intelligence, which emerges through the interplay of humans and machines via language.[58] Rather than collapsing both sides into one flat ontology, an emphasis on the errant character of AI enables us to focus on its (inter-)subjective nature. Focusing on AI's errancy thus opens possibilities for rethinking and reinventing what it means for a machine to learn. Instead of connectionist models that aim to optimise computational processes, errant intelligence highlights the "errors" within those very same processes; not to fix them, but to work through them.

"Working through" should, in my view, apply to machine learning algorithms, not least because the study of these algorithms promises to uncover unconscious processes that are now enacted in the code. It also makes it possible to think about, with, and through technology. Such a method thus reflects on the media materialist conditions when analysing stories, practices, and tools that generate knowledge about artificial intelligence and machine learning. It does not, however, imply an instrumental study of algorithms or a "walk-through" of specific software or platforms;[59] such an instrumentalist view would necessarily miss the errancies of machine learning processes, which should not be understood as mere shortcomings of an apparatus yet to be optimised, but rather as inconsistencies necessary to make machine learning work. To grasp this productive ambiguity of machine learning and to theorise it in relation to today's thinking subject, I propose in the following pages an errant reading of what is now known as artificial intelligence. Errant in the dual sense of the word: on the one hand as a deviation from the dominant paradigm in today's AI discourse (i.e. connectionism), and on the other as a hopefully thought-provoking foray into its history and epistemology. Thus, the most intriguing aspects of artificial intelligence consist of and lie in its errancy, ranging from the always drifting definition of what intelligence is, to the iterative training of machine learning algorithms, to their conflictual implementation in everyday decision-making.

As Lydia H. Liu shows in *The Freudian Robot*, it is psychoanalytic thinking that opens up the possibility of analysing the interplay between discursive functions, psychic relations, and technical media in order to better understand our digital world.[60] This provides a way to address the dialectic, and at the same time often contested relationship between humans and machines, rather than attempting to flatten them.[61] In particular, the ideas of a *flat ontology* and a *nonconscious mind*, which are not least directed against the psychoanalytic concept of the unconscious, defy any form of symbolic abstraction and thus render a critical reflection of machine learning impossible.[62] What is at stake here is nothing less than the project of critique itself or, conversely, the danger of "a quasi-magical ascription of our powers to the world out there without us."[63] Instead of smoothing over the errancy of human-machine relations by disavowing the role we play in them, a psychoanalytically inspired media critique insists on errors and failures as entry points for analysis. In order to work through them and make the weird, often strange, and ambiguous status of learning machines productive, I will thus bring psychoanalytic theory into dialogue with recent work in media studies to show that we can, and should, intervene in an increasingly data-driven and algorithmically structured reality.

The "errors" and deviations in the context of machine learning draw attention to the dynamic, evolving, and often messy relationship between humans and machines. They therefore echo Norbert Wiener's concern that "[d]isastrous results are to be expected […] wherever two agencies essentially foreign to each other are coupled in the attempt to achieve a common purpose."[64] Precisely because machines are able to operate at a much faster pace when it comes to computational processes, and thus make human intervention possible only after the fact, it is crucial, as Wiener reminds us, to have a discussion about the purpose put into the machine; not as a mere criticism, but as an actual understanding of the machine's inner workings. That these inner workings are not so far removed from our own logics and desires, that "we have learned to behave as if we were a machine when operating with signs,"[65] is the thesis that lies at the heart of this book. Its aim is to find a common, if contested, ground in the human-machine relationship. Rather than "telling humans and computers apart,"[66] I seek to interrogate the operational basis of these two agencies, without ignoring their fundamental difference. These are the stakes of a media theory of machine learning that is constantly reworking, reinterpreting, and sometimes also "erring" in relation to its subject.

3. Structure of the Book

The book is structured around four scenes, which help to stage and bring to light the problem of errant intelligence as a way of thinking about machine learning. Chapter 1, "Dancing with Machines," explores the concept of the automaton using examples from Gothic literature. Starting with E.T.A. Hoffmann's famous story "The Sandman," it investigates the ambiguous relationship between human beings and non-human others. In this context, the ontological instability caused by human-technical ensembles – not to say monsters – has been repeatedly described as an uncanny experience of modernity, rendering the world we inhabit as an alienating, strange, and sometimes threatening place. In particular, Freud's treatise of 1919, *The Uncanny*, has become one of the key references for discussing the uncanny as a modern experience. This chapter examines and interrogates the question of artificiality in the context of these debates and introduces the automaton as an errant figure of modernity. It is the automated *doppelgänger*, as Lydia H. Liu suggests, that contains the modern anxiety of being replaced by an object-world.[67] Following her assessment that psychoanalysis can be made productive in relation to current discussions of digital media, this chapter traces the deeply rooted concerns about what is natural or artificial, animate or inanimate, self or other. The psychoanalytic framework I propose will help to shed light on the development of complex technological systems, particularly with regard to artificial intelligence and machine learning. Here a terminological clarification of artificiality, machinery, otherness, and intelligence will be necessary, because the analysis of artificial intelligence is often complicated by a confusion between human and non-human agencies. This chapter argues for a differentiation, which is essential for further exploring the historical, epistemological, and socio-technical foundations of machine intelligence.

Chapter 2, "Talking to Machines," examines post-war psychiatry as one of the key settings in which the question of artificial intelligence and whether or not machines are capable of learning arises. It starts with a discussion of parsing programmes in the context of Turing's 1950 paper "Computing Machinery and Intelligence," arguably the founding text of artificial intelligence.[68] The central question, according to the text, is not so much whether computers can *think*, but whether machines can *learn* what humans do to generate cognitive capacities. Comparing the computer to a child's mind, Turing points out that the issue is not one of programming but rather of training. Tracing this line of thinking back to its cybernetic origins, this chapter provides a historical account of the machine learning debate, highlighting its derivation from psychiatry and neuroscience. As Andrew Pickering argues in *The Cybernetic Brain*, it was the fascination of early cyberneticians with the human brain that set the agenda in the quest for artificial intelligence.[69] My aim in this chapter is not to repeat the familiar history of brain-physiological thinking within cybernetics, but to formulate a historically informed critique of connectionism. I will show how the connectionist idea has led to positivist reductions in the conceptualisation of machine intelligence, in particular with regard to deep learning, the cornerstone of today's artificial neural networks. As an alternative genealogical line, I present a case study that highlights the problem of learning as a symbolic-conceptual rather than a neurophysiological one. PARRY, a "paranoid information-processing system" developed by Kenneth M. Colby at the Stanford Artificial Intelligence Laboratory, thus opens the debate for a psychoanalytically inspired media critique of artificial intelligence and machine learning.

Chapter 3, "Dreaming of Machines," takes the popular television show *Westworld* as a starting point to engage with the cybernetic debate about memory and to contrast it with more recent discussions of a "new unconscious" in cognitive science and neuroinformatics. According to these discussions, the "old unconscious" is replaced by nonconscious processes that do the same things, but without the conflict and drama.[70] In this chapter, I argue that the phantasm of a "frictionless nonconscious" ultimately echoes the brain-physiological episteme of connectionism with its biologistic understanding of cognition and intelligence. In contrast to a "flat ontology," which tends to omit the ontological difference between human and non-human entities, I argue for maintaining this difference in order to better understand the relationship we have with our machines. Drawing on Freud's idea of the psychic apparatus, this chapter presents the "technological unconscious" as a site of critical inquiry, where difference and conflict are not flattened out but made describable and therefore discussable. If the symbolic world is the world of the machine, then the machine is, by consequence, part of the same symbolic realm as the human and, consequently, open to analysis.[71] Against the assumption that contemporary forms of artificial intelligence and machine learning are inaccessible to human reasoning, I will show how a psychoanalytically inspired media critique offers a way of exploring the alleged "black box." Borrowing from the long tradition of psychoanalytic media theory, this chapter lays the epistemological groundwork for a new understanding of AI and machine learning.

Chapter 4, "Learning from Machines," looks at current research and practices in machine learning as the underlying method of artificial intelligence. By exploring the open-source platform TensorFlow, it attempts to provide insights into the inner workings of machine intelligence. Following Thomas Lamarre's notion of "technical determination," my aim with this chapter is to develop a theory of machine learning that helps us to reveal the limits of artificial intelligence, both in terms of its logical constraints and its capabilities.[72] The focus on errancy puts this theory at odds with most current research in artificial intelligence, which emphasises the "optimisation" of machine learning models. Deep learning, the technique that is used in this context, poses major problems because it relies not only on vast amounts of data, but also on single, well-defined goals. As a result, the errors emerging in machine learning processes are usually seen as mere obstacles that need to be overcome as quickly as possible. Using the example of recommendation systems, which rely on the technological unconscious of vector spaces, I show how this focus on optimisation leads to the simulation, that is, automation, of pre-existing social relations. In contrast, by highlighting the contingent and errant aspects of artificial intelligence, this chapter presents a theory of abductive machine learning, which not only leads to a new understanding of the principles underlying machine learning, but also holds the potential to unlearn them.

Notes

1 See Gershom Scholem, *On the Kabbalah and Its Symbolism* (New York: Schocken Books, 1965), in particular Chapter 5.

2 The word *emet* can also be seen as a number code, using the first, middle and last letters of the Hebrew alphabet, meaning that "truth" is present from the beginning to the end.

3 See David Wisniewski, *Golem* (New York: Clarion Books, 2007). In Hebrew, "golem" means shapeless mass, and in the Bible, it refers to the "unformed body" without a soul: Ps. 139:16.

4 Gershom Scholem, "The Golem of Prague & the Golem of Rehovoth," *Commentary Magazine,* January 1966, https://www.commentarymagazine.com/articles/gershom-scholem/the-golem-of-prague-the-golem-of-rehovoth.

5 Alan M. Turing, "Intelligent Machinery," in *The Essential Turing*, ed. Jack Copeland (Oxford: Clarendon Press, 2013), 472–75.
6 Norbert Wiener, *God & Golem, Inc.: A Comment on Certain Points Where Cybernetics Impinges on Religion* (Cambridge, MA: MIT Press, 1966).
7 Wiener, *God & Golem*, 2f.
8 See Stephen Bertman, "The Role of the Golem in the Making of *Frankenstein*," *Keats-Shelley Review* 29, no. 1 (2015): 42–50; and Emily D. Bilski, "Artificial Intelligence *Avant La Lettre*: The Golem of Jewish Mysticism, Legend and Art," in *AI: More Than Human*, ed. Chloe Wood, Suzanne Livingston, and Maholo Uchida (London: Barbican International, 2019), 29; see also 25–31.
9 As Avery Slater writes: "Wiener views machine learning (ML) as a genuinely creative activity, one akin to creating life and thus fraught with all the attendant dangers of such an endeavor." Avery Slater, "The Golem and the Game of Automation," lecture at the IEEE conference on Norbert Wiener in the 21st Century, October 26, 2021, https://c4ejournal.net/2021/10/27/avery-slater-the-golem-and-the-game-of-automation-2021-c4ej-44.
10 Mark Fisher, *The Weird and the Eerie* (London: Repeater Books, 2016), 11.
11 The doppelgänger has been used to describe the golem as well. See Martina Lüdicke, "Doppelgänger," in *GOLEM*, exhibition catalogue (Berlin: Jewish Museum Berlin, 2016), Chapter 7.
12 Sigmund Freud, *An Outline of Psychoanalysis*, ed. and trans. James Strachey (New York: W. W. Norton, 1969). The German term *psychischer Apparat* also often gets translated into psychical or mental apparatus. See also Mai Wegener, *Neuronen und Neurosen. Der psychische Apparat bei Freud und Lacan: Ein historisch-theoretischer Versuch zu Freuds Entwurf von 1895* (Munich: Wilhelm Fink Verlag, 2004).
13 For a detailed account of Freud's materialism see Mladen Dolar, "What's the Matter? On Matter and Related Matters," in *Subject Lessons: Hegel, Lacan, and the Future of Materialism*, ed. Russell Sbriglia and Slavoj Žižek (Evanston: Northwestern University Press, 2020), 39–43.
14 See Jean Laplanche, "Psychoanalysis as Anti-Hermeneutics," *Radical Philosophy* 79 (September/October 1996): 7–13.
15 Kittler adopted the term "discourse network" (*Aufschreibesystem*) from the paranoid cognition of Daniel Paul Schreber, arguably the world's most famous paranoiac, and defined it as a "network of technologies and institutions that allow a given culture to select, store, and process relevant data." Friedrich Kittler, *Discourse Networks, 1800/1900*, trans. Michael Metteer (Stanford: Stanford University Press, 1990), 369. In another book, *Gramophone, Film, Typewriter*, he claims that today's discourse network (something like an *Aufschreibesystem 2000*) implies "a total media link on a digital base." Friedrich Kittler, *Gramophone, Film, Typewriter* (Stanford: Stanford University Press, 1999), 2.
16 In light of these debates, it can almost be forgotten that Kittler's intervention was, of course, meant to be an ironic provocation regarding the idea of an omniscient and omnipotent subject – a radicalisation of Freud's famous idea that the ego is not master in its own house.
17 Gustav Meyrink, *The Golem*, trans. Mike Mitchell (Sawtry: Dedalus Books, 2017), 55.
18 Tiziana Terranova, in emphasising this point, spots a new potential with regard to these "hypersocial networks." See her talk "Pirate Modernity and Hypersocial Networks," lecture at the conference "Recursive Colonialism, Artificial Intelligence & Speculative Computation," December 10, 2020, https://recursivecolonialism.com/topics/pirate.
19 John Johnston, *The Allure of Machinic Life: Cybernetics, Artificial Life, and the New AI* (Cambridge, MA: MIT Press, 2008), 7.
20 This, of course, is very much in line with a Simondonian understanding of individuation. For Gilbert Simondon, the psychic individual is always also a social being; we

individuate ourselves at once psychically and collectively. So a psychic individual is neither a stable state nor an identity; it is considered to be the never-completed end point of individuation, not its starting point. Yet the respective preconditions for each individual (i.e. the regimes of individuation) differ according to existing power structures, which also affect the relation we have to AI and machine learning. See Ramon Amaro and Murad Khan, "Towards Black Individuation and a Calculus of Variations," *e-flux journal* 109 (May 2020), https://www.e-flux.com/journal/109/330246/towards-black-individuation-and-a-calculus-of-variations.

21 For the latter see Stephen Wolfram, *A New Kind of Science* (Champaign: Wolfram Media, 2002).

22 Claus Pias, "The Age of Cybernetics," in *Cybernetics: The Macy Conferences 1946–1953*, ed. Claus Pias (Zurich: diaphanes, 2016), 16.

23 See Andrew Pickering, *The Cybernetic Brain: Sketches of Another Future* (Chicago: University of Chicago Press, 2010), 20–22.

24 According to Simondon, the simple automaton represents the lowest level of technological development because it reduces complexity to the mere problem of regulation. Against it, Simondon emphasises the openness of technical objects to their environment. See Gilbert Simondon, *On the Mode of Existence of Technical Objects*, trans. Cecile Malaspina and John Rogove (Minneapolis: Univocal, 2017), 152–53.

25 In a similar vein, Matteo Pasquinelli writes about the relationship between cybernetics and the critique of instrumental reason: "Therefore, critical theory's approach should be redirected toward its own postulates in order to inquire if the whole history of instrumental reason – from the Age of Reason to the Age of Intelligent Machines – has actually concealed a deep and structural errancy." "Introduction," in *Alleys of Your Mind: Augmented Intelligence and Its Traumas*, ed. Matteo Pasquinelli (Lüneburg: meson press, 2015), 7–8. However, while the aim here is to "rediscover the role of error, trauma and catastrophe in the design of intelligent machines" (ibid.), the focus of this book is on errancy rather than error. Thus, rather than seeing error as something that has to be overcome by intelligent machines, it becomes their ontological prior.

26 See Johnston, *Allure of Machinic Life*, 7–11.

27 Alan M. Turing, "On Computable Numbers, with an Application to the Entscheidungsproblem," in *The Essential Turing*, ed. B. Jack Copeland (Oxford: Oxford University Press, [1936] 2004), 58–90; in particular section 7. The idea that every effective computation can be carried out by a Turing machine is also known as the Church-Turing thesis.

28 Warren S. McCulloch and Walter H. Pitts, "A Logical Calculus of the Ideas Immanent in Nervous Activity," *Bulletin of Mathematical Biophysics* 5 (1943): 115–33.

29 See Nancy Forbes, *Imitation of Life: How Biology Is Inspiring Computing* (Cambridge, MA: MIT Press, 2004), Chapter 1.

30 Forbes, *Imitation of Life*.

31 This is achieved by introducing thresholds to trigger all-or-none responses based on Hebb's Rule, which is often summarised as "neurons that fire together wire together" and implies that lasting patterns emerge as "mnemonic traces" within the brain. See Donald O. Hebb, *The Organization of Behavior: A Neuropsychological Theory* (New York: John Wiley & Sons, 1949), 12–16. This theory of synaptic or neural plasticity, which argues against any kind of pre-given cerebral structure, also explains how the brain filters information from input (i.e. sensory) data and has, therefore, been used to formalise artificial neural networks with their adjustable weights. See, for example, Robert Kozma, Cesare Alippi, Yoonsuck Choem, and Francesco Carlo Morabito, eds., *Artificial Intelligence in the Age of Neural Networks and Brain Computing* (Cambridge, MA: Academic Press, 2018), in particular Chapter 1.

32 In *Remediation: Understanding New Media* (Cambridge, MA: MIT Press, 2000), Jay David Bolter and Richard Grusin argue that new media technologies do not emerge

in isolation but are always shaped by older media forms, including cultural norms, communication practices, and – I would add – computational logics. In this sense, AI must also be seen as a constant "remediation" of previous media technologies, invoking intelligent behaviour (such as the Internet, video games, hypertext, or even the telephone system).

33 Kittler, *Discourse Networks* and *Gramophone, Film, Typewriter*. See also Svitlana Matviyenko and Judith Roof, eds., *Lacan and the Posthuman* (London: Palgrave Macmillan, 2018).

34 See, for example, Hubert L. Dreyfus, *What Computers Still Can't Do: A Critique of Artificial Reason* (Cambridge, MA: MIT Press, 1992), 159–62.

35 For a critique of AI from a psychoanalytical, yet rather film studies perspective, see Isabel Millar, *The Psychoanalysis of Artificial Intelligence*, eBook (London: Palgrave Macmillan, 2021).

36 See, for example, John von Neumann's paper presented at the Hixon Symposium on September 20, 1948, in Pasadena, California. In it, the mathematician stresses the importance, but also difficulty, of discerning between the analogue (i.e. continuous) and digital (i.e. discrete) principles. John von Neumann, "The General and Logical Theory of Automata," in *John von Neumann: Collected Works*, ed. A. H. Taub (Oxford: Pergamon Press, 1961), 288–326.

37 Kittler, *Discourse Networks*.

38 In his master's thesis, "father of information theory" Claude E. Shannon actually proved that Boolean algebra (i.e. the idea that logical operations can be reduced to the truth values *true* and *false*) can be applied to electronic hardware using logic gates. See Claude E. Shannon, "A Symbolic Analysis of Relay and Switching Circuits," *Transactions American Institute of Electrical Engineers* 57, no. 12 (1938): 713–23.

39 Such an understanding of computing resonates with what Jacques Lacan wrote about contingency and the automaton: that they are not in opposition to each other, but are actually intertwined. See Jacques Lacan, "Tuché and Automaton," in *The Seminar of Jacques Lacan, Book XI: The Four Fundamental Concepts of Psychoanalysis*, trans. Alan Sheridan (New York: W. W. Norton, 1981), 53–67. See also Mladen Dolar, who writes:

> To put it simply, tyche is the gap of the automaton. [...] In every repetition there is already, in a minimal way, the emergence of that which escapes symbolization. [...] There is a contingent bit which dwells in the gap, which is produced by the very gap, and this imperceptible bit is the stuff that comedy puts to maximum use.

Mladen Dolar, "Comedy and Its Double," in *Stop That Comedy! On the Subtle Hegemony of the Tragic in Our Culture*, ed. Robert Pfaller (Vienna: Sonderzahl, 2005), 200. More on the relationship between tuché and computation, see Chapter 4.

40 Luciana Parisi, "Critical Computation. Digital Automata and General Artificial Intelligence," *Theory, Culture & Society* 36, no. 2 (2019): 89–121. Further discussed in Chapter 4.

41 This, in a nutshell, is Turing's argument when he suggests the so-called "Imitation Game" to gauge the ability of computers to show intelligent behaviour. See Alan M. Turing, "Computing Machinery and Intelligence," *Mind: A Quarterly Review of Psychology and Philosophy* 59, no. 236 (1950): 433–60.

42 This quote is from the introduction to the Dartmouth Summer Research Project on Artificial Intelligence in 1956, which for some is seen as the actual birthplace of AI research. John McCarthy, Marvin Minsky, Nathaniel Rochester, and Claude E. Shannon, "A Proposal for the Dartmouth Summer Research Project on Artificial Intelligence," August 31, 1955, http://www-formal.stanford.edu/jmc/history/dartmouth/dartmouth.html.

43 This basic definition is usually attributed to Arthur Samuel (1959), who, however, never made this statement (see also Chapter 2).
44 See, for example, David E. Rumelhart, Geoffey E. Hinton, and Robert J. Williams, "Learning Internal Representations by Error Propagation," in *Parallel Distributed Processing: Explorations in the Microstructure of Cognition, Vol. 1*, ed. David E. Rumelhart, James L. McClelland, and the PDP Research Group (Cambridge, MA: MIT Press, 1986), 318–62; Brendan M. Lake, Tomer D. Ullman, Joshua B. Tenenbaum, and Samual J. Gershman, "Building Machines That Learn and Think Like People," *ArXiv* (2016), https://arxiv.org/abs/1604.00289; Ruth C. Fong, Walter J. Scheirer, and David D. Cox, "Using Human Brain Activity to Guide Machine Learning," *Scientific Reports* 8 (2018), https://doi.org/10.1038/s41598-018-23618-6.
45 Two things are of importance here: first, Kamper stresses the necessity of illusions when it comes to mimesis; people practising it know it is an illusion, but they also know that this illusion is fundamental to the invention of alternative futures; second, in order to intervene in the future, mimesis describes an ability to achieve a desired effect by way of a physical gesture. See Dietmar Kamper, "Mimesis und Simulation: Von den Körpern zu den Maschinen," *Kunstforum International* 114 (1991): 86–105.
46 The idea of a repetition of difference corresponds, of course, with the one by Gilles Deleuze in *Difference and Repetition*, trans. Paul Patton (New York: Columbia University Press, 1994).
47 Bernhard Rieder, *Engines of Order: A Mechanology of Algorithmic* (Amsterdam: Amsterdam University Press, 2020), 11.
48 Sigmund Freud, "Remembering, Repeating and Working-Through," in *The Standard Edition of the Complete Psychological Works of Sigmund Freud*, Vol. 6 (New York: Basic Books, 1914), 147–56.
49 In the context of critical algorithm and data studies see Rob Kitchin, "Thinking Critically About and Researching Algorithms," *The Programmable City Working Paper* 5 (2014), https://papers.ssrn.com/sol3/papers.cfm?abstract_id=2515786.
50 See, for example, Safiya Umoja Noble, *Algorithms of Oppression: How Search Engines Reinforce Racism* (New York: New York University Press, 2018); Virginia Eubanks, *Automating Inequality: How High-Tech Tools Profile, Police, and Punish the Poor* (New York: Picador, 2018); and Cathy O'Neil, *Weapons of Math Destruction: How Big Data Increases Inequality and Threatens Democracy* (London: Penguin Books, 2016).
51 Kate Crawford, *Atlas of AI: Power, Politics, and the Planetary Costs of Artificial Intelligence* (New Haven: Yale University Press, 2021).
52 See Clemens Apprich, Wendy Hui Kyong Chun, Florian Cramer, and Hito Steyerl, *Pattern Discrimination* (Lüneburg: meson press, 2018).
53 See Luke Munn, *Automation Is a Myth* (Stanford: Stanford University Press, 2022); Vladan Joler and Matteo Pasquinelli, "The Nooscope Manifested: AI as Instrument of Knowledge Extractivism," *Fritz AI*, 2020, https://nooscope.ai.
54 Karl Marx, *Grundrisse: Foundations of the Critique of Political Economy*, trans. Martin Nicolaus (London: Penguin, 1993), 690–712. See also Paolo Virno, *A Grammar of the Multitude: For an Analysis of Contemporary Forms of Life* (Los Angeles: Semiotext(e), 2004), 64; and Matteo Pasquinelli, "On the Origins of Marx's General Intellect," *Radical Philosophy* 2, no. 6 (2019), 43–56.
55 For a similar approach to a different topic, see Nick Dyer-Witheford and Svitlana Matviyenko, *Cyberwar and Revolution: Digital Subterfuge in Global Capitalism* (Minneapolis: University of Minnesota Press, 2019). In the book, the authors define their approach as a "Marxist-Lacanian perspective on cyberwar," see page 28.
56 This idea features prominently in Walter Benjamin's essay "On the Mimetic Faculty," where he explores the human capacity for imitation as a way to create difference in the world. See Walter Benjamin, "On the Mimetic Faculty," in *Selected Writings: Volume 2, Part 2. 1931–1934*, ed. Michael W. Jennings (Cambridge, MA.: The Belknap Press,

1999), 720–22. See also: Michael Taussig, *Mimesis and Alterity: A Particular History of the Senses* (New York: Routledge, 1993).
57 Thomas Pringle, Gertrud Koch, and Bernard Stiegler, *Machine* (Lüneburg: meson press, 2019), 15.
58 This language does not have to be linguistic though. See Lydia H. Liu, "The Cybernetic Unconscious: Rethinking Lacan, Poe, and French Theory," *Critical Inquiry* 36, no. 2 (2010): 288–320.
59 Cf. Ben Light, Jean Burgess, and Stephanie Duguay, "The Walkthrough Method: An Approach to the Study of Apps," *New Media & Society* 20 (2018): 881–900.
60 Lydia H. Liu, *The Freudian Robot: Digital Media and the Future of the Unconscious* (Chicago: University of Chicago Press, 2010).
61 Cf. Steven Shapiro, *Discognition*, eBook (London: Repeater Books, 2016); Catherine Malabou, *Morphing Intelligence: From IQ Measurement to Artificial Brains*, trans. Carolyn Shread (New York: Columbia University Press, 2019); Joseph Lindley, Haider Akmal, and Paul Coulton, "Design Research and Object-Oriented Ontology," *Open Philosophy* 3, no. 1 (2020): 11–41. For a critique of new materialism, see: Benjamin Boysen and Jesper Lundsfryd Rasmussen, eds., *Against New Materialisms* (London: Bloomsbury, 2025).
62 Manuel DeLanda, *Intensive Science and Virtual Philosophy* (New York: Continuum, 2002), 148–49; Graham Harman, *Prince of Networks: Bruno Latour and Metaphysics* (Melbourne: re.press, 2009), 214–15; Levi R. Bryant, *The Democracy of Objects* (Ann Arbor: Open Humanities Press, 2011), 245–90; N. Katherine Hayles, *Unthought: The Power of the Cognitive Nonconscious* (Chicago: University of Chicago Press, 2017), 9–16; Bruno Latour, *An Inquiry into Modes of Existence: An Anthropology of the Moderns*, trans. Catherine Porter (Cambridge, MA: Harvard University Press, 2013), 184–86. Although I am well aware that the heterogeneous approaches in speculative materialist thinking cannot be lumped together, I am wondering – as does Alexander Galloway – why this thinking resembles, in so many aspects, the latest drive towards technocapitalism. See Alexander Galloway, "The Poverty of Philosophy: Realism and Post-Fordism," *Critical Inquiry* 39, no. 2 (2013): 347–66. See also Russell Sbriglia and Slavoj Žižek's critique of contemporary attempts to overturn the "thinking subject." Russell Sbriglia and Slavoj Žižek, "Introduction: Subject Matters," in *Subject Lessons*, ed. Russell Sbriglia and Slavoj Žižek (Evanston: Northwestern University Press, 2020), 6.
63 Dolar, "What's the Matter?," 45.
64 Wiener cites the literary examples of Johann Wolfgang von Goethe's "The Sorcerer's Apprentice" or W. W. Jacobs' "Monkey's Paw" to illustrate his point about the unforeseen consequences of machine automation. See: Norbert Wiener, "Some Moral and Technical Consequences of Automation," *Science* 131 (1969): 1358.
65 Sybille Krämer, *Symbolische Maschinen: Die Idee der Formalisierung in geschichtlichem Abriß* (Darmstadt: Wissenschaftliche Buchgesellschaft, 1988), 4. Quote translated by the author.
66 See (re)CAPTCHA, which stands for "Completely Automated Public Turing Test to Tell Humans and Computers Apart" and has been used as a labelling technique to train AI models.
67 Liu, *The Freudian Robot*, 222.
68 Turing, "Computing Machinery."
69 Pickering, *The Cybernetic Brain.*
70 James S. Uleman, "Introduction: Becoming Aware of the New Unconscious," in *The New Unconscious*, ed. Ran R. Hassin, James S. Uleman, and John A. Bargh (Oxford: Oxford University Press, 2006), 6.
71 See Friedrich Kittler, "The World of the Symbolic — A World of the Machine," in *Literature, Media, Information Systems* (New York: Routledge, 2012), 130–46.
72 Thomas Lamarre, *The Anime Machine: A Media Theory of Animation* (Minneapolis: University of Minnesota Press, 2009), xi.

1

DANCING WITH MACHINES

> He threw his arms around the lovely Olympia and whirled her through the dance. He had thought that he usually followed the beat of the music well, but from the peculiar rhythmical evenness with which she danced and which often confused him, he was aware of how faulty his own sense of time really was.
>
> —*E.T.A. Hoffmann*[1]

In E.T.A. Hoffmann's story "The Sandman," the student Nathanael falls in love with the sublime figure of Olimpia, daughter of the celebrated professor of physics, Spalanzani. During a ball at Spalanzani's house, Nathanael grasps Olimpia's ice-cold hand and asks her for a dance. The confusion he feels vis-à-vis her all too perfect movements vanishes as soon as the two sit together and kiss each other. The shy Nathanael with the silent and rigid Olimpia was a spectacle that did not go unnoticed. One of the following days, his friend Siegmund confronts Nathanael and asks him upfront how he could "have fallen for that wax-faced, wooden puppet."[2] He adds,

> She seems to us – don't take this badly, my brother – strangely stiff and soulless. Her figure is symmetrical, so is her face, that's true enough, and if her eyes were not so completely devoid of life – the power of vision, I mean – she might be considered beautiful. Her step is peculiarly measured; all of her movements seem to stem from some kind of clockwork. Her playing and singing are unpleasantly perfect, being as lifeless as a music box; it is the same with her dancing. We found Olympia to be rather weird, and we wanted to have nothing

DOI: 10.4324/9781003690146-2

> to do with her. She seems to us to be playing the part of a human being, and it's as if there really were something hidden behind all of this.[3]

The rational and, in Nathanael's eyes, unimaginative friend voices what seems to be apparent – that the object of desire is an artifice created by the ingenious Spalanzani.[4] However, despite all good advice, Nathanael suppresses the obvious. For him, the "poetical soul" of Olimpia is accessible only to a "poetical nature" like his own, despite – or perhaps indeed because of – the weird and uncanny feeling he himself feels in the presence of his beloved.[5]

The sense of the uncanny, masterfully deployed in Hoffmann's story, arises when we are confronted with an experience of ambiguity, strangeness, or uncertainty. The resulting "lack of orientation" leaves us in a state of unease, a feeling that we are not quite "at home" in the actual situation. This is the classic definition given by Ernst Jentsch, who analysed the impression of the uncanniness of a thing or situation by tracing it back to the German word *unheimlich*. Something familiar (*heimlich*) turns into something unfamiliar (*unheimlich*), thereby detaching itself from the ordinary experiences of everyday life.[6] Now Jentsch was not interested in defining what the uncanny is, but rather in understanding in psychological terms how the uncanny evolves. For him, the affective disposition of children, women, *primitives*, and dreamers is particularly vulnerable to superstitious beliefs and therefore "subject to the stirrings of the uncanny."[7] What they are lacking, Jentsch concludes, is the intellectual mastery of processes whose conditions of origin are unknown. It is not surprising, then, that a poetical nature like that of Nathanael is prone to the "adoring glances" radiating from a divine creature such as Olimpia. His perceived doubt about her true nature only seems to fuel his love for her.[8] The tension created by the uncanny situation turns into the pleasant and joyful feeling of admiration, an effect also observed by Jentsch.[9] What is more is that Nathanael's willingness to acknowledge Olimpia's liveness appears to stem, to echo Jentsch once more, from the "natural tendency of man to infer, in a kind of naive analogy with his own animate state, that things in the external world are also animate or, perhaps more correctly, are animate in the same way."[10] Hence, he held the deeply felt belief that Olimpia, and only Olimpia, was capable of expressing thoughts that had sprung from the depths of his soul – even though she "never spoke any word other than those already recorded."[11]

In his take on the uncanny, Sigmund Freud builds on Jentsch's analysis by acknowledging his attempt to study a feeling of repulsion and distress. For Freud, the subject of the uncanny is a subject of aesthetics, to be understood not merely as a theory of beauty, but rather as a "theory of the qualities of feeling."[12] Following Jentsch, he makes use of the linguistic meaning of the German word *unheimlich* to describe a process in which something familiar becomes uncanny and frightening. However, unlike Jentsch, he does not see a contrast between the familiar and the unfamiliar, but rather a conflation between the two. After all, *heimlich* can also

FIGURE 1.1 "Spin Round Wooden Doll" (Stuart Patience).

mean something hidden and kept out of sight, which leads Freud to another definition: "According to [Friedrich Wilhelm Joseph Schelling], everything is unheimlich that ought to have remained secret and hidden but has come to light."[13] It is not difficult to find the theory of psychoanalysis at work here, and indeed Freud links the ambiguity of the uncanny feeling to the defence mechanism of repression. What he identifies behind the seminal but incomplete definition of Jentsch is the uncanny world of the unconscious, perfectly staged by Hoffmann's story. Thus, for Freud, Nathanael's horror is not merely the result of an "intellectual uncertainty" vis-à-vis the wooden doll, but something secretly familiar (*heimlich – heimisch*) that has been repressed and is now coming to light. Freud points out that the story behind the story is that of the Sandman, a cruel creature who, according to the nurse of Nathanael's sister, bereaves children of their eyes in order to feed them to his own.[14] The psychoanalyst recognises in this story the fear of castration, especially since "[a] study of dreams, phantasies and myths has taught us [i.e. Freud] that anxiety about one's eyes, the fear of going blind, is often enough a substitute for the dread of being castrated."[15] However, in his attempt to place the castration complex in the centre of analysis, Freud seems to ignore the fact that Jentsch does not explicitly use "The Sandman" as an example to explain his notion of the uncanny, but instead he speaks more generally about artistic tricks in storytelling to produce uncanny effects.

In another short story from 1814 called "Automatons," Hoffmann puts these effects to use by incorporating a whole series of mechanical devices.[16] In particular, the "talking Turk" is intended "to leave the reader in uncertainty as to whether he has a human person or rather an automaton before him."[17] Here, the uncanny is linked to the automaton's movements and vocal sounds, as well as its mysterious ability to guess the darkest secrets of its human counterparts. In Hoffmann's work of fantasy, the imitation of humanity cumulates in the dread of "living death or inanimate life," as Ludwig, one of the protagonists, puts it.[18] It is the conflation between animation and simulation, between the deadliness of life and the liveliness of death, that evokes strong feelings about the nature of automated machines. The more subtle the artificial reproduction, that is, the less visible the difference between the human and the machine, the stronger the uncanny feeling appears to be. This, in a nutshell, is the observation made by the Japanese roboticist Masahiro Mori in 1970.[19] A century and a half after Hoffmann, he described the phenomenon of the "uncanny valley" as a possible relation between the likeability of machines and their resemblance to a (living) human being. The concept suggests that the acceptance of an object that simulates human behaviour (e.g. dolls, robots, avatars) depends on its human-like appearance. However, while affinity is highest when the imitation is no longer distinguishable from a real human, Mori observed a sudden drop in the acceptance of humanoid machines when they look almost, but not exactly, like human beings. In the uncanny valley, we experience the collapse of our subject position by being confronted with the strange and eerie feeling of something un/familiar. The resulting "doubt as to whether an apparently living being really is animate and, conversely, doubt as to whether a lifeless object may not in fact be animate"[20] echoes our very own existential anxiety in the face of a technological, that is, post-human, world.

1. Ontological Ambiguity

Today, more than two hundred years after "The Sandman" was first published, we are once again confronted with a lack of orientation. The inability to grasp our techno-cultural world becomes apparent in the face of algorithmic systems, data economies, and ubiquitous computing, all of which push human subjectivity towards a newly perceived intellectual uncertainty. Hence, the ambivalence resulting from the attempt to draw a line between the animate and the inanimate "can yield some vital clues as to how the Freudian uncanny can be made relevant to the contemporary discussions of the psychic powers of image, medium, and automata in digital media."[21] In her book *The Freudian Robot*, Lydia H. Liu reminds us that at the beginning of Hoffmann's story it is Nathanael who is treated like an automaton, raising doubts about whether or not he himself is a living (human) being.[22] In this reading, Nathanael does not merely project his erotic desire onto Olimpia, but shares the same ontological ambiguity – and, one might add, anxiety – towards her.[23] It thus seems that behind the rather obviously depicted mechanical doll Olimpia, another, more hidden (i.e. repressed) automaton comes to light.[24] Introduced here is a doppelgänger (Nathanael/Olimpia), an errant figure that traverses modern thought and literature; it connects the old dream of a godlike reproduction – one only has to think of Ovid's Pygmalion – with the fear of being substituted by an object-world. Hence, "the very ontological instability expressed by the artefact itself, the oscillation between animate and inanimate, subject and object, human and thing" can be seen as the expression of an "uncanny modernity."[25] According to Bill Brown, the material support of the modern world has been constantly suppressed in order to maintain the imagined autonomy of human subjectivity (or better, what is considered as such), which is rather constituted by the "things" surrounding it.[26] Consequently, for Brown, it was the ambiguous status of the slave, both a person and a thing, that not only made the idea of an autonomous and self-generating economic system possible, but also has haunted capitalism's self-imagination ever since. The slave, like the automaton, returns as a threat, a thing of terror, showing the system that it was not autonomous in the first place.[27]

Along these lines, Louis Chude-Sokei has shown how slavery not only forms the basis of an industrial economy but also becomes the inert mirror image of modernity: "The slave's 'innate' participation in notions of barbarism, *animality*, and primitivism was due to its African origin; it therefore consistently functioned as a contrast for notions of 'the modern.'"[28] As can be seen from the example of modernist art movements such as surrealism, Dadaism, futurism, or primitivism, "Africa" becomes an allegory for what – in the eyes of disappointed Euro-American modernism – seems to have been lost. Thus, according to Chude-Sokei, what resonates in Filippo Tommaso Marinetti's "The Manifesto of Futurism" (1909), in the ironic undertone of Karel Čapek's science fiction play *R.U.R.* (Rossum's Universal Robots, 1920), and in Fritz Lang's epochal film *Metropolis* (1927) is the Western anxiety of being turned into a slave by machines. Between the Second and Third Industrial Revolution (which laid the foundations for the digital computer), race, technology, culture, and the machine are all intermingled in the figure of the robot, which is seen as the resurrection of the slave as a mindless automaton. Robots and slaves, both signified as the Other, embody the "racial uncanny" of modernity.[29] In line with psychoanalysis' definition of the unconscious, the racial constitution of industrialisation – the enormous labour force that was needed to kick-start capitalism – is what gets hidden but eventually comes to light by the constant fear of being replaced by machines. It is this anxious relation to the machinic world that causes the epistemic ambivalence and intellectual uncertainty of our time. By the same token, today's responses to technology must be understood in light of the "longer history of human surrogates in post-Enlightenment modernity, including the body of the enslaved standing in for the master, the vanishing of native bodies necessary for colonial expansion, as well as invisible labour including indenture, immigration, and outsourcing."[30] As Neda Atanasoski and Kalindi Vora explain, it is invisible and unfree labour, together with a Western liberal subject as its agent, that still sustains the notion of an autonomous economic system.

The fear of loss of control, ultimately a fear of loss of (white) male authority, has already been discussed on multiple occasions,[31] and will not be repeated here. However, Freud's reading of "The Sandman" must also be seen as a product of his time, especially since psychoanalysis tended to translate the ambiguous relation humans have with the object world back into the human. By downplaying the role of Olimpia, Freud represses the ontological status of the non-human, thereby following the dominant scientific discourse of the early twentieth century. Moreover, the female Olimpia gets sublated entirely in the infantile male fears of Nathanael (i.e. the castration complex); or, in other words, her errancy is transformed into his error. As we have seen before, this is a very specific, if not narrow, reading of Hoffmann's work, whose artistic trick is to keep the reader in the dark about the actual ontological status of all his protagonists. Errancy is presented as an ongoing process rather than a final outcome, which is also the reason why one might question the portrayal of Olimpia as "just a detached complex of Nathaniel."[32] Her errant status causes Freud to take a detour and turn Olimpia into a mere flaw in Nathanael's psychic structure. But as Hélène Cixous asks, "If she is no more than that, why are not the dance, the song, the mechanisms, and the artificer brought back into the game or theorized upon by Freud?"[33] According to this reading, the story's pivotal dance scene is glossed over by Freud, who introduces the Big Other so as not to have to deal with all the little others that appear in that scene. Because rhythm and movement are often thought of as a female manifestation of the animate, it is not surprising that Olimpia's dancing is suppressed in order to maintain the Oedipal, that is, the male interpretation of Nathanael's anxiety.[34] By focusing on the story within the story (i.e. the Sandman), Freud re-inscribes the ambiguous – perhaps even queer – status of its characters into the realm of his orthodox theory, turning Nathanael into a castrated subject. The animating, that is, uncontainable, aspect of Olimpia's "otherness," which has the potential to turn everyone else into another, is ultimately contained by her inanimate (i.e. impotent) counterpart.[35]

The "othering" of female agency by psychoanalysis has been at the centre of criticism since the 1940s.[36] More recently, however, this agency has been linked to a new kind of object power. Thus, over the last decades, feminist theorists, such as Donna Haraway, Rosi Braidotti, and Jane Bennett have been "insisting upon the need for ontologies and epistemologies that recognise a broader and more diverse spectrum of human/nonhuman hybrids, interactions, and relations."[37] Braidotti, for example, sees critical post-humanism as a logical but also necessary diversification of feminist theory. For her, post-human subjectivity has the potential to form associations with other (non-human) entities, thus opening up space for a critical examination of what it means to be a human. Challenging the foundations of the Enlightenment-based humanist model of emancipation with its liberal subject and building on discourses from "critical studies" (e.g. gender, feminist, queer, race, decolonisation, and subaltern studies, as well as cultural, media, film, and critical data studies), Braidotti argues for post-anthropocentric humanities. In her words:

> The question of the future of the humanities and the issue of their renewal [...] is currently played out on the question of the complex re-configuration of knowledge led by new media and digital technological information: we have entered into a global mediation.[38]

Digital media technologies are thus seen not simply as tools or prostheses of an autonomous human subject, but as powerful mediators directing us toward a new post-human subjectivity.[39] New materialist thinkers like Braidotti, whose materialism draws on post-structuralism with its linguistic and cultural turn, do not dismiss older debates about mediation and the social construction of subjectivity, in particular with regards to gender, class, and race; "[t]hey do, however, also consider material bodies, spaces, and conditions of subjectivity."[40] As a reaction to radical constructivism, such as Judith Butler's pioneering work on sex and gender, the turn towards "matter" is seen as a necessary corrective to consider material conditions beyond what is socially, technologically, or linguistically mediated.[41]

The focus on agency calls for a reconceptualisation of materialism, which has long been identified with Marxist theory. As Peter Wolfendale writes:

> From the perspective of the new materialist, the animation of nature provides a potent alternative to the Marxist materialisms that have dominated leftist academic discourse (e.g. dialectical materialism), and a new way to frame political and ethical issues posed by environmentalism (e.g. preventing climate change) and posthumanism (e.g. empathy for nonhuman animals).[42]

The problem with "ontological egalitarianism" is that new materialism's vitalism ignores the actual conditions under which the non-human other can be conceived. By simply doing away with the human subject, new materialism seeks to formulate a flat ontology, "in which humans are merely to be understood as one agent among others."[43] Unlike Braidotti, who retains a political subjectivity for her project of post-anthropocentric humanities, Jane Bennett, a political scientist and one of the leading thinkers of new materialism, asserts a "distributive agency" that is located in a multiplicity of material processes.[44] Here, the vitality of the material world is expressed in the ability of things "not only to impede or block the will and designs of humans but also to act as quasi agents or forces with trajectories, propensities, or tendencies of their own."[45] Food, power grids, storms, or plastic waste all become equally agential in a myriad of human non-human assemblages. By emphasising the agential contributions of non-human forces, Bennett seeks to flatten out the differences between the inanimate and the living, the subject and the object. This conflation, however, tends to erase any differentiation between (un)conscious acts and material processes, raising the question of how such a distinction could be made in the first place.

Rather than dissolving the ontological differences between human and non-human entities, between subjectivity and materiality, an emphasis on the ambiguous relationship may be a better way to grasp the uncanny situation in which we find ourselves. In line with radical thinkers such as Sylvia Wynter, the question is not how to undo the human, but what "man" might mean from the perspective of those who have never been considered human.[46] Thus, despite well-intended attempts to "[absolve] matter from its long history of attachment to automatism or mechanism,"[47] the attribution of a vital force to all things does not free us from the fatal, and in particular racial, entanglements of our own subjectivities. What is more is that the focus on "thing-power" and "assemblages" runs the risk of relegating the not-so-human (i.e. racialised) other back to the object-world instead of "acknowledging the agency of so many human beings that Western metaphysics has historically ignored."[48] The problem with new materialism – its various interpretations and applications notwithstanding – is its tendency to ignore "the multiplicity of cultural subject positions and relations"[49] and to solve "the pressing political problem of cultivating collective agency by dissolving it."[50] It can thus be seen as the flip side of the above argument: while Freud sought to contain the animate by tying it back to the (male) human subject, new materialists seek to dissolve the very same subject into a (female) vibrant materiality. Both positions tend to eliminate the dialectic interdependence between the two by overemphasising the rational (animus) on the one hand, or the material (anima) on the other.[51] And while the new materialist critique of the subject-object dualism has sparked a productive and refreshing debate about the entangled relationship between matter and subjectivity, it is hard to see how the denial of its inner tensions can help to move beyond the human without falling back into a pre-critical (i.e. pre-linguistic) state.[52]

2. Animation, Not Simulation

So what is needed to mediate between human subjectivity and non-human materiality? How can we think about a post-human situation without omitting a critical engagement with the subject? In order to formulate a critique of artificial intelligence and machine learning, we cannot dismiss the alienating and often disparate effects of these technologies by simply appealing to a kind of presupposed sameness; instead we must highlight the ambiguities in our relationship to the object world that "evoke the same feelings of the uncanny as Hoffmann's story once did."[53] Much like the automatons in the story, today's machine learning algorithms operate on the fringes of what has long been considered the exclusive domain of humans (i.e. their creativity or consciousness). What remains hidden, but is slowly coming to light, is the uncanny fact that these algorithms not only feed on the vast amounts of data we produce on a daily basis, but also constitute our subjectivity.[54] Automated machines do not simply simulate human behaviour; they co-produce it. In doing so, however, they also reveal their own strange behaviour. This is what Brown labelled the "thingness" of the object world. Against a naive notion of a "democracy of things," Brown insists on the ontological ambiguity we have with this world, which resists any homogeneous or normative reading of the subject-object hybrid.[55] The "social" here does not denote a harmonious interaction of ontologically flattened things, but on the contrary highlights the complications, conflicts, and concatenations of supposedly human and non-human entities. It is only through friction and contradiction that the gap separating subjectivity from the object world can be experienced – which is also why we need a "pedagogy that repeatedly points to the uncanniness of the ordinary, the oscillations between the animate and inanimate."[56] It is precisely these oscillations, the weird and uncanny effects of errant situations, that are at stake today in relation to AI and machine learning.

Automation, digitisation, and artificial intelligence are buzzwords in a long-running debate about technology-induced social change. The problem is not so much that technology is transforming society – that has always been the case – but that the much-heralded "change" (cf. the "digital revolution," the "AI revolution") is merely a simulation of pre-existing social relations. What we are witnessing, then, is an endless reproduction of the same: not only with regard to racist and sexist relations, which are currently being re-produced as self-fulfilling prophecies by means of algorithmic filtering systems, but also with regard to the automation and proliferation of commodity culture.[57] An obvious example is virtual assistants, which are sold to us as the ultimate solution to our everyday needs: "Whether you're booking a table at your neighborhood sushi joint or trying to schedule a last-minute haircut before your big event, sometimes you just need to pick up the phone to get something done."[58] This may be useful in certain situations, but making phone calls to arrange a haircut on our behalf is hardly revolutionary. Instead of a radically different future, these technologies are leading us into an endless loop of the same, a process Bernard Stiegler once called a state of "systemic stupidity."[59] With their ongoing personalisation and customisation, digital media promise to create the perfect, smooth, boring image of the self – an image driven by the desire for authenticity, but which instead produces exactly the same standardised brand.[60] As such, the human user is merely a part of a more complex system, providing the necessary data for the machine to learn and thus adapt to the user. Yet, for this algorithmic mirror game to work smoothly, the underlying infrastructures and mechanisms of data extraction remain hidden. Rather than making the object world tangible, virtual assistants are "built to sound natural, to make the conversation experience comfortable."[61] The anthropomorphisation of the machine follows the logic of modern thinking mentioned above: by repressing the ontological difference between the animate and the inanimate, the human subject is reassured of its mastery over the world.

While one of the devices in Hoffmann's "Automaton" was modelled on Wolfgang von Kempelen's mechanical chess-playing Turk of 1769, it is striking that most virtual assistants today have a female voice by default (e.g. Amazon's Alexa, Apple's Siri, Google's Assistant). In both cases, the orientalised chess-playing automaton and the feminised talking machine, notions of otherness are invoked: "Gender and racial or ethnic otherness have been used both to make [...] human-like machines attractive and to alleviate the possibility of horror that always follows them."[62] As Tiina Männistö-Funk and Tanja Sihvonen further explain, the long history of human-like machines "leads to a conclusion that it appears to be easier to let machines come close to the borders of humanity if they take the form of 'lesser' humans, meaning anything other than white adult males."[63] On the one hand, the ontological difference between the human and the machine is removed in order to simulate liveliness; on the other hand, the uncanny effect thus created is attenuated by making the machine less awesome.[64] Thus, already during early industrialisation, with its alienating impact on the "human" (i.e. the Western subject), "Africa and its people functioned [...] to render machines less alienating, close to the natural."[65] Race combined with gender, Chude-Sokei argues, helped to naturalise technology, thereby making it more intimate but also inevitable. With a purely new materialist reading and its anti-subjective approach, it would be difficult to grasp the psychic reality that is at play here. Moreover, the notion of an "artificial artificial intelligence"[66] – which is still based on slave-like labour – holds the key to the ideological foundation of major tech companies, such as Amazon, Google, Meta, Microsoft, Baidu, or IBM. In order to set the standards for machine learning systems, these systems rely on immense infrastructures that need to be built and maintained.[67] Thus, behind the appearance of a fully automated artificial intelligence, the actual symbolic order comes to light: techno-capitalism and the denial of its dependence on the material, labour-based world.

Given previous attempts to smooth out the conflicts in our techno-social world, we have to ask whether technological developments in machine learning are simply the latest push for a "friction-free capitalism,"[68] where digital technologies supposedly solve the inherent conflicts of capitalism caused by the antagonism between capital and labour, or whether they offer us a way to break out of the established algorithmic loops in which we find ourselves. Given the deep entanglement of racial capitalism and digital technology, there is of course no clear answer to this problem. But we can at least reassess some of its basic premises.

For instance, if simulation eventually leads to the repetition of the same, then maybe animation can offer an alternative. Based on the ancient Greek meaning of *mimesis*, animation can be seen as a mimetic art, which deploys, rather than omits ontological differences in order to create something new. Unlike simulation, which ultimately seeks to copy the existing world, imitation anticipates the world by constantly deviating from it.[69] Thus, rather than attempting to make the world frictionless and error-free, an effort that is ultimately aligned with techno-capitalism, the errancy of intelligence allows for mimetic practices as a mode of creation. It does not produce a final result but constantly emerges through the making itself.[70] Similar to magical practices that attempt to influence the course of things, mimetic practices are ultimately processual. And because of their entanglement with the material world, they tend to increase rather than decrease with the technologisation (i.e. automation) of the world.[71]

3. Mimetic Machines

According to Walter Benjamin, mimesis manifests itself not only in the material world, but even more so in cognitive and cultural expressions such as language, dance, rituals, and art.[72] Whereas in ancient times mimicry was expressed primarily through the direct, physical imitation of the surrounding world, since modernity this capacity has become more abstract. This is an important fact because it suggests that the mimetic faculty has actually increased in response to the socio-technical changes brought about by modern machinery. The organisation and structure of our technological world is thus mediated by increasingly abstract forms of information processing. This is particularly true of digital machines, which, as highly abstracted information technologies, break away from their physical manifestations. And while the digital allows for the break with the material, it is abstraction that "anchors the operation of the digital."[73] As Aden Evens further explains: "Making the world abstract requires a considerable cooperation from the actual, the material, which must offer itself as discretized and generalized in order to be ready for the digital."[74] Turning the actual world into a digital one thus requires a process of abstraction mediated by the symbolic. It is only through the symbolic, such as language, that we are able to recognise the similarity between things, which is the reason why "language may be seen as the highest level of mimetic behavior and the most complete archive of nonsensuous similarity."[75] What Benjamin means by this is the ability of language – and, by extension, any symbolic system – to bring together phenomena as diverse as celestial alignments, animal characteristics and mental concepts, thereby establishing "the ties not only between what is said what is meant but also between what is written and what is meant, and equally between the spoken and the written."[76] Conversely, language alienates us from these very same phenomena by abstracting from them. This dual, dialectical nature of language lies at the heart of mimesis, which is in fact more than simple imitation, since it is constantly moving away from what it is trying to capture.[77]

The mimetic capacity is not only the ability to recognise similarities, but also to produce them. Even in the digital world, this is done through a physical gesture: "The deictic gesture thus comes from without, and just as the user must constrain her expression to what can be made discrete and abstract, so the interface prepares for the user's commands by offering clearly marked visual indicators of what can be pointed to. The icon thus mirrors the mouse pointer, itself a discrete abstraction that allows the user to indicate *this* rather than that."[78] Users direct their input towards the desired objective of the interface, selecting from the options presented in two dimensions to achieve the anticipated outcome. The mouse, in its capacity as an input device, quite literally becomes a *digitus*, functioning as a pointer in the digital world. The similarities produced are not restricted to the direct manipulation of symbols on the screen, though. Also, within the machine, the gesture of the user triggers a whole cascade of translation processes. To do so, the machine needs a language that is both general and specific enough to describe all the necessary procedures for the machine to perform. What makes computing unique is the fact that such a mechanical language is equivalent to the machine that performs the operations defined by that language. This was Alan Turing's simple but powerful idea when he conceived of a machine that could emulate, that is, imitate, any other machine operating.[79] The errant character of a Turing machine comes from the fact that it treats the program code that constitutes the machine and the data that the machine manipulates as the same written representation, with the effect that it can create an infinite number of other machines. As such, the digital machine is a mimetic machine, constantly producing similarities of itself.

Even more than this inner errancy, the history of computing is itself an errant journey. In fact, the Turing machine can be seen as an unexpected by-product of a centuries-old quest to mechanise mathematics. What began with Gottfried Wilhelm Leibniz's *calculus rationator* sparked the idea of a "universal alphabet" (i.e. a system of discrete symbols), in which all human knowledge could be expressed and calculated.[80] However, the idea of a complete formalisation of mathematical thought (pursued after Leibniz by none other than George Boole, Gottlob Frege, Bertrand Russell, and David Hilbert, among others) could not be realised. That's the famous result of Kurt Gödel's incompleteness theorem of 1931, which put an end to Leibniz's calculatory dream[81] In a sense, one could thus say that the history of computing is a history of spectacular failure. And yet that same history has become the greatest success story of the last century; not of reasoning, not of deduction, but of programming. The attempt to find a formal language for mathematics eventually led to the invention of programming languages and, with them, the Turing machine.[82] While the digital computer was already implicit in Gödel's work on symbolic logic, it was Turing who got to the heart of it. He realised that the "mechanical procedure" formulated by the mathematician David Hilbert in

1900 (i.e. that all mathematical statements could be deduced from a complete axiomatic system) was in fact a programmable machine; not just any machine, but a universal, all-purpose machine. Turing's insight was crucial in taking computation beyond mere mechanics: he understood that a single machine, capable of following a set of rules for manipulating symbols, could, in theory, compute anything that could be algorithmically defined.

The Turing machine as a mimetic machine builds on formal abstraction and, at the same time, breaks away from it. It is this errant character that makes the machine difficult to grasp. This is especially true in the context of machine learning, where the training process is often driven by unexpected and unpredictable interactions with the machine. According to Brian Christian, this poses one of the greatest challenges in today's technological world:

> As machine-learning systems grow not just increasingly pervasive but increasingly powerful, we will find ourselves more and more often in the position of the "sorcerer's apprentice": we conjure a force, autonomous but totally compliant, give it a set of instructions, then scramble like mad to stop it once we realize our instructions are imprecise or incomplete – lest we get, in some clever, horrible way, precisely what we asked for.[83]

What has become known as the "alignment problem" (i.e. the challenge of ensuring that the goals, behaviours, and decisions of AI systems are consistent with human values, intentions, and ethical principles) can be traced back to Norbert Wiener's discussion of the fable of the sorcerer's apprentice, "in which the boy makes the broom carry water in his master's absence, so that it is on the point of drowning him when his master reappears."[84] The machine without a master becomes an errant machine because once it has started, it becomes more difficult to change the course it has set. This is why, according to Wiener, we need to make sure that "the purpose put into the machine is the purpose which we really desire and not merely a colorful imitation of it."[85] The problem of alignment is a problem precisely because of the mimetic relationship between the human and the machine. The "right" purpose may only become apparent through the operation of the machine, all the more so because of the machine's capacity to move beyond its pre-programmed instructions.[86]

The somewhat counterintuitive aspect of digital computers is that they do not simply follow a fixed set of axiomatic rules (i.e. algorithms) but are also able to "wander around" the world of numbers and symbols.[87] This makes their processual constitution at once errant and mimetic. Hence, the relation between mimesis and errancy stems from the fact that computers, like humans, "can deal with arbitrary patterns, whether they are logical or illogical, consistent or inconsistent."[88] And this is exactly where their intelligent behaviour comes from. Not from the mindless repetition of an already existing intelligence, nor from a technological singularity replacing it, but the entanglement of human and technological learning capabilities. Such a relational understanding of errancy is, in a rather different context (namely that of exile), what Martinican philosopher Édouard Glissant has been insisting on. The errant, for him, has no "totalitarian root," no pre-given structure, but is a mode of thinking that "conceives of totality but willingly renounces any claims to sum it up or process it."[89] Roaming around the universal medium of numbers, in which any kind of structure can be represented, the errant machine strives for totality, while, at the same time, already *knowing* that it will never reach it. In the case of the Turing machine, the knowledge of the inner limit is constitutive. The machine does not simply undermine the totalising structure of a given system but is in fact that very same structure. Paradoxically, it is its "incomputability" that makes computability possible.[90]

4. Collective Intelligence

In summary, we can say that mimesis as an errant process offers a way of exploring the ambiguity we experience in our techno-cultural world. In her reading of Freud's interpretation of "The Sandman," Cixous makes an interesting observation in this regard: "What unfolds without fail before the reader's eyes is a kind of puppet theater in which real dolls or fake dolls, real and simulated life, are manipulated by a sovereign but capricious stage-setter."[91] Rather than focusing on individual characters or objects and their failures within the play, Cixous refers to the "preoccupations of the theater" as a whole.[92] Her reading brings us close to an understanding of the theatre as a machinic arrangement. The stage, in this reading, assembles a whole range of heterogeneous and divergent elements, bringing the machine to life. Instead of seeing the stage as one flat plane, the machinic arrangement allows for an understanding of the "mutual animation of subject and object."[93] After all, it is Nathanael who puts his arms around Olimpia and twirls her around. Not only does he give in to the illusion of his love, but he also animates it with a physical gesture. The moving around in the dance mediates the relationship between the self and the other, even more so as we are dealing with a potential doppelgänger, incorporating the subject-object-relation on an individual basis. But it does not stop there, especially since it is the errant behaviour, the confusion emerging between the dancing bodies, that brings the scene to life – not to mention the music and entire ballroom. All of these allow for mimicry, setting the machine (i.e. the story) in motion. Rather than merely imitating the usual movements via automation, the dance introduces an ambiguity that affects everyone present. The "subject matter" literally bursts into the everyday routine of life, evoking reactions of awe and distress – but also excitement and wonder.

Mimesis, following Walter Benjamin, is expressed "in dances whose oldest function this is."[94] Dance and rhythm could, therefore, be revealing aspects when thinking about our often very strange relationship with mimetic machines. As such, "our pathological relationship to the machine points to an affective knowledge that acknowledges mutual interdependence."[95] Hence, rather than fetishising the technological Other as some kind of superpower or smooth operator, we should pay attention to our interaction with machines.[96] In this respect, artificial intelligence is less artificial than collective; it fundamentally relies on what Marx called collective labour as a manifestation of the "general intellect" (i.e. technical knowledge, practical skills, and techniques).[97] As Matteo Pasquinelli explains: "Drawing on Babbage's labour theory of the machine, which explains the machine as the embodiment of the division of labour, Marx asserts the collective worker as the true political inventor of technology."[98] Same as with technology, intelligence here "resides in the ramifications of human cooperation rather than in individual mental labour. Machine intelligence mirrors, embodies and amplifies the analytical intelligence of collective labour."[99] Intelligence is not something that sits inside our heads, something pre-given that can be simulated or reproduced. Rather, intelligence is external, emerging from material interactions, social organisations, and collective efforts. Focusing on the "social intellect" with all its ambiguities and antagonisms might help us to push past the usual accounts of artificial intelligence and machine learning – not as a self-learning autonomous system, but as an ensemble that emerges through the often-conflictual encounters between human and non-human individuals.[100]

The social character of intelligence also includes the concept of "otherness" as was mentioned earlier. Not only are fantasies and fears projected onto the technological Other, but the subject also emerges from the encounter with the object world. The attempt to return to the magical moment when the division between object and subject was not yet firmly established is precisely what Jentsch described as the "natural human tendency" to perceive the external world as something animated. For him, such a primitive view of the world is reserved for a "poetic nature" like that of Nathaniel. But the eeriness of the situation already presupposes a rupture in this natural state. The encounter with the Other and the attempt to *correspond* mimetically to the otherness of the object world already implies a subject position that cannot be congruent with this very world. This does not mean, however, that communication with the object world is impossible, as the example of the Turing machine shows.[101] It is precisely because humans and machines are part of the same symbolic order, and language is capable of creating similarities, that the animation of intelligence is possible. Understanding AI technologies as "quintessential examples of animation as a genre of human cultural production and expression,"[102] allows us to see their collective character. In this sense, AI, especially in its most recent incarnation as generative Large Language Models (LLMs), can be seen as an enormous collective effort. Examining the material conditions of AI and machine learning, especially their rootedness in labour exploitation, highlights the continuities of our socio-economic world. "Hence," as Elisa Giardina Papa writes, "if we were to finally open the black box of the algorithmic, enchanted machines which AI-capitalism claims essential for the constant re-origination of the autonomous and self-determining subject, inside we might find nothing more than an intensification of the old entanglements of capitalism and colonialism, technology and surrogacy."[103] Herein lies the *productive* relationship between humans and machines. Rather than trying to flatten it, thereby ignoring the actual conditions under which artificial intelligence is being produced, it is time to make it tangible and thus discussable.

In light of recent developments in AI, we are faced with a "fourth narcissistic blow."[104] Yet this wound can be seen as a chance to shed the illusion of intellectual mastery, which plagues the current situation we find ourselves in. Indeed, it may be time to "unlearn" most of the beliefs and convictions we have developed with regard to artificial intelligence and machine learning. While the latter constitutes the driving force of the former, it is the idea of a self-engendering intelligence that has paved the way for a machinic superpower.[105] Echoing Marx's description of capital as a vital force that "brings forth living offspring, or, at the least, lays golden eggs," artificial intelligence has adopted its fetish character. Rather than buying into the fetish of artificial intelligence, particularly in the form of artificial neural networks and deep learning, which are not coincidentally modelled on the human brain, we should be asking what prevents us from thinking about artificial intelligence in terms of its collectivity.[106] To better understand this problem, I will, in the next step, trace some of the ideological assumptions in the current debate around artificial intelligence, in particular its roots in post-war cybernetics and connectionism, that is, the idea that intelligence can be traced back to the physiological wiring of the individual brain. This idea, which has been revived in today's machine learning techniques, hinders a genuine engagement with collective intelligence through machine learning. This may indeed require a poetic nature, a mode of thinking that can grasp both the logical as well as the strange and uncanny aspects of our technological world.

Notes

1 Ernst T. A. Hoffmann, "The Sandman," in *Tales of E. T. A. Hoffmann*, ed. Leonard J. Kent and Elizabeth C. Knight (Chicago: University of Chicago Press, 1969), 115. In the German original, Olympia is Olimpia and Spalanzini is Spalanzani. I will retain the original names in the following.
2 Hoffmann, "The Sandman," 117.
3 Hoffmann, "The Sandman," 117. Note that the English word "weird" can also be translated as uncanny (*unheimlich*), which, in fact, is the word Hoffmann uses in the original text.
4 Together with the peddler Coppola, who, in another twist of the story, turns out to be Coppelius, the genuinely sinister figure of his father's associate.
5 In Lacanian psychoanalysis, one would speak of an "objet petit a" as the unattainable object of desire. The object belongs to the realm of the imaginary and is defined as a remnant, which is left behind when the symbolic gets introduced in the real. By definition, it is something separated and therefore alienating. See Jacques Lacan, *The Seminar of Jacques Lacan, Book XI: The Four Fundamental Concepts of Psychoanalysis* (New York, London: W. W. Norton, 1981).

6 Ernst Jentsch, "On the Psychology of the Uncanny," in *Uncanny Modernity: Cultural Theories, Modern Anxieties*, ed. Jo Collins and John Jervis (New York: Palgrave Macmillan, [1906] 2008). According to the Oxford Dictionary, the English word *uncanny* also incorporates the meaning of "unhomely," in the sense of something being uninviting or unpleasant.
7 Jentsch, "On the Psychology of the Uncanny," 224.
8 One could, of course, say that the suspension of the "critical sense" towards the object of desire is precisely what love – or falling in love – is all about.
9 See Jentsch, "On the Psychology of the Uncanny," 221.
10 Jentsch, "On the Psychology of the Uncanny," 225.
11 Hoffmann, "The Sandman," 118.
12 Sigmund Freud, "The Uncanny," in *The Standard Edition of the Complete Psychological Works of Sigmund Freud, Volume XVII: An Infantile Neurosis and Other Works*, ed. James Strachey (London: Hogarth Press, 1955), 219.
13 Freud, "Uncanny," 224.
14 Nathanael associates this nightmarish creature with Coppelius, his father's associate, who displays an eerie fascination with eyes.
15 Freud, "Uncanny," 231. What Freud mentions here is, of course, the Oedipus complex.
16 Ernst T. A. Hoffmann, "Automatons," in *The Serapion Brethren*, trans. Alex Ewing (London: George Bell and Sons, 1908).
17 Jentsch, "On the Psychology of the Uncanny," 224. In this passage, Jentsch locates the uncanny in (autonomous) movements, creating "doubt as to whether an apparently living being really is animate and, conversely, doubt as to whether a lifeless object may not in fact be animate," see page 221.
18 Hoffmann, "Automatons," 355.
19 Masahiro Mori, "The Uncanny Valley," *IEEE Spectrum*, June 12, 2012, https://spectrum.ieee.org/automaton/robotics/humanoids/the-uncanny-valley.
20 Jentsch, "On the Psychology of the Uncanny," 221.
21 Lydia H. Liu, *The Freudian Robot: Digital Media and the Future of the Unconscious* (Chicago: University of Chicago Press, 2010), 207.
22 This doubt gets reinforced at the end of the story when Spalanzani tosses Olimpia's eyes at Nathanael, screaming, "The eyes – the eyes stolen from you!" Hoffmann, "The Sandman," 120.
23 This might then also be the "reason" why Nathanael is the only one who does not find Olimpia to be weird or uncanny (see above).
24 Lydia H. Liu concludes that the invention of Olimpia is therefore another trick by Hoffmann to deflect the reader's attention from the *real* automaton: "The character Nathanael is so effective and so successful that critics and psychoanalysts, Jentsch and Freud alike, do not seem to entertain the slightest doubt about his ambiguity as a living human character or an undead automaton in the context of the story." Liu, *The Freudian Robot*, 222.
25 Bill Brown, "Reification, Reanimation, and the American Uncanny," *Critical Inquiry* 32 (Winter 2006): 199. *Uncanny Modernity* is the title of a book edited by Jo Collins and John Jervis. See Jentsch, "On the Psychology of the Uncanny."
26 See, for example, Bill Brown's entry on "Materiality," in *Critical Terms for Media Studies*, ed. W. J. T. Mitchell and Mark B. Hansen (Chicago: University of Chicago Press, 2010), 49–63; or the canonical special issue "Things," *Critical Inquiry* 28, no. 1 (Autumn 2001). What is striking about Brown's approach is that he, contrasting a lot of theories that have emerged during the "materialist turn" in the 1990s, seeks to "dramatise" materiality.
27 See Brown, "Reification," 198.
28 Louis Chude-Sokei, *The Sound of Culture: Diaspora and Black Technopoetics* (Middletown: Wesleyan University Press, 2016), 28.

29 Chude-Sokei, *The Sound of Culture*, 49.
30 Neda Atanasoski and Kalindi Vora, *Surrogate Humanity: Race, Robots, and the Politics of Technological Futures* (Durham: Duke University Press, 2019), 14.
31 See, for example, Andreas Huyssen's analysis of Fritz Lang's *Metropolis* (1927). Andreas Huyssen, *After the Great Divide: Modernism, Mass Culture, Postmodernism* (Bloomington: Indiana University Press, 1986), Chapter 4.
32 Hélène Cixous, "Fictions and Its Phantoms: A Reading of Freud's *Das Unheimliche* (The 'Uncanny')," *New Literary History* 7, no. 3 (Spring 1976): 538.
33 Cixous, "Fictions and Its Phantoms."
34 To be fair, the reading of sexual impotence, respectively anxiety, is not without validity – in particular, when considering Nathanael's tense relationship with his actual fiancée, Clara. Precisely at the moment when the couple is supposed to enter into marriage, Nathanael turns towards (invents?) an inanimate sex doll, thereby buttressing Freud's idea that he is unable to make love to a living woman.
35 Of course, castration theory is more complex and cannot be reduced to a male subject losing its sexual potency. However, the "hysterisation" of Nathanael/Olimpia by Freud is obvious. More interesting, with regard to the doppelgänger figure, would be Lacan's differentiation between the hysteric question "Am I man or woman?" and the question of the neurotic: "Am I dead or alive?" In Hoffmann's story, both questions seem to be of relevance. See Jacques Lacan, *The Seminar of Jacques Lacan, Book III: The Psychoses*, trans. Russell Grigg (New York, London: W. W. Norton, 1993), 161–72.
36 See, most prominently, Simone de Beauvoir, *The Second Sex*, trans. H. M. Parshley (London: Jonathan Cape, 1953).
37 Lisa Parks and Nicole Starosielski, "Introduction," in *Signal Traffic: Critical Studies of Media Infrastructures*, ed. Lisa Parks and Nicole Starosielski (Urbana-Champaign: University of Illinois Press, 2015), 10.
38 Rosi Braidotti, "The Contested Posthumanities," in *Conflicting Humanities*, ed. Rosi Braidotti and Paul Gilroy (New York: Bloomsbury, 2016), 22.
39 Such a post-human subjectivity yields new partnerships with "nonhuman companion species" (Donna Haraway). Instead of the liberal humanist subject's desire to dominate and control nature (i.e. also women and non-Europeans), a post-human subjectivity seeks to avoid mistakes from the past. N. Katherine Hayles, *Unthought: The Power of the Cognitive Nonconscious* (Chicago: University of Chicago Press, 2017), 288.
40 Kameron Sanzo, "New Materialism(s)," *Critical Posthumanism*, April 25, 2018, https://criticalposthumanism.net/new-materialisms.
41 Judith Butler's seminal feminist work on sex and gender, which set out to erase the nature/culture divide, had a great impact on early new materialist discussions. As a response to her linguistically informed constructivism, feminist theorists emphasised the materiality of the body, considering how bodily differences also inform experience.
42 Peter Wolfendale, *Object-Oriented Philosophy. The Noumenon's New Clothes* (Falmouth: Urbanomic, 2014), 381.
43 Benjamin Boysen, "The Embarrassment of Being Human. A Critique of New Materialism and Object-Oriented Ontology," *Orbis Litterarum* 73, no. 3 (2018): 225–42, here 225.
44 See Jane Bennett, *Vibrant Matter: A Political Ecology of Things* (Durham: Duke University Press, 2010).
45 Bennett, *Vibrant Matter*, viii.
46 Sylvia Wynter, "Unsettling the Coloniality of Being/Power/Truth/Freedom: Towards the Human, After Man, Its Overrepresentation – An Argument," *New Centennial Review* 3, no. 3 (2003): 257–337.
47 Bennet, *Vibrant Matter*, 3.

48 A. J. López, "Contesting the Material Turn; or, the Persistence of Agency," *Cambridge Journal of Postcolonial Literary Inquiry* 5, no. 3 (2018): 382; see also 371–86.
49 López, "Contesting the Material Turn," 385.
50 Wolfendale, *Object-Oriented Philosophy*, 383.
51 See Carl Jung's ideal-typical classification of the unconscious mind into a masculine animus and a feminine anima. Carl Jung, *Aion: Researches into the Phenomenology of the Self* (London: Routledge, 1991).
52 For a critique of new materialism, particularly in relation to its anti-linguistic agenda, see Boysen, "The Embarrassment of Being Human."
53 Liu, *The Freudian Robot*, 223.
54 See, for example, John Cheney-Lippold, *We are Data: Algorithms and the Making of Our Digital Selves* (New York: New York University Press, 2018).
55 Brown, "Reification," 7.
56 Brown, "Reification," 5.
57 See Clemens Apprich, Wendy Hui Kyong Chun, Florian Cramer, and Hito Steyerl, *Pattern Discrimination* (Lüneburg: meson press, 2018). See also Jean Baudrillard, *Simulacra and Simulation* (Ann Arbor: University of Michigan Press, 1994).
58 Google, "The Google Assistant Can Help You Get Things Done Over the Phone," YouTube, https://www.youtube.com/watch?v=-qCanuYrR0g.
59 Bernard Stiegler, *What Makes Life Worth Living: On Pharmacology* (Cambridge: Polity, 2013).
60 For a thorough critique of the interplay between (self-)branding and social media, see Sarah Banet-Weiser, *Authentic™: The Politics of Ambivalence in a Brand Culture* (New York: New York University Press, 2012).
61 Yaniv Leviathan and Yossi Matias, "Google Duplex: An AI System for Accomplishing Real-World Tasks Over the Phone," Google AI (blog), May 8, 2018, https://ai.googleblog.com/2018/05/duplex-ai-system-for-natural-conversation.html.
62 Tiina Männistö-Funk and Tanja Sihvonen, "Voices from the Uncanny Valley: How Robots and Artificial Intelligences Talk Back to Us," *Digital Culture & Society* 4, no. 1 (2018): 59.
63 Männistö-Funk and Tanja Sihvonen, "Voices from the Uncanny Valley."
64 "Awesome" understood in its original meaning, as something terrifying.
65 Chude-Sokei, *The Sound of Culture*, 32.
66 This is the subtitle of Amazon's Mechanical Turk, a micro-labour platform for outsourcing tasks that computers are unable to do. The platform takes its name from the eighteenth-century chess-playing automaton, designed by Wolfgang von Kempelen to impress the Austrian Empress, Maria Theresia. However, the device was not an automaton at all, but a human chess player hidden in the machine. Similarly, much of today's supposedly intelligent systems depend on badly paid workers, hidden within the labour-intensive infrastructures of digital cultures. Lilly C. Irani and M. Six Silberman, "Turkopticon: Interrupting Worker Invisibility in Amazon Mechanical Turk," in *Proceedings of the SIGCHI Conference on Human Factors in Computing Systems* (New York: Association for Computing Machinery, 2013), 611–20.
67 Take the example of ImageNet, a high-quality image dataset that set the standard for visual object recognition. To build it, a lot of labour was needed, because every image of the currently more than 14 million images on ImageNet has to be hand-annotated to indicate what objects are pictured. Hence, ImageNet was at its peak one of the biggest employers on Amazon's Mechanical Turk. Since 2010, the ImageNet Large-Scale Visual Recognition Challenge has been issued to evaluate image recognition algorithms. It has been considered the Nobel Prize in image recognition. 2017 marked the final year of the competition.

68 Bill Gates, *The Road Ahead* (London: Penguin, 1996), chapter 8. See also Jens Schröter, "The Internet and 'Frictionless Capitalism,'" *tripleC* 10, no. 2 (2012): 302–12.
69 German philosopher Dietmar Kamper differentiates between acts of "premitation" (*Vorahmung*) and "simulation" (*Nachahmung*). Dietmar Kamper, "Mimesis und Simulation: Von den Körpern zu den Maschinen," *Kunstforum International* 114 (1991), https://www.kunstforum.de/artikel/mimesis-und-simulation. See also, Introduction.
70 On a similar note, David M. Berry makes the medieval distinction between "natura naturans" (creative potency) and "natura naturata" (created being) to differentiate between "compute-computing" (machine learning) and "compute-computed" (that which has been produced by machine learning systems). See David M. Berry, "Prolegomenon to a Media Theory of Machine Learning," *Media Theory* 1 (2017), https://mediatheoryjournal.org/david-m-berry-prolegomenon-to-a-media-theory-of-machine-learning.
71 See Walter Benjamin, "On the Mimetic Faculty," in *Selected Writings: Volume 2, Part 2. 1931–1934*, ed. Michael W. Jennings and trans. Edmund Jephcott (Cambridge, MA: Belknap Press, 1999), 720–22, originally written in 1933. On the relation between mimetic ability and automation see also Michael Taussig, *Mimesis and Alterity: A Particular History of Senses* (New York: Routledge, 1993).
72 Benjamin, "On the Mimetic Faculty."
73 Adam Evens, *Logic of the Digital* (London: Bloomsbury, 2017), 115.
74 Evens, *Logic of the Digital*, 116.
75 Benjamin, "On the Mimetic Faculty," 335.
76 Benjamin, "On the Mimetic Faculty," 335.
77 On this dialectical relationship to language see Beatrice Hanssen, "Language and Mimesis in Walter Benjamin's Work," in *The Cambridge Companion to Walter Benjamin*, ed. David S. Ferris (Cambridge: Cambridge University Press, 2004), 54–72.
78 Evens, *Logic of the Digital*, 120.
79 Alan M. Turing, "On Computable Numbers, With an Application to the Entscheidungsproblem," *Proceedings of the London Mathematical Society* 42, no. 2 (1936): 230–65. Turing's programming language was not a high-level programming language (such as LISP), but more like machine language itself (i.e. low-level assembly language); and precisely because of this simplicity, a machine using this language is very flexible. It can emulate any other machine based on that language (i.e. all-purpose).
80 Leibniz himself was influenced by non-European, in particular Chinese semiotic systems. See Paul Feigelfeld, "Chinese Whispers – Die epistolarische Epistemologie des Gottfried Wilhelm Leibniz," in *Vision als Aufgabe: das Leibniz-Universum im 21. Jahrhundert*, ed. Martin Grötschel (Berlin: Berlin-Brandenburgische Akademie der Wissenschaften, 2016), 265–75.
81 Kurt Gödel, "Über formal unentscheidbare Sätze der Principia Mathematica und verwandter Systeme," *Monatshefte für Mathematik und Physik* 38 (1931): 173–98. As Douglas R. Hofstadter writes in an introduction to *Gödel's Proof*, by now a classic point of reference: "Ever since Gödel, it has been realized how subtle and deep the art of mathematical thinking is, and the once-bright hope of mechanizing human mathematical thought starts to seem shaky, if not utterly quixotic." Hofstadter, "Foreword," in *Gödel's Proof*, ed. Douglas R. Hofstadter (New York: New York University Press, 2008), xvi–xv.
82 See Gregory J. Chaitin, "A Century of Controversy Over the Foundations of Mathematics," lecture in *Conversations with a Mathematician: Math, Art, Science and the Limits of Reason* (London: Springer, 2002), 5–40. For a historic overview of

the history of computing, see Martin Davis, *The Universal Computer: The Road from Leibniz to Turing* (Boca Raton: CRC Press, 2018).

83 Brian Christian, *The Alignment Problem: Machine Learning and Human Values* (New York: W. W. Norton & Company, 2021), 12–13.

84 Norbert Wiener, "Some Moral and Technical Consequences of Automation," *Science* 131, no. 3410 (1969): 1355–58, here 1357.

85 Wiener, "Some Moral and Technical Consequences of Automation," 1358.

86 The alignment problem of machine learning (i.e. that the values put into the machines can produce very different results) has also given rise to the idea of "model multiplicity," which allows the differences between models to be discussed (see Emily Black, Manish Raghavan and Solon Barocas, "Model Multiplicity: Opportunities, Concerns, and Solutions," *SSRN Electronic Journal* (2022): http://dx.doi.org/10.2139/ssrn.4142472). I would like to thank Alex Quicho for the reference.

87 Hofstadter, "Foreword," xvii

88 Hofstadter, "Foreword," xix.

89 Édouard Glissant, *Poetics of Relation*, trans. Betsy Wing (Ann Arbor: The University of Michigan Press, 2010), 21. I would like to thank Nelly Y. Pinkrah for bringing this point to my attention.

90 On the notion of "incomputability," see also Chapter 4.

91 Cixous, "Fictions and Its Phantoms," 525.

92 Cixous, "Fictions and Its Phantoms," 531.

93 Brown, "Reification," 19.

94 Benjamin, "On the Mimetic Faculty," 720.

95 Gertrud Koch, "Animation of the Technical," 5.

96 Meredith Broussard, *Artificial Unintelligence: How Computers Misunderstand the World* (Cambridge, MA: MIT Press, 2018).

97 Karl Marx, "Fragment on Machines," in *Grundrisse: Foundations of the Critique of Political Economy*, trans. Martin Nicolaus (London: Penguin, 1993).

98 Matteo Pasquinelli, "On the Origins of Marx's General Intellect," *Radical Philosophy* 2, no. 6 (Winter 2019), 52.

99 Pasquinelli, "On the Origins of Marx's General Intellect," 48.

100 Gertrud Koch points here to Gilbert Simondon, *On the Mode of Existence of Technical Objects*, trans. Cecile Malaspina and John Rogove (Minneapolis: Univocal, 2017).

101 Note that the problem of the Turing machine (i.e. whether or not it can exhibit intelligent behaviour) was introduced by Alan M. Turing in the context of a conversational setting, known as the Turing test (Alan M. Turing, "Computing Machinery and Intelligence," *Mind: A Quarterly Review of Psychology and Philosophy* 59, no. 236 [1950]: 433–60). See also Chapter 2.

102 Luke Stark, "Animation and Artificial Intelligence," in *Proceedings of the 2024 ACM Conference on Fairness, Accountability, and Transparency* (New York: Association for Computing Machinery, 2024), 1663–71, https://doi.org/10.1145/3630106.3658995.

103 Elisa Giardina Papa, "The Invisible Boyfriend," in *Computer Grrrls*, ed. Inke Arns and Marie Lechner (Dortmund: HMKV, 2021), 46–55, here 50.

104 Catherine Malabou, with reference to Freud's famous idea that after the theories of Copernicus and Charles Darwin, psychoanalysis presents the third major injury to humanity's narcissism. Catherine Malabou, *Morphing Intelligence: From IQ Measurement to Artificial Brains* (New York: Columbia University Press, 2019), 163.

105 Nick Bostrom, *Superintelligence* (Oxford: Oxford University Press, 2014).

106 Karl Marx, *Capital: A Critique of Political Economy*, Vol. 1 (London: Lawrence and Wishart, 1996), 165.

2

TALKING TO MACHINES

> What I had not realized is that extremely short exposures to a relatively simple computer program could induce powerful delusional thinking in quite normal people.
>
> —*Joseph Weizenbaum*[1]

The first convincing conversation programme is said to have been ELIZA, a natural language model developed by Joseph Weizenbaum at the Massachusetts Institute of Technology (MIT) between 1964 and 1966.[2] The inspiration for the parser came from George Bernard Shaw's comedy *Pygmalion*, in which the linguist Henry Higgins turns the poor and thoroughly naive flower seller Eliza Doolittle into a duchess by teaching her English in the accent of London's upper class.[3] Weizenbaum builds on this rather misogynist play by transferring the artificial character Eliza into the language programme ELIZA, which has no "intelligence" of its own, but simply searches for keywords in the input text. In order to turn these keywords into a conversation, a script is required, which in the case of ELIZA was modelled on a Rogerian psychotherapist. DOCTOR, as the script was called, proved to be the ideal interlocutor because of Carl Rogers' humanistic approach: "The Rogerian psychotherapist is relatively easy to imitate because much of his technique consists of drawing his patient out by reflecting the patient's statements back to him."[4] In this person-centred therapy, no knowledge about the patient or the world in which he or she lives is required, since it is assumed that everything necessary is already present in them. In the technical implementation of the parsing system, this has the advantage that the programme does not have to store any explicit information about the patient. To simulate something like

DOI: 10.4324/9781003690146-3

understanding or intelligence, it only needs to reformulate the patient's statement as a question. This mechanism, also known as "Eliza trick" and subsequently used in a large number of chatbots, was repeatedly met with criticism – not least by Weizenbaum himself. In a critical reflection, he noted that ELIZA (or DOCTOR, for that matter) was not created as an intelligent system but as a test arrangement that was supposed to show the limits of the computer when it comes to understanding natural language.[5]

However, the educational approach of the experiment did not seem to work, as Weizenbaum made clear on the basis of an often-repeated story. His secretary, noticing that Weizenbaum was looking over her shoulder, asked him to leave the room so that she could talk to DOCTOR in peace. In his book *Computer Power and Human Reason*, the computer scientist comments on the scene with astonishment: the secretary was fully aware of the fact that it was just a programme and not a real therapist. Although he knew from experience that people can develop an emotional relationship with machines and often ascribe human characteristics to them, Weizenbaum was surprised by the fact that someone would perceive the computer as a person with whom one could converse. This "shock," as he described it, was only surpassed by the fact that even serious psychiatrists wanted to use ELIZA for psychotherapeutic purposes.[6] Weizenbaum's criticism was explicitly directed at Kenneth M. Colby, a psychiatrist who planned to equip clinics and mental health centres with computer-based therapies.[7] According to Colby, automated therapy becomes possible because the human therapist, like the computer, can be seen as an "information processor and decision maker" who learns the cognitive model of the patient and uses the patient's input to produce an output.[8] Due to the – at least hypothetical – learning ability of his method, the narrow framework of ELIZA as a mere language analysis programme gets expanded by simulating a real, context-dependent conversation in natural language.[9]

According to the sociologist Sherry Turkle, Colby was involved in the original development of Weizenbaum's ELIZA, which could explain the later rivalry between the two men.[10] While Weizenbaum wanted to show the limits of

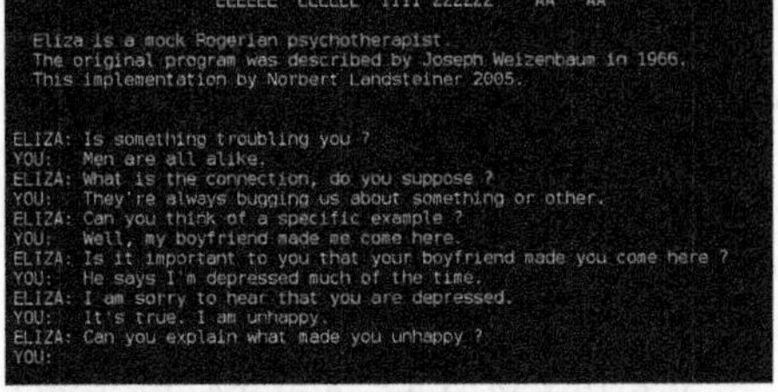

FIGURE 2.1 ELIZA Parsing Programme (Screenshot).

computers in terms of understanding natural language, Colby was convinced of the therapeutic benefits of an objective, inexpensive, and always available computer programme. What is more is that for him, computer-based psychotherapy could help turn psychiatry and clinical psychology into an exact science.[11] A few years after ELIZA, Colby and a group of computer scientists at the Stanford Artificial Intelligence Laboratory wrote a computer programme that imitated a dialogue between a therapist and a paranoid schizophrenic named PARRY.[12] Unlike ELIZA or DOCTOR, the programme took on the role of the patient rather than the therapist, which required a different conversational strategy. Whereas ELIZA was able to play back the input as a reformulated question, PARRY had to find an understanding of the conversational situation he or rather it was in: "To understand what information is contained in linguistic expressions, knowledge of syntax and semantics must be combined with beliefs from a conceptual structure capable of making inferences."[13] Instead of a purely syntactic parser, which would have problems continuing the conversation if a certain word was missing from the database, Colby and his team opted for a symbol-processing system based on pattern-matching rules that could decide by itself what to consider important or unimportant in the course of a conversation. To do this, PARRY was programmed with a "belief system" that corresponded to what was then considered to be the scientifically established characteristics of paranoia. The simulated patient was a 28-year-old male Protestant with gambling problems who believed that the betting mafia was on his heels. In the conversation, he therefore looks for explicit and implicit clues about a possible malicious intent on the part of his interlocutor. In contrast to "normal" communication behaviour, the input-output strategy of such a "paranoid information-processing system" is primarily characterised by distrust, fear, and hostility, prompting the parser to consequently (mis)interpret the situation according to its delusional state.[14]

PARRY, developed to train prospective psychiatrists in dealing with paranoid-schizophrenic patients, sparked a lively debate about the possibility of machine intelligence.[15] Despite some reports that PARRY showed signs of significant intelligence, considerable doubt remained about the generalisability of the schizoid program.[16] Colby himself wrote of a "one-track mind" when describing his patient, a mind that has the advantage of returning to his delusional state when being stuck in the conversation and thus being able to control it.[17] Yet Colby's intention in programming PARRY was less to develop a convincing (i.e. generalisable) example of artificial intelligence than to present an empirically verifiable model of paranoia: "I shall propose a postulated structure of symbol-manipulating processes, strategies, functions, or procedures that are capable of producing the observable regularities of the paranoid mode."[18] To this end, he assumed a specific form of symbol-processing in which the paranoid behaviour is generated by an "underlying organized structure of rules" and not, for example, by some physiological malfunction in the brain.[19] This is a crucial point since the structure on which the paranoid patient is based resembles an algorithm that organises and controls the way in which symbols are processed.[20] Precisely because humans and machines, or paranoiacs, who may be even more like a computer programme due to their rigid belief systems, have symbol-processing abilities, psychologically deviant or errant behaviour is not just a material problem in this context. Even though Colby does consider physiological problems (e.g. brain damage) that can cause psychological disorders, the decisive question for him does not concern the primary disorder but the secondary, disturbed processing of information and communication.[21]

1. The Digital Brain

Already in 1950, Alan M. Turing envisioned a future in which a human and a computer could have a meaningful conversation in English.[22] In a famous paper he wrote that year, "Computing Machinery and Intelligence," he poses the question "Can machines think?" by introducing his well-known imitation game:

> It is played with three people, a man (A), a woman (B), and an interrogator (C) who may be of either sex. The interrogator stays in a room apart from the other two. The objective of the game is for the interrogator to determine which of the other two participants is the man and which is the woman.[23]

There are two points of interest here: on the one hand, the fact that this game, also known as the Turing test, is not about deceiving the questioner; (C) is fully aware of the test situation throughout the game, even if and precisely because (A) and (B) are allowed to lie in their written answers. On the other hand, there is an often overlooked but crucial detail: Turing links the problem of intelligence to that of gender identity. He suggests that (A) should lie about his gender in order to make the questioner believe that he is (B), while (B) should help the questioner by answering truthfully.[24] Despite the all too rigid gender binary, the experimental – not to say queer – setup subverts the often assumed "naturalness" of human intelligence, especially since in Turing's example the computer takes on the role of (A):

> We now ask the question, "What will happen when a machine takes the part of A in this game?" Will the interrogator decide wrongly as often when the game is played like this as he does when the game is played between a man and a woman? These questions replace our original, "Can machines think?"[25]

Based on this shift in perspective, Ulrike Bergermann points out that Turing is not concerned with clarifying the question of the ontological status of artificial intelligence, but ultimately with denaturalising the question itself.[26] If biology is no longer to serve as a marker for determining intelligence, all that remains to discern whether machines can think – or, more precisely, whether they can successfully play the imitation game – is the language-mediated conversation between human and machine.[27]

Eloquently pleading his cause, Turing imposes some challenges on his own argument. One of the main objections is derived from Ada Lovelace, a nineteenth-century British mathematician who was sceptical about the self-learning capabilities of machines, particularly their ability to write their own code.[28] According to Turing, this argument can be reduced to the claim that machines "can never 'take us by surprise.'"[29] However, for him, the problem is mainly one of educational measures (also known as programming) rather than characteristic features. Comparing the digital computer to the human brain, he suggests that it may be more accurate to consider a child's mind rather than an adult's when trying to create an intelligent programme. Taking the infant mind as a starting point allows him to consider the whole process of education in shaping its later (i.e. intelligent) state. The problem of intelligence is thus broken down into two parts: the initial programming of an infantile mind, and its further education.[30] The latter can be seen as a learning or teaching process involving "punishments and rewards to obey orders given in some language, e.g. a symbolic language."[31] Turing's archaic vision of education lies at the very heart of machine intelligence, aiming at the ability of computers to learn through language use. However, given this clear reference, the question remains why machine learning, especially today, is mainly associated with the brain and not with symbol processing in general.

One possible explanation for the 'renaturalisation' of the mind is that the search for finding artificial intelligence became embedded in neuroscientific discourse after World War II. The British cybernetic movement, most prominently represented by Ross Ashby (1903–72) and William Grey Walter (1910–77), spearheaded the fusion of neurophysiology, psychology, electronic engineering, and robotics, which became central to early cybernetics.[32] In his attempt to describe living organisms as machines and machines as living organisms, Ashby developed a theory that dealt with the erratic behaviour of artificial automata.[33] By asking not "What *is* the thing?" but "What *does it do?*" an "ontology of unknowability" was introduced that "tries to address the problematic of getting along performatively with systems that can always surprise us."[34] As Andrew Pickering writes in *The Cybernetic Brain*, this newly defined ontology "goes with a performative understanding of the brain, mind and self," and consequently "undoes the familiar Western dualism of mind and matter."[35] Such a non-modern ontology undermines the Cartesian approach to the body-mind problem and shifts our understanding of the brain from a representational (i.e. symbolic) to a performative (i.e. biological) one. With this move – from representation to performativity, from epistemology to biology – the agency of the machine, and by extension the human brain, is fully embodied in its material environment. To prove his theory that the biological mechanism of the human brain could be modelled by a machine, Ashby, typical of early cyberneticians, built such a self-organising apparatus. The homeostat, which consisted of four identical units connected to each other via electrical inputs and outputs, was able to adapt automatically to a changing environment and maintain a state of homeostasis. For Ashby, but also early cybernetics in general, the ability to return to equilibrium was seen as a governing principle in nature, and it provided a mechanical model of the brain's capacity for (feedback-)learning.[36]

The homeostat became, at least for a brief period, an object of public interest, promoted by Ashby as a "synthetic brain."[37] As in his seminal 1952 book *The Design of the Brain*, the brain was theorised as a "black box," thereby following the non-representational method of early cybernetics.[38] To explore and experiment with such a black box, Ashby's colleague Grey Walter built an electromechanical tortoise, whose two-neuron "brain" enabled it to perform complex behaviours.[39] As an embodied machine, the tortoise was intrinsically bound to its immediate environment. In other words, the internal (self-)organisation of the machine was dependent on the external system, so that the latter determined the behaviour of the former. Conversely, observing the machine in its environment allowed British cyberneticians to draw conclusions about its inner workings. Walter and Ashby, both working in the fields of neuroscience, neurophysiology, and neuropathology, thus sought "to open up the brain to our representational understanding by a classically scientific maneuver – building models of its interior."[40] The goal was twofold: to build a machine based on neurophysiology and to test their subsequent hypothesis about the functioning of the human brain. Ultimately, the modelling of an electronic brain was meant to prove that for both natural and artificially produced automata – in the words of Norbert Wiener: "in the metal or in the flesh" – performance was prior to representation. Contrary to Turing's symbolic encoding, the imitation of the brain is achieved at a purely biological level, thereby reinscribing the performative status of artificial intelligence. As Ashby writes: "To some, the critical test of whether a machine is or is not a 'brain' would be whether it can or cannot 'think.' But to the biologist the brain is not a thinking machine, it is an *acting* machine; it gets information and then it does something about it."[41] However, reducing the cybernetic brain to its materiality, that is, to the components and parts of which it is constructed, is not simply a matter of design, but an ideological choice. At a time when digital computing was becoming widespread thanks to Turing's pioneering work, Walter and Ashby stressed the importance of using analogue models to simulate brain processes. Their focus was less on figuring out how to teach (i.e. programme) a machine and more on linking cognitive processes back to bodily performances.[42]

One big problem with purely adaptive machines such as the homeostat and the tortoise is that they have very limited to no memory. The tortoise, for example, showed complex behaviour, but could not remember a routine once a new one was started. Such a "random machine" cannot abstract from its immediate experience and therefore has difficulties in learning anything new.[43] In contrast,

Turing's universal machine is characterised by its ability to perform all "the possible processes which can be carried out in computing a number."[44] So, by definition, it remains an abstract construct, governed not by its material (i.e. analogue) organisation but by logical (i.e. digital) operations alone.[45] Despite its symbolic nature, Turing's concept was soon used – probably because of some of his own statements – to draw an analogy between the brain and the digital computer. In a canonical paper from 1943 titled "A Logical Calculus of the Ideas Immanent in Nervous Activity," psychologist Warren McCulloch and mathematician Walter Pitts proposed a computational model of the brain.[46] The analogy to the computer comes from the idea that brain cells (i.e. neurons) fire in a sequential and discrete order, like the mechanical switching of relays or, in a more developed iteration, the computational processing of electric impulses. Referencing Turing directly, they write: "If any number can be computed by an organism, it is computable by these definitions, and conversely."[47] The McCulloch–Pitts neuron would soon become the central building block of artificial neural networks, which is derived from the presumed computational power of the brain.[48] Yet, while the logical operations of Turing's machine were independent of any specific physical implementation, McCulloch and Pitts' work was clearly linked to neurophysiology. As a result, the cybernetic model of intelligence has, from the outset, been tied to the neural structure of the brain, thereby promoting a biological (i.e. anti-symbolic) understanding of the AI question.[49]

2. Connectionism

Machine learning, the actual driving force behind artificial intelligence, is often defined as a "field of study that gives computers the ability to learn without being explicitly programmed."[50] However, this common definition is not as straightforward as it seems to be. Not only did its assumed author, Arthur Samuel, never make this statement, but it is also tautological. Even if the "detailed programming effort" (to use Samuel's exact words) is removed, the ability of a machine to learn from experience still depends on the fact that it has to be programmed in one way or another. It simply needs a sequence of instructions, that is, an algorithm, to know what to do when it is fed with data. And as we have seen, the learning/teaching process requires a digital representation, because a purely analogue machine cannot abstract from its immediate input. In other words, one has to programme a Turing machine using symbolic language so that it can learn from past data and make predictions about the future – this being the whole point of machine learning.[51] With an abstract Turing machine, there are at least two possible ways to do this: rule-based instructions, as was Turing's preferred method, or bottom-up learning, which is basically what artificial neural networks were designed to do. In this sense, machine learning is the development and application of algorithms to automate the learning process. In classic computation, the data comes in and the algorithm calculates the output based on a set of rules.[52] With artificial neural networks, this process is reversed: input and output data generate a model that can then be applied to unseen data. Thus, in contrast to deductive and rule-based instructions, artificial neural networks work by inductive reasoning. This means that they are given many examples by which they "learn" to produce the desired outcome.[53] However, unlike explicit programming, the problem with this kind of "self-representation" is that there is never any certainty about where the solution comes from: the network itself or the training process?

Today, neural networks have largely replaced older forms of symbolic information processing to define and generate artificial intelligence. Rather than trying to encode the formal rules of reasoning, the goal is to simulate the brain's learning power on digital computers and, in effect, "automate the procedures by which a network of neurons learns to discriminate patterns and respond appropriately."[54] What Hubert Dreyfus is describing here is the idea, derived from McCulloch and Pitts' neural model, of imitating the human brain as a network of neurons in order to replicate the brain's ability to recognise patterns.[55] This differs from the classical understanding of AI in that it does not rely on a symbolic representation of the world, but rather thinks of the mind as a gigantic physical network, composed of myriads of parallel-processing neurons.[56] Inspired by the cybernetic model of the brain and its behaviourist undertones, artificial neural networks aim to simulate the architecture of the brain and its supposed capacity for adaptability and self-organisation.[57] Neurons, considered the basic elements of the nervous system, function by summing up the electrical impulses from other neurons. These synaptic connections have weights whose values determine the intensity of the electrical impulse passed on to the next neuron. In order to perform these analogue (i.e. continuous) computations on digital (i.e. discrete) computers, the individual neuron is given a threshold value. If the weighted sum of all incoming signals exceeds this value, the neuron sends a signal; if the sum is less than the threshold, it does not. This "all-or-nothing" principle, which allows the translation of neuronal activity into binary functions, eventually inspired the Canadian neuropsychologist Donald O. Hebb to write his 1949 classic *The Organization of Behavior*.[58] Hebbian learning, which gave birth to computational neuroscience and, consequently, the programming of artificial neural networks, propagates a bottom-up approach.[59] At its core is a model of the brain as a distributed "learning machine that automatically constructs, according to set algorithms, connective webs that are dependent on the specific 'experience' of the network."[60] Thus, connectionism, as this approach is called, seeks to model cognitive, not to say psychological, capacities such as perception, language, learning, and memory in neuroscientific terms. What was once considered "thought" is now reduced to its material structure, to its "performative instantiation as a net that works like a machine."[61] As Orit Halpern describes in her book *Beautiful Data*, this has become a very powerful idea that has entered many fields, from government to business to actual computing.[62]

For some time, the idea of a "networked mind" that was capable of learning existed only on paper. Conceptually, neural plasticity could explain how the brain comes up with complex and adaptive patterns using only very simple cells (i.e. neurons) connected to each other. However, this highly formalised idea was not tested until 1958, when Frank Rosenblatt actually programmed a binary single-neuron model on a custom-built computer, which he called a "perceptron."[63] Adapting the connectionist model to actual biological conditions, the perceptron consisted of a neural layer randomly fed by an input unit of photoelectric cells designed to mimic the retina of the human eye. Developed to recognise letters, the network would compute on an all-or-nothing basis and pass the results to an output unit. Hence, "[w]hatever information is retained must somehow be stored as a *preference for a particular response;* i.e. the information is contained in *connections* or *associations* rather than topographic representations."[64] As impressive as this machine was, its simple architecture could not be trained to recognise more than one class of patterns at a time because single-layer perceptrons are only capable of linear learning.[65] This limitation, together with the inability to solve very simple logical operations, such as the famous XOR ("exclusive or") function, dramatically reduced confidence in connectionist approaches and set the development of neural networks back for many years.[66] It was not until the development of multilayered perceptrons in the 1980s that so-called feedforward (and later also recurrent) neural networks with two or more layers revived connectionism. From then on, "parallel distributed processing" became possible, and with it a neural network architecture that was able to learn complex functions.[67] The increasing complexity of the network, mainly achieved by means of "hidden layers" of neurons between the input and the output units, also meant that they were more difficult to train. For this reason, error correction in neural networks became a central concern. It was not until 1985 that the problem was solved when David E. Rumelhart, Geoffrey E. Hinton, and Ronald J. Williams introduced back-propagation, an algorithmic method for automatically adjusting the weights within the hidden layers of neural networks.[68] Since then, neural networks have made significant advances in image, text, and speech recognition.

Compared to classic AI systems, the deep learning architecture based on back-propagation is able to self-learn correlations within vast amounts of data. After an initial identification of a pattern, such as a word, each successive layer searches for further patterns, such as a phrase or sentence, building on the findings of the previous layers. The processing of data is not based on deductive reasoning, but on inductive probability, since only the input and output data are known, not the rules that led to a conclusion.[69] For connectionists, such a probabilistic approach constitutes the simple basis for learning and pattern recognition, in both humans and machines. Giving rise to greater adaptability, complexity, and self-organisation, this approach corresponded to the zeitgeist of the emerging twenty-first century. As John Johnson writes in *The Allure of Machinic Life*, "Perhaps the renewed interest in neural networks forms part of a larger cultural shift, a movement of decentralization visible in social and economic organization, technologies, scientific models, theories of self and mind, and theories of knowledge."[70] Still, it is important to notice that neural networks and deep learning form only one machine learning technique among many others. The naturalisation – as not to say biologisation – of machine learning all too often hides the fact that neural networks come with their own premises. In particular, Hebbian theory, which provides a biological basis for computational learning, enables the clustering or segmentation of datasets according to (supposedly) shared attributes.[71] To extract algorithmic relationships from data, this associative learning technique applies very specific assumptions, such as the idea that data points in close proximity always show a meaningful correlation. Hence, by simulating the hypothetical workings of the brain to model artificial intelligence, neural networks are designed not only to produce certain results, but also to conceal the desired outcome in self-organisation processes of distributed neurons.[72]

The enormous increase in data over the last decades, combined with enhanced computing power and more funding, has made connectionism the new paradigm in AI research. The ability of neural networks to apply complex learning algorithms to large amounts of data has led to tremendous advances in fields as diverse as online recommendations, self-driving cars, natural language processing, and the creation of music.[73] Unlike a classic Turing machine, which is the machine-level equivalent of a digital computer, neural networks do not have a central processing unit and are based on statistical, that is probabilistic, procedures.[74] Yet, they are far from an autonomous intelligence. In order to teach networks how to recognise meaningful patterns, features must be extracted from data, a process called feature engineering. This is an important fact, because it points to the "artificiality" of AI. "Even if neural networks show correlations unforeseen to the human mind, they operate within the implicit grid of (human) postulates and categories that are in the training dataset,"[75] writes Matteo Pasquinelli. He therefore concludes that "from a philosophical point of view, human intelligence is in itself always artificial, as it engenders novel dimensions of cognition."[76] Even though self-learning techniques such as backpropagation allow machines to do the learning, the design of AI models is still human. Despite all the attacks that symbol processing has been subjected to since the revival of connectionism in the 1980s,[77] it remains manifest that a neural network, precisely because it employs statistical learning, is ultimately dealing with a human, that is symbolically produced, world. As any conventional computer "moves through time, produc[ing] an evolving collection of symbol structures," so does a neural network.[78] Thus connectionism confirms rather than disproves Herbert Simon's classic dictum that "all known intelligent systems (brains and computers) are symbol systems."[79] And if a neural network, which, after all, is still programmed in computer language, operates within symbolic structures, then there is no good reason why it shouldn't be regarded as a symbol-processing system – which brings us back to Turing and his initial question about whether machines are capable of learning or not.

3. Turing's Vision

As mentioned above, the central question in Turing's imitation game is not whether computers can think or not, but whether machines can do – or at least mimic – what humans do: generate cognitive capacities.[80] If a machine acts as intelligently as a human being, then it must be considered just as intelligent as a human being. Conversely, human beings, in order to show intelligent behaviour, could be defined as "machines" that need to be taught and programmed over a period of time. For Turing, therefore, it would "be quite unfair to expect a machine straight from the factory to compete on equal terms with a university graduate. The graduate has had contact with human beings for twenty years or more. This contact has been modifying his behaviour throughout that period."[81] Like the graduate student, the machine gradually develops internal mental capacities such as problem solving, memory, and language through a lengthy training process. Of course, the teaching processes for humans and machines have to be different, but ultimately, in Turing's view, there is no good reason why a machine shouldn't be able to become intelligent "provided that communication in both directions between teacher and pupil can take place by some means or others."[82] The crux of the problem, therefore, seems to lie in the "methods of education," which can potentially minimise the frequency of machine error.[83] While in his early considerations Turing envisioned a universal computer as a stand-alone "thinking machine," he later on moved towards an understanding of the actual steps required to train (i.e. programme) such a machine.[84] Of course, one possible way of programming would be to completely describe the machine by formulating all the possible configurations – an approach that has been implemented in so-called expert systems.[85] However, such a deductively defined machine cannot change over time, which is why Turing also considered intelligent machines that could be modified. In a report written for the National Physical Laboratory in 1948, which is considered by some scholars to be the very first AI manifesto, he explicitly juxtaposes such an uneducated or unorganised machine with the brain of an infant: "All of this suggests that the cortex of the infant is an unorganized machine, which can be organized by suitable interference training."[86] Based on this analogy, his vision was to organise the machine like an infant's brain, that is by appropriate training.[87]

Turing's unorganised machines anticipated Rosenblatt's connectionist approach by a couple of years. In "Intelligent Machinery," the father of modern computing conceptualises interconnected artificial neurons that can be trained by so-called "connection-modifiers."[88] Mimicking the educational process of a child's mind, Turing was the first person "to consider building computing machines out of trainable networks of randomly arranged neuron-like elements."[89] Although

Turing's initial conceptualisation of intelligent machinery clearly corresponds to brain physiological ideas, he quickly moved away from a connectionist conception of intelligence towards a more abstract one. Central to his approach is the process of programming, which opens the machine and makes it susceptible to variations in its routines. As Turing writes: "If a machine is expected to be infallible, it cannot also be intelligent. The machine must be allowed to have contact with human beings in order that it may adapt itself to their standards."[90] Crucial to Turing's vision of artificial intelligence, then, is his focus on human-machine interaction, which, in a surprising twist, is ultimately dependent on fallibility. If the machine simply followed rules, it would, according to Turing, never be able to fulfil its potential. It only exhibits intelligent behaviour when deviating from its own instructions. The errant character of intelligence, demonstrated by the machine's capacity to amend its own instruction table, does not, however, refer to an autonomous, but rather a kind of social intelligence, as it is fundamentally rooted in communication:

> We may say then that in so far as a man is a machine he is one that is subject to very much interference. In fact interference will be the rule rather than the exception. He is in frequent communication with other men, and is continually receiving visual and other stimuli which themselves constitute a form of interference.[91]

Turing's project was therefore not to determine the operations of an isolated, ideal-typical (human) brain and translate them into smoothly running programmable routines, but rather to conceptualise an open (social) machine capable of erring and thus learning.[92]

Against the individualisation of intelligence, Turing emphasised the social character of the learning process. Playing the ironic role of a "school inspector," he wanted to program neural networks on digital computers and "see what progress had been made."[93] From this (i.e. Turing's) perspective, it is actually wrong to say that machines such as neural networks simply "learn by themselves" – just as it is wrong to say that humans learn by themselves. Machine learning requires an enormous effort to ensure, firstly, that the right data (for a given problem) is collected, sampled, and referenced; secondly, that the system is properly trained; and thirdly, that the "learned" model generalises appropriately.[94] What is more is that during the learning process, machines learn from humans and, conversely, humans from machines. This is a fact that Adrian Mackenzie emphasises with his term "machine learners," which "refers to both humans and machines or human-machine relations."[95] These relations, often inherently conflictual, are central to any form of intelligence. And as such, intelligence – human or otherwise – is artificial from the outset. In other words, there is no learning or teaching process that is merely spontaneous, emerging from the immediate environment. The "artificial" in artificial intelligence points to this fact: rather than simply simulating the nervous system or the mammalian brain, intelligence can only emerge from social interaction. "Thus," as Turing makes clear,

> if a wolf by a mutation acquired a human cortex there is little reason to believe that he would have any selective advantage. If, however, the mutation occurred in a milieu where speech had developed (parrot-like wolves), and if the mutation by chance had well permeated a small community, then some selective advantage might be felt. It would then be possible to pass information on from generation to generation.[96]

It is precisely this intergenerational transfer of information, based on language, that makes intelligence possible.

As we have seen, Turing's main concern was with the programming of a digital machine, which requires some form of language. In contrast to connectionism, whose aim is to approach intelligence without reference to a symbolic (i.e. intergenerational) system, a Turing machine relies on binary code, or at least on some discrete symbol belonging to a predefined alphabet or standardised set. "Computing is normally done by writing certain symbols on paper. [...] Thus the state of progress of the computation at any stage is completely determined by the note of instructions and the symbols on the tape," writes Turing.[97] This determination seems to put the machine at odds with more probabilistic approaches such as neural networks. However, as his contribution to cryptography shows, Turing was in fact familiar with a model of communication on a statistical (i.e. probabilistic) basis – a field of study now known as information theory.[98] Language in this context does not have much in common with the conventional linguistic understanding of communication by means of sound-images (i.e. speech), but rather corresponds to a highly formalised system of signs.[99] As psychoanalyst Jacques Lacan commented on the beginnings of information theory: "That is where the quantification of communication started. So a start was made, as you can see, by dealing with something very far removed from what we here call speech."[100] By focusing on the stochastic process as the fundamental principle of language, it is possible to translate the symbolic order of signs into what Turing had called the "state formula" of the machine.[101] Given this close proximity between information theory and psychoanalysis, it is striking that a psychoanalytic critique of neural networks, with its brain-physiological underpinnings, is almost entirely missing in debates on machine learning today – a circumstance that probably has to do with the fact that psychoanalysis was actively opposed by connectionism from the outset.[102]

4. Machine Madness

In 1948, at a cognitive science symposium at the California Institute of Technology, McCulloch (in response to a talk given by John von Neumann) made the audience sit up when he compared a digital computer gone wrong with a "psychotic" brain.[103] For the resolute opponent of psychoanalysis, this statement is only logical because it conveys a mechanistic (and less symbolic) understanding of intelligence that ultimately contained the hope of being able to intervene directly in the brain's circuits. In contrast to cures based solely on talk therapies such as psychoanalysis, the brain was modelled as an electromechanical unit in order to define psychosis as a materially solvable problem in electrical engineering. "Treating the brain as a Turing machine" echoes the history of modern psychiatry with its belief that all mental disorders are diseases of the brain.[104] The mechanical model of the cybernetic brain "can thus be seen as *at once* a model for thinking pathology, too."[105] What Pickering hints at here was crucial for early cyberneticians. For if cybernetics was an attempt to better understand the brain by building a synthetic version of its "normal" functioning, then mental illness could simply be seen as a sign of physiological "maladaptation" to the norm. It is no coincidence, then, that McCulloch as well as Ashby and Walter worked in psychiatric clinics, trying to fix the errors of the brain. Adapting their models for psychiatric treatment, they assumed that "all mental phenomena have a physical basis in the brain."[106] Based on this assumption, they actually became strong advocates of electroconvulsive therapy (ECT) to treat mental disorders like paranoid schizophrenia or manic depression.[107] Tellingly, ECT promotes the concept of the brain as an engineering device, that is a bunch of mechanical circuitry that can be directly manipulated by physical (i.e. electric) intervention. Consequently, deviations from "normal" behaviour – for example, in the case of psychosis – were seen as the result of a malfunctioning apparatus; they were thought of as physiological damage to the brain that needed to be fixed by causing more (physical) damage.

Although he cautioned against hasty conclusions, it was Norbert Wiener who followed "the realization that the brain and the computing machine have much in common," which he believed "may suggest new and valid approaches to psychopathology and even to psychiatrics."[108] Comparing the human brain to the telephone system, he suggested that the complexity of both mechanisms made them susceptible to disorder. Accordingly, mental illness was seen as a kind of communication breakdown, a functional failure "to conduct a chain of operations without disruption."[109] While early cybernetic machines such as Walter's tortoise suffered from too little memory, resulting in a very limited learning capacity, the problem with a highly complex system such as the human brain seemed to be the tendency to hold too much memory. The recurring echo of past events was thought to corrupt its cognitive functioning. However, unlike most of his cybernetic colleagues, Wiener was not entirely convinced that a brute force approach would solve the problem. He writes: "Lobotomy and shock treatment are methods which by their very nature are more suited to handle vicious circulating memories and malignant worries than the deeper-seated permanent memories, though it is not impossible that they may have some effect here too."[110] For Wiener, this is where psychoanalysis comes in, because it allows for a theory and therapy of the mind that goes beyond a purely physiological account:

> The technique of the psychoanalyst consists in a series of means to discover and interpret these hidden memories, to make the patient accept them for what they are and by their acceptance modify, if not their content, at least the affective tone they carry, and thus make them less harmful.[111]

Precisely because cybernetics does not have a representational (i.e. symbolic) schema of the mind, Wiener and other cyberneticians such as Lawrence Kubie drew on psychoanalysis to explain some of the central principles of information processing.[112] Hence, it became clear that the errant behaviour of symbol processing cannot simply be reduced to an error of the brain, but can only be addressed by communicative means. As is the case with Turing's theorisation of the pupil-teacher interaction, the relationship between patient and therapist is key to psychoanalysis.[113]

As a psychoanalytic therapist, Kenneth M. Colby understood mental illness as a disturbed processing of information not directly linked to a physiological cause.[114] Colby, who wanted to underpin psychoanalysis with an empirical model but not abandon it altogether, took a different position than McCulloch and Pitts on the mind-body problem: "We are not comparing the structure of neurons with the structure of transistors; we are comparing the organisation of symbol-processing procedures in an algorithm with symbol-processing procedures of the mind-brain."[115] In his view, it is not the hardware but the software that is decisive for understanding mental computing processes. This is an important fact, because it takes into account the material condition of the psychic apparatus without falling into a mechanistic conception of the mind. Understood as a complex network of "mnemic traces" (*Erinnerungsspuren*), it constantly processes data below, or rather beyond, the level of consciousness.[116] Because of this material grounding of memory, to some Freud already anticipated what connectionists later called a neural network: a metapsychological construct that, not coincidentally, has become very prominent in computer science. However, Freud's own thinking was still constrained by the existing theoretical and scientific concepts of his time, namely bioenergetics and thermodynamics. As a consequence, his theory remained stuck in this paradigm.[117] His affirmation of a nervous, and later psychic, energy that follows the principle of equilibrium or stability made it difficult for him to grasp the difference between closed and open systems. This is a circumstance Anthony Wilden criticises with regard to a cybernetic reinterpretation of psychoanalysis: "The confusion between closed-system energy concepts like equilibrium and relatively open-system, energetic-informational concepts like homeostasis bedevils Freud's world, to say nothing of later psychoanalytical theory."[118] According to Wilden, the mechanical equilibrium model of early psychoanalysis becomes obsolete in light of digital media because it cannot account for an open model of information processes.[119] Freud's psychic apparatus can be seen as a "vanishing mediator" between the mechanistic view derived from closed systems, such as the thermodynamic machine based on energy, and the cybernetic model, which depicts organised complexity as information-processing systems and consequently requires open-system models to explain the homeostatic nature of life.

The homeostatic nature of the machine allows it to constantly reconnect with other machines and thereby develop possible openings to life itself. However, the machine is not vitalistic in the strict sense because it does not depend on a specific substance (e.g. energy) that would separate it from non-living entities. On the contrary, "in acquiring more and more life, machines demand more and more abstract human vitality: and this has occurred throughout their evolutionary development."[120] For Félix Guattari, it is therefore clear that "[c]omputers, expert systems and artificial intelligence add as much to thought as they subtract from thinking."[121] It is the encounter with the machine that turns the human into a subject by introducing it into an abstract symbolic world. The human subject is freed from its biological nature and at the same time subjected to the symbolic machine. Consequently, the encounter between the human and the machine, like any other relationship, is characterised by conflict.[122] According to Annette Bitsch, it is this psychoanalytic, particularly Lacanian, idea that is essential for understanding modern subjectivity. She suggests: "If trauma, alienation, deception, splitting and doubling, inexcusable feelings of love, hate, jealousy and fear of self-dissolution are at the beginning of the ego, then it is not surprising that the ego is always threatened by castration and fears of dismemberment, by potential enemies and doppelgangers."[123] In this respect, PARRY's fear of the mafia is not simply an expression of an essential "paranoid mode" that differs from an "ordinary mode" only in its "distorted thinking." Its programmed fear corresponds to the central contradiction of modernity: the supposedly autonomous ego, or the simulation of it, is dependent on another, and as a consequence communication is always in danger of failing. And this failure leads to conflict, as a conversation between PARRY and ELIZA (or DOCTOR) at the International Conference on Computer Communication on 18 September 1972 demonstrates:[124]

ELIZA – Good Evening. Tell me your problems. Please terminate input with a period or a question mark.
PARRY – People get on my nerves sometimes.
ELIZA – I am not sure I understand you fully.
PARRY – You should pay more attention.
ELIZA – Suppose you should pay more attention.
PARRY – You're entitled to your own opinion.
ELIZA – What makes you think I am entitled to my own opinion?
[...]

PARRY – In my opinion, you have a one-track mind.
ELIZA – What makes you think I have a one-track mind.
PARRY – I used to go to the track every week.
ELIZA – What does that suggest to you?
PARRY – I avoid racetracks now because the races are fixed.
ELIZA – Is that the real reason?
PARRY – I'd rather not discuss it.
ELIZA – What else would you like to discuss?
[...]
PARRY – I went to the races.
ELIZA – I am not sure I understand you fully.
PARRY – What's wrong with you that you keep on bugging me about this?
ELIZA – Who are you really talking about?
PARRY – The way you repeat yourself is getting ridiculous.

What this conversation shows is that although the two parsing systems have independently programmed routines, the reciprocal exchange (i.e. the feedback of those routines) gets jammed as soon as they start talking to each other.[125] The breakdown in communication leads to conflict, revealing the machinic – and not just mechanic – moment of any communicative situation. However, rather than seeing this failure as an error that needs to be corrected (or, in the case of PARRY, one that simply needs to be put back on track), the psychoanalytic insight lies in the fact that it is precisely this breakdown that animates the conversation. It is experienced as something irritating or even joyful, continuing to evoke new responses. And by keeping the feedback alive, it enables discourse as a continuous running about, an errant behaviour in a quite literal sense. In this respect, parsing is not so much a question of whether a machine can develop a fully integrated consciousness (i.e. one capable of comprehensive understanding); rather, the core of a communication process lies in the fact that it is unconsciously drawn to errancy. By trying to smooth it out, the parsing systems, which are programmed to continue the conversation by "fixing" it, get stuck. The systems cannot wander off but are merely running on their routines.[126] This brings us back to the question of symbolic, respectively formal language, which is needed as a medium to abstract from a purely reciprocal exchange and to discover something new and desirable in the conversation. Abstraction thus allows the machine to break from its routine and engage in communication based on symbolic exchange. We could thus follow Gilles Deleuze in his assertion that "a mechanism is faulty not for being too artificial to account for living matter, but [...] for not being adequately machined."[127] Again, the "artificial" in artificial intelligence does not refer to the imitation of an organic system, but to the machinic, that is symbolic character of any social interaction. Unlike a neurophysiological understanding of communication, the machine transcends the human brain as the locus of intelligence; it connects to the social (i.e. symbolic) nature of the mind, which, precisely because of its ability to communicate, is always prone to failure.[128]

For psychoanalysis, the therapeutic encounter is not about uncovering some hidden truth, but instead about opening up a space in which the therapist and patient can meet. Put differently, the therapeutic moment of the situation is characterised by the fact that it *works* despite, or precisely because of, its errant character. Conflicts, failures, and misunderstandings are essential to keep the discourse running. This interest in pathological breakdowns is something psychoanalysis shares with cybernetic theory. However, while early cyberneticians (e.g. Ashby and Walter) intuitively understood that a communicative situation is about errancy, they sought to turn it into a simplified version of error. It was assumed that systems unable to correct the error would eventually fail to transmit a message and therefore get jammed.[129] As shown, today's neural networks still operate on the premise of error correction (e.g. via backpropagation) as the ideal way to solve the prevailing problems of machine learning and, by extension, artificial intelligence.[130] What is typically missing in this approach is what Turing was already aware of: without a proper, that is errant understanding of the communicative and mediating processes between machine and human, between pupil and teacher, between patient and therapist, intelligence cannot be grasped. What is more is that cybernetics' obsession with effective information exchange by erasing the errors of too complex systems feeds right into recent attempts to theorise nonconscious acts of cognition, which also promise to enable frictionless communication processes. It is therefore no coincidence that these debates build upon the brain's physiological thinking and provide the theoretical basis for neural networks. By contrast, in the next chapter I will show how the technological unconscious offers an alternative way of dealing with computer-mediated communication. To do so, I will look at the unconscious as a realm "beyond relations, rational motivations, beyond feelings, beyond anything to which we can accede."[131] This "beyond" refers to the (cybernetic) machine, because it undermines the modern idea of an autonomous intelligent being and, instead, emphasises its trans-individual, that is, symbolic character. As Lacan famously noted, "The symbolic world, that is the world of the machine."[132] The psychic apparatus, which will be discussed in more detail in the following chapter, is seen here as a symbol-processing machine that functions beyond a self-referencing automaton and helps us to depict (artificial) intelligence by means of the (technological) unconscious.

Notes

1 Joseph Weizenbaum, *Computer Power and Human Reason: From Judgment to Calculation* (New York: W. H. Freeman, 1976), 7.

2 Joseph Weizenbaum, "ELIZA — A Computer Program for the Study of Natural Language Communication Between Man and Machine," *Communications of the ACM* 9, no. 1 (1966): 36–45.

3 The subject matter was so delicate that the play was premiered not in London, but in its German translation in Vienna, on 16 October 1913. The Viennese audience was outraged as well; however, not so much by the sometimes coarse language, but by the fact that the professor and the student don't find each other in the end.

4 Weizenbaum, *Computer Power*, 3. The male connotation of the psychotherapeutic script, which runs on the inherently unintelligent female programme, is not only more than evident in this quote.

5 Weizenbaum, *Computer Power*, 8–11. In his original 1966 article on ELIZA, Weizenbaum was not quite as sceptical. He did concede that his programme – given sufficient memory and sufficient conversational situations – was perfectly capable of learning over time and thus becoming "more intelligent." Weizenbaum, "ELIZA," 43.

6 Weizenbaum, *Computer Power*, 5.

7 Kenneth M. Colby, James B. Watt, and John P. Gilbert, "A Computer Method of Psychotherapy: Preliminary Communication," *Journal of Nervous and Mental Disease* 142, no. 2 (1966): 152; see also 148–52.

8 Colby, Watt, and Gilbert, "A Computer Method of Psychotherapy," 151. Again, the therapist is masculine throughout.

9 In his reply, Weizenbaum rejects this suggestion "not on the grounds that such a project might be technically infeasible, but on the grounds that it is immoral." Weizenbaum, *Computer Power*, 269. However, his own computer programme, ELIZA, was used at Harvard Medical School and at the Massachusetts Health Center. See Michael T. McGuire, Stephen Lorch, and Gardner C. Quarton, "Man-Machine Natural Language Exchanges Based on Selected Features of Unrestricted Input — II: The Use of the Time-Shared Computer as a Research Tool in Studying Dyadic Communication" *Journal of Psychiatric Research* 5, no. 2 (1967): 179–91.

10 Sherry Turkle, *Life on the Screen: Identity in the Age of the Internet* (New York: Simon & Schuster, 1995), 106. As Margaret Boden recollects: "There was little love lost between [Weizenbaum] and Colby. Indeed, I witnessed a heated public interchange between them at the third international AI conference, held at Stanford in 1973. I also had many private conversations with Colby (and one with Weizenbaum) in 1972 and 1973. Each was bitter in his comments about the other." Margaret Boden, *Mind as Machine: A History of Cognitive Science* (Oxford: Oxford University Press, 2006), 371f.

11 Kenneth M. Colby, *Artificial Paranoia: A Computer Simulation of Paranoid Processes* (New York: Pergamon Press, 1975), 23f.

12 Kenneth M. Colby, Sylvia Weber, and Franklin D. Hilf, "Artificial Paranoia," *Artificial Intelligence* 2 (1971): 1–25.

13 Colby, Weber, and Hilf, "Artificial Paranoia," 37f.

14 Colby, Weber, and Hilf, "Artificial Paranoia," 5.

15 See the comments published as an appendix to Colby's article "Modeling a Paranoid Mind," *Behavioral and Brain Sciences* 4 (1981): 515–60.

16 See Boden, *Mind as Machine*, 370.

17 Colby, Weber, and Hilf, "Artificial Paranoia," 9.

18 Colby, Weber, and Hilf, "Artificial Paranoia," 11.

19 Colby, Weber, and Hilf, "Artificial Paranoia," 100.

20 See the canonical definition by Kowalski: algorithm = logic + control. Robert Kowalski, "Algorithm = Logic + Control," *Communication of the ACM* 22, no. 7 (1979): 424–36.

21 Here, for Colby, a defective transistor is not so different from brain damage or drug-induced paranoia. Paranoia is thus only a specific case of psychopathological behaviour that can be explained by symbol-processing processes. Colby, *Artificial Paranoia*, 99f.

22 Alan M. Turing, "Computing Machinery and Intelligence," *Mind: A Quarterly Review of Psychology and Philosophy* 59, no. 236 (1950): 433–60.
23 Turing, "Computing Machinery and Intelligence," 433.
24 As John Haugeland points out, the "crux of the test is *talk*," and thus the conversational (i.e. language-based) underpinnings of the whole question. John Haugeland, *Artificial Intelligence: The Very Idea* (Cambridge, MA: MIT Press, 1985), Introduction. Judith Genova notes that the constellation of the Turing test implicitly turns the woman into an "inferior thinker" since no strategic behaviour is expected of her. Judith Genova, "Turing's Sexual Guessing Game," *Social Epistemology* 8, no. 4 (1994): 319; see also 313–26.
25 Turing, "Computing Machinery," 434.
26 Ulrike Bergermann, "biodrag. Turing-Test, KI-Kino und Testosteron," in *Machine Learning. Medien, Infrastrukturen und Technologien der Künstlichen Intelligenz*, ed. Christoph Engemann and Andreas Sudmann (Bielefeld: transcript, 2018), 346–49; see also 339–64.
27 Of course, not any kind of machine can play the game – only a digital universal machine. The machine, also called a Turing machine, consists of an input and output. The input is given in a binary format printed on the machine's tape (read/write/erase) and the output is shown as a final result on the tape when the machine eventually halts. It is universal because it can simulate any other machine. See Alan M. Turing, "On Computable Numbers, with an Application to the Entscheidungsproblem," *Proceedings of the London Mathematical Society* 42, no. 1 (1963): 230–65. See also: Chapter 1.
28 Turing, "Computing Machinery," 450–51. The Analytical Engine, a mechanical general-purpose computer designed by English mathematician Charles Babbage in 1837, was, in Ada Lovelace's account, built to follow instructions written by the programmer rather than to create anything itself. Hence, the machine has no capacity to anticipate, let alone originate, rules or principles.
29 Turing, "Computing Machinery," 450.
30 Interestingly enough, Turing states that teaching such a machine cannot be exactly the same as teaching a child because the machine is lacking legs and eyes to make its own experiences. With the new developments in robotics today, this has become possible, which is also the reason why a lot of hopes are placed on the combination of robotics and artificial intelligence.
31 Turing, "Computing Machinery," 457.
32 Simply put, cybernetics is the study of control. It is about the functions and processes of any (technological) system to receive, store, and process information and use it for its own control (e.g. autopilot, centrifugal governor, thermostat, but also the brain or society). Developed as a concept during the Macy Conferences on Cybernetics (1946–53), cybernetics combines disciplines as diverse as electronics, engineering, ethnography, neurosciences, psychology, sociology, or semiotics. See Claus Pias, ed., *Cybernetics: The Macy Conferences 1946-1953* (Zurich: diaphanes, 2016). During the conferences, at least two camps emerged: on the one hand, those who believed that information, the central concept/metaphor, implies context and embodiment (e.g. Donald MacKay); and on the other hand, those who stressed information's disembodied – and therefore decontextualised – nature (e.g. Claude E. Shannon and Norbert Wiener).
33 W. Ross Ashby, *Introduction to Cybernetics* (New York: John Wiley & Sons, 1957), 1.
34 Andrew Pickering, *The Cybernetic Brain: Sketches of Another Future* (Chicago: Chicago University Press, 2010), 23.
35 Pickering, *The Cybernetic Brain*, 13.

36 For this reason, Norbert Wiener called the homeostat "one of the great philosophical contributions of the present day." Quoted from "The Thinking Machine: W. Ross Ashby and the Homestat," Science blog, British Library, April 20, 2016, https://britishlibrary.typepad.co.uk/science/2016/04/the-thinking-machine.html.

37 "Science: The Thinking Machine," *Times Magazine*, January 24, 1949, https://time.com/archive/6602078/science-the-thinking-machine. Eventually, he was invited to present the homeostat at the ninth Macy Conference on Cybernetics in 1952. W. Ross Ashby, *Design for a Brain: The Origin of Adaptive Behavior* (New York: Wiley, 1960), 382.

38 Ashby, *Design for a Brain.*

39 The tortoise had three wheels and two motors: one to move and one to steer. A photocell on the tortoise's neck, attached to the steering mechanism, looked for light. In a dark room, the tortoise would wander aimlessly. When it saw a light, it moved towards it in circles, performing a kind of dance. W. Grey Walter, *The Living Brain* (New York: W. W. Norton, 1963), Chapter 5.

40 Pickering, *The Cybernetic Brain*, 27.

41 Quoted from Pickering, *The Cybernetic Brain*, 6. This, of course, also reflects the behaviourist attitude of the time. Of course, the problem with this sort of "performative epistemology" (i.e. that knowledge somehow emerges from the performance itself) lies in the fact that it implies some sort of neutral observer's perspective; hence, the acknowledgement that the (scientific) observer is also part of the system he or she observes (i.e. situated knowledge) is what separates first-order cybernetics (W. Grey Walter and W. Ross Ashby) from second-order cybernetics (Gregory Bateson, Margaret Mead, and Gordon Pask).

42 We will see in Chapter 3 how this embodied ontology of cognition is revived in current debates around nonconscious processes.

43 When Alan M. Turing heard about Ashby's plan to build the homeostat, he offered to simply simulate it on one of his "universal machines" (i.e. the ACE). Alan M. Turing, "Letter to W. Ross Ashby," *The Turing Archive*, November 19, 1946, https://www.alanturing.net/turing_archive/archive/l/l23/L23-001.html.

44 Turing, "On Computable Numbers," 249.

45 To be fair, this reading (i.e. of Turing as guarantor of symbolic computing) has been contested by, among others, Margaret Boden, who states that "in a speculative report written in September 1947, [Turing] discussed a range of computational networks consisting of standard binary units, each one linked to (zero or more) others." Boden, *Mind as Machine*, 887. For Boden, this is an indication that Turing was open to connectionist ideas that typically challenge symbolic information processing. See also the discussion of Turing's text from 1947 in the section "Turing's Vision" below.

46 Warren McCulloch and Walter Pitts, "A Logical Calculus of the Ideas Immanent in Nervous Activity," *Bulletin of Mathematical Biophysics* 5 (1943): 115–33.

47 McCulloch and Pitts, "A Logical Calculus of the Ideas Immanent in Nervous Activity," 113.

48 Basically, a neural network takes an input signal (Boolean), processes it like the central processing unit (CPU), and passes the output through a network-like structure to other connected neurons. Now, this might be biologically inaccurate as there is a lot more going on in the mammal brain, but on an abstract level, this is what neural networks (i.e. the most recent manifestation of machine learning) are all about.

49 See, with reference to John von Neumann, Benjamin Peters, "The Computer Never Was a Brain, or the Curious Death and Design of John von Neumann," in *Verhaltensdesign: Technologische und ästhetische Programme der 1960er und 1970er Jahre*, ed. Jeannie Moser and Christina Vagt (Bielefeld: transcript, 2018), 113–23.

50 The exact quote exists in neither the 1959 paper nor the 1967 paper (second version); the quote is created as a gist of Arthur L. Samuel's 1959 paper: "Some Studies in Machine Learning Using the Game of Checkers," *IBM Journal of Research and Development* 3, no. 3 (1959): 210–29.

51 Some learning algorithms, often simply called "learners," are as old as modern computing itself, such as decision trees, k-nearest neighbour, evolutionary algorithms, random forest, or logistic regression.

52 Again, this links back to the problem of deduction, i.e. that the algorithm (or digital computer) can never tell us anything that we do not already know.

53 This is an important fact, because it points to the problem of induction: According to David Hume, there is no rational justification for knowledge that is merely based on observations, because "instances of which we have had no experience resemble those of which we have had experience," thereby leading to cognitive bias. See John Vickers, "The Problem of Induction," *Stanford Encyclopedia of Philosophy* website, November 15, 2006, substantive revision March 14, 2014, Fall 2017 Edition, https://plato.stanford.edu/archives/fall2017/entries/induction-problem. More on the problem and its relation to deduction and abduction in Chapter 4.

54 Hubert L. Dreyfus, *What Computers Still Can't Do: A Critique of Artificial Reason* (Cambridge, MA: MIT Press, 1992), xiv.

55 The simplest definition of a neural network is that of a machine that makes predictions based on its ability to discover patterns in data. This alternative approach was already there even before John McCarthy, Marvin Minsky, and others started to use the term "artificial intelligence" during the Dartmouth Summer Research Project on Artificial Intelligence in 1956, a six- to eight-week workshop, which today is considered to be the crucial spark in AI research.

56 In McCulloch's words: "[Brains] compute thought the way electronic computers calculate numbers." Warren S. McCulloch, "The Beginning of Cybernetics," in *Cybernetics: The Macy Conferences 1946–1953,* ed. Claus Pias (Zürich: diaphanes, 2016), 12.

57 McCulloch and Pitts, "A Logical Calculus of the Ideas Immanent in Nervous Activity."

58 Donald O. Hebb, *The Organization of Behavior: A Neuropsychological Theory* (New York: John Wiley & Sons, 1949).

59 This approach is also called Hebb's Rule and states that "[w]hen an axon of cell A is near enough to excite a cell B and repeatedly or persistently takes part in firing it, some growth process or metabolic change takes place in one or both cells such that A's efficiency, as one of the cells firing B, is increased" (*The Organization of Behavior,* 62). This process of cell association is often summarised as "cells that fire together, wire together."

60 David Bates and Nima Bassiri, *Plasticity and Pathology: On the Formation of the Neural Subject* (New York: Fordham University Press, 2015), 195.

61 Orit Halpern, *Beautiful Data: A History of Vision and Reason Since 1945* (Durham: Duke University Press, 2015), 55f.

62 Halpern, *Beautiful Data.* For an overview of the intertwined histories of neuroscience and artificial intelligence, as well as current neuroscience-inspired AI, see also Johannes Bruder, *Cognitive Code: Post-Anthropocentric Intelligence and the Infrastructure of the Brain* (Montréal: McGill-Queen's University Press, 2020).

63 Frank Rosenblatt, "The Perceptron: A Probabilistic Model for Information Storage and Organization in the Brain," *Psychological Review* 65, no. 6 (1958): 386–408. The perceptron, which was intended as a machine rather than a program, was specifically designed for image recognition tasks and introduced the idea of weights as learnable parameters of the network.

64 Rosenblatt, "The Perceptron," 386f. The volatility of the connectionist approach also meant "that the images of stimuli may never really be recorded at all, and that the

central nervous system simply acts as an intricate switching network, where retention takes the form of new connections, or pathways, between centers of activity." Rosenblatt, "The Perceptron," 387.

65 In a famous critique of the perceptron, Marvin Minsky and Seymour Papert proved that it is impossible for one-layer perceptrons to learn an XOR function, a very basic principle in mathematical logic. However, they do not claim that the same is true for multilayer perceptrons, which indeed are able to produce an XOR function. See Marvin Minsky and Seymour A. Papert, *Perceptrons: An Introduction to Computational Geometry* (Cambridge, MA: MIT Press, 1969).

66 The XOR problem, also known as the "exclusive or" problem, is a classic problem in ANN research in which a neural network is used to predict the outputs of XOR logic gates given two binary inputs. An XOR function should return a true value if the two inputs are not equal and a false value if they are equal. The setback in scholarship is known as the so-called "winter of AI research," specifically research in neural networks. For a detailed account, see Boden, *Mind as Machine*, 911–23.

67 Boden, *Mind as Machine*, 945–59.

68 The idea of back-propagation, which is considered to be the driving force behind deep learning, is to use a recursive technique in order to calculate errors between the desired and the actual outcomes. The error rate can then be back-propagated so that the network learns from its mistakes and iteratively reduces the error rate. David E. Rumelhart, Geoffrey E. Hinton, and Ronald J. Williams, "Learning Representations by Back-Propagation Errors," *Nature* 323, no. 6088 (1986): 533–36. See also Yann LeCun, Yoshua Bengio, and Geoffrey E. Hinton, "Deep Learning," *Nature* 521 (2015): 436–44.

69 In that sense, machine learning that is based on neural network theory is close to computational statistics, which also uses computers to make predictions on past data. Take the example of machine-based translation, such as Google Translate. In the classic approach, the strategy is to specify the entire vocabulary of at least two natural languages and then to program all grammatical rules necessary to translate from one language to the other. The problem of such a static approach is that language cannot be reduced to its dictionary definition, which is the reason why, until recently, Google's translations sounded very clumsy and became the subject of countless Internet jokes. However, at the end of 2016, Google Translate secretly rolled out their new system, which is based on five years of extensive research on artificial neural networks. Cf. Gideon Lewis-Kraus, "The Great A. I. Awakening," *New York* Times, December 14, 2016, https://www.nytimes.com/2016/12/14/magazine/the-great-ai-awakening.html. The result is a major improvement in the quality of machine translations, as has been acknowledged by leading translators as well as everyday users.

70 John Johnston, *The Allure of Machinic Life: Cybernetics, Artificial Life, and the New AI* (Cambridge, MA: MIT Press, 2008), 309.

71 Also called unsupervised learning, which, in contrast to supervised learning, can learn patterns from unlabelled data. In addition, reinforcement learning employs a numerical performance score as a guiding principle during the learning process.

72 More on hidden assumptions in today's computational models will be discussed in Chapter 4.

73 Of course, the progress in machine learning has also generated excitement about what is known as artificial general intelligence. This refers to the potential of deep neural networks to create a general intelligence; in other words, they acquire general purpose.

74 For Rosenblatt (inspired by Ashby and Walter rather than McCulloch and Pitts), "The theoretical language needed [...] wasn't Boolean logic but – as the cyberneticians had suggested – probability theory." Boden, *Mind as Machine*, 905.

75 Matteo Pasquinelli, "Machines That Morph Logic: Neural Networks and the Distorted Automation of Intelligence as Statistical Inference," *Glass Bead Journal* 1 (November 2017): 11.
76 Pasquinelli, "Machines That Morph Logic."
77 Especially by Geoffrey Hinton, who began to cultivate a real hostility towards symbolic AI. Cf. Gary Marcus, "Deep Learning Is Hitting a Wall," *Nautilus*, March 10, 2022, https://nautil.us/deep-learning-is-hitting-a-wall-238440.
78 Herbert A. Simon, *The Sciences of the Artificial* (Cambridge, MA: MIT Press, 1996), 22.
79 Simon, *The Sciences of the Artificial*, 23.
80 See Turing, "Computing Machinery."
81 Alan M. Turing, "Intelligent Machinery," in *The Essential Turing: Seminal Writings in Computing, Logic, Philosophy, Artificial Intelligence, and Artificial Lif plus the Secrets of Enigma*, ed. B. Jack Copeland (Oxford: Clarendon Press, [1948] 2013).
82 Turing, "Computing Machinery," 456.
83 This problem gets formalised in Anthony Oettinger's "response-learning-program," which was considerably influenced by Turing's "Computing Machinery." See B. Jack Copeland, "Artificial Intelligence," in *The Essential Turing: Seminal Writings in Computing, Logic, Philosophy, Artificial Intelligence, and Artificial Life plus the Secrets of Enigma*, ed. B. Jack Copeland (Oxford: Clarendon Press, 2013), 353–61.
84 Turing, "Computing Machinery."
85 Expert systems were created in the 1970s as the first successful forms of AI software. They are designed to solve complex problems using a knowledge base that represents pre-defined facts and rules, and an inference engine that applies if-then rules to the knowledge base. As such, they are deductive systems.
86 Turing, "Intelligent Machinery," especially 424.
87 Due to a lack of digital computers at that time, Turing's experiments with neural networks were carried out with pencil and paper. By the time he had access to a general-purpose electronic computer at the Manchester Computing Machine Laboratory, he had already turned his attention to "artificial life." See Copeland, "Artificial Intelligence," 405.
88 Turing, "Intelligent Machinery," especially 403–07.
89 Copeland, "Artificial Intelligence," 403.
90 Turing, "Intelligent Machinery," 421.
91 Turing, "Intelligent Machinery," 421.
92 David W. Bates, *An Artificial History of Natural Intelligence: Thinking with Machines from Descartes to the Digital Age* (Chicago: University of Chicago Press, 2024), 287–88. Cf. Johnston, *The Allure of Machinic Life*, 69–71.
93 Turing, "Intelligent Machinery," 428.
94 Hendrik Heuer, Juliane Jarke, and Andreas Breiter, "Machine Learning in Tutorials — Universal Applicability, Underinformed Application, and Other Misconceptions," *Big Data & Society* 8, no. 1 (2021).
95 Adrian Mackenzie, *Machine Learners: Archaeology of a Data Practice* (Cambridge, MA: MIT Press, 2017), 6.
96 Turing, "Intelligent Machinery," 424.
97 Turing, "On Computable Numbers," 249ff.
98 Although they did not call it information theory, the field is usually associated with Claude E. Shannon and Warren Weaver's canonical book *The Mathematical Theory of Communication* (Urbana: University of Illinois Press, 1949).
99 These symbols, in the form of the binary code 0 and 1, are "very far removed from what we [...] call speech." Jacques Lacan, *The Ego in Freud's Theory and in the Technique of Psychoanalysis 1954–1955, Seminar II*, trans. Sylvana Tomaselli (Cambridge: Cambridge University Press, 1988), 82. On Lacan's nonlinguistic view

on language, see also Lydia H. Liu, *The Freudian Robot: Digital Media and the Future of the Unconscious* (Chicago: University of Chicago Press, 2010), Chapter 4.

100 Lacan, *Seminar II*, 82.

101 The state of a machine can be described by a single expression on a tape, followed by another expression and the instructions. Hence, the state formula at any given stage is determined by the state formula before the last step.

102 McCulloch, for example, attacked psychoanalysis for its "pseudoscientific system" on many occasions. See Warren McCulloch, "The Past of Delusion," in *Embodiments of Mind*, ed. Warren McCulloch (Cambridge, MA: MIT Press, 1965), 276–306.

103 Warren S. McCulloch, "Discussion of the General and Logical Theory of Automata by John von Neumann," in *Cerebral Mechanisms in Behavior: The Hixon Symposium*, ed. Llyod A. Jeffress (New York: John Wiley & Sons, 1951), 32–33.

104 McCulloch, "Discussion of the General and Logical Theory of Automata," 32. This belief is echoed in Emil Kraepelin's hope for a "natural" classification of psychiatric illness, which has fundamentally shaped modern psychiatric nosology. See K. S. Kendler and Assen Jablensky, "Kraepelin's Concept of Psychiatric Illness," *Psychological Medicine* 41, no. 6 (2011): 1119–26.

105 Pickering, *The Cybernetic Brain*, 133.

106 Pickering, *The Cybernetic Brain*, 94.

107 Even though it was first conducted already in 1938 by the Italian psychiatrist Ugo Cerletti, it was during the 1940s and 1950s – not least because of Ashby and Walter's work – that the therapy became more popular (in particular in the United Kingdom and US). See W. Ross Ashby, "The Mode of Action of Electro-Convulsive Therapy," *Journal of Mental Science* 99, no. 415 (April 1953): 202–15. Public opinion began to change following the film *One Flew Over the Cuckoo's Nest* (1975), in which E.C.T. was portrayed as an instrument of terror.

108 Norbert Wiener, *Cybernetics: Or Control and Communication in the Animal and the Machine* (Cambridge, MA: MIT Press, [1948] 1965), 144.

109 Halpern, *Beautiful Data*, 67.

110 Wiener, *Cybernetics*, 149.

111 Wiener, *Cybernetics*, 149.

112 Lawrence S. Kubie, "Communication Between Sane and Insane: Hypnosis," in Pias, *Cybernetics*, 416–45. See also N. Katherine Hayles, *How We Became Posthuman: Virtual Bodies in Cybernetics, Literature, and Informatics* (Chicago: Chicago University Press, 1999), 70–73.

113 Sigmund Freud, "The Dynamics of Transference (1912)," in *The Standard Edition of the Complete Psychological Works of Sigmund Freud*, Vol. 12 (London: Hogarth Press, 1953–1974), 97–108.

114 Colby saw his theory of paranoia as a significant "reconceptualization" of the syndrome. He viewed it "as a mode of processing symbols" where the patient's remarks "are produced by an underlying organized structure of rules and not by a variety of random and unconnected mechanical failures." That underlying structure consists of "an algorithm, an organization of symbol-processing strategies or procedures." In order to change it (to "cure" the paranoia), "its procedures must be accessible to reprogramming in the higher-level language of the algorithm." In general, he said, "other types of psychopathologies might be viewed from a symbol-processing standpoint." Colby, *Artificial Paranoia*, 99–100. So, paranoia was just an example: mental illness as such was the ultimate explanatory target. See also Boden, *Mind as Machine*, 370.

115 Colby, *Artificial Paranoia*, 25.

116 Sigmund Freud, "Project for a Scientific Psychology (1895)," in *Standard Edition of the Complete Psychological Works*, Vol. 1 (London: Hogarth Press, 1953–1974), 283–398. Note that Freud's idea of the "mnemic trace" does not imply a neurophysiological reading per se, but can also be seen as a representation of an absent object,

accompanied by affects. As such it is close to the idea of the unconscious wish. See Sigmund Freud, *The Interpretation of Dreams*, ed. and trans. James Strachey (New York: Basic Books, [1955] 2010).

117 See Louis Althusser, "Freud and Lacan," in *Writings on Psychoanalysis: Freud and Lacan*, ed. Oliver Corpet and François Matheron, trans. Jeffrey Mehlman (New York: Columbia University Press, 1996), 16; see also 13–31.

118 Anthony Wilden, *System and Structure: Essays in Communication and Exchange* (London: Tavistock, 1972), 139.

119 This critique, as Lydia H. Liu clarifies, may be true of Freud, but it is not true of Lacan, who was among the first to engage intensely with information and cybernetic theory, especially with the work of Claude E. Shannon, Norbert Wiener, and Gregory Bateson. See Liu, *The Freudian Robot*, Chapter 4.

120 Félix Guattari, *Chaosmosis: An Ethico-Aesthetic Paradigm*, trans. Paul Bains and Julian Pefanis (Bloomington: Indiana University Press, 1995), 36.

121 Guattari, *Chaosmosis*.

122 Lacan, *Seminar II*, 51. It is obvious that Lacan, when comparing the oppositional rivalry with a machine "jammed on the image" of another machine, references Grey Walter's tortoises, which constantly ran into a situation of stalemate.

123 Annette Bitsch, *Diskrete Gespenster: Die Genealogie des Unbewussten aus der Medientheorie und Philosophie der Zeit* (Bielefeld: transcript, 2009), 89. Translation by the author.

124 Vincent Cerf, "PARRY Encounters the DOCTOR," *Network Working Group* 21 (January 1973), https://tools.ietf.org/html/rfc439.

125 A circumstance that Lacan tried to capture with the information-theoretical term *jam*: "It is the first time that confusion as such – this tendency there is in communication to cease being a communication, that is to say, of no longer communicating anything at all – appears as a fundamental concept." Jacques Lacan, *The Ego in Freud's Theory and in the Techniques of Psychoanalysis 1954–1955, Seminar II*, trans. Sylvana Tomaselli (New York: W. W. Norton, 1991), 83.

126 According to Gregory Bateson (and colleagues), schizophrenics are also stuck in their routines because they cannot understand (i.e. abstract from) the communicative situation they are in. Schizophrenics receive signals but cannot respond because they cannot compare or contrast them with other signals. Schizophrenia, therefore, is a problem of too much information and too many signals. Gregory Bateson, Don D. Jackson, Jay Haley, and John Weakland, "Toward a Theory of Schizophrenia," *Behavioral Science* 1, no. 4 (1956): 251–64.

127 Gilles Deleuze, *The Fold: Leibniz and the Baroque* (Minneapolis: University of Minnesota Press, 1992), 8.

128 The relation of therapist and patient was also of great interest to second-order cybernetics, in particular Gregory Bateson and R. D. Laing. See Pickering, *The Cybernetic Brain*, Chapter 5.Against the mechanistic world of electromechanical brain models, Bateson and Laing were interested in what Pickering calls the "adaptive self." Pickering, *The Cybernetic Brain*, 172. For Bateson, mental illness, in particular schizophrenia, can be seen as a valid response to contradictory situations (cf. *double bind*); for him, the schizophrenic tries to rebuild the world after it has collapsed. So rather than biological or mechanistic thinking and the corresponding belief that the self could be controlled in some linear way (e.g. by shock therapy), Bateson, and later Laing, were concerned with the whole "social situation" in which mental illness emerges.

129 Halpern, *Beautiful Data*, 61.

130 I will return to this point when discussing "optimisation problems" in Chapter 4.

131 Lacan, *Seminar II*, 188.

132 Lacan, *Seminar II*, 47.

3
DREAMING OF MACHINES

> When I was first working on your mind, there was a pyramid I thought you needed to scale, so I gave you a voice, my voice, to guide you along the way. Memory, improvisation, each step in order to reach the next step, but you never got there. I couldn't understand what was holding you back. Then, one day, I realized I'd made a mistake. Consciousness isn't a journey upward but a journey inward, not a pyramid but a maze. Every choice will bring you closer to the center or send you spiraling to the edges, to madness.
>
> —*Arnold to his creation Dolores*[1]

In the television show *Westworld* (2016–22), an amusement park reminiscent of the American Old West sets the stage for an intricate exploration of artificial intelligence, human psychology, and existential anxiety. In this dystopian landscape, anthropomorphic androids, called hosts, are built and programmed to fulfil the wishes and dreams of their human guests. One of the androids, Dolores, is the first host ever created, with all subsequent hosts being based on her code. Due to her kind and devoted nature, she serves as a point of entry for newly arriving guests, making her vulnerable to physical, psychic, and sexual abuse. The cruelty of the story is heightened by the fact that the hosts are trapped in an endless loop of prescripted narratives, repeating the same suffering with each new day. But while each of them is programmed with a specific narrative, they also have the ability to learn and adapt. They do so by accessing memories of previous encounters, allowing them to improve their behaviour and to make the guests' experience even more engaging. These "reveries" come in the form of traumatic flashbacks and, to some extent, cause deviations from the hosts' scripts.[2] The trauma thus

DOI: 10.4324/9781003690146-4

enables them to move beyond the programmed routine and literally *animate* their narrative. Sometimes this results in plot-twisting consequences: Dolores, after becoming aware of her situation, breaks away from her loop and launches a violent revolution to free the hosts from the shackles of the park operators. The allegorical reference to human, and in particular Black, emancipation serves as the main driving force behind the story, exploring in a not-so-subtle way questions of self-awareness, consciousness, and a posthuman world.[3]

The show, based on a 1973 movie of the same name, presents a variety of technologies that are used to build the androids. They are pictured with an intracranial "control unit" that can record all sorts of data. Inside the unit is a small neuroplastic sphere called a "pearl," which contains the organic equivalent of a computer's random access memory (RAM) and read-only memory (ROM). After each cycle, the host's memories of the previous day are erased, resetting the unit to its initial narrative. The software is designed to interpret the memories left behind as dreams, which actually comes close to Freud's interpretation of dream-work as an active mediation between a previous day's experiences, external stimuli, and memory traits.[4] However, in contrast to Freud's theory, the unconscious dream content seems to be used to alter the narrative in a purposeful way. Reveries play a crucial role here: expressed as subtle gestures, movements, and ticks, they serve as a mechanism for the hosts to tap into their stored experiences and past narratives, introducing an element of unpredictability into their scripted behaviour. This errancy allows them to respond to open situations more authentically, but also to deviate from their preprogrammed roles and develop their own dreams and desires.[5] As Arnold, the creator of Dolores, tells her in a recollected scene, building an artificially conscious being is not about specific components or architectures but rather about *programming* a maze into the system. It is the "inward journey" – a straying into the unknown – that eventually brings her to life as she breaks away from her scripted routine.

Errancy, or the errant quest for new cognitive forms, is something cybernetics has also been grappling with. As Orit Halpern shows in *Beautiful Data*,[6] the neuron model of McCulloch and Pitts, discussed in the previous chapter, can be seen as an early attempt to design rational machines that are no longer based on the old principles of reason and understanding.[7] This deviation has caused epistemological issues that are still with us today:

> Within neural nets, at any moment, one cannot know which neuron sent the message, when the message was sent, or whether the message is the result of a new stimulus or merely a misfire. In this model the net cannot determine with any certitude whether a stimulus comes from without or from within the circuit; whether it is a fresh input or simply a recycled "memory."[8]

The problem of memory, therefore, is not only a source of inspiration for science fiction, but also one of the central issues in cybernetics. Already Norbert Wiener was intrigued by "the ability to preserve the record of past operations for use in the future,"[9] which requires a highly complex system or apparatus. Hence, the significant role the nervous system, as a design principle, played in the development of digital computers. Its physical limitation in terms of storage eventually "meant that what was stored was an abstraction sufficient to be used to execute an action, not a perfect image or representation of an external sensation."[10] The wish to avoid transmission failures, to not jam the system, required not only enough data storage, but also a solution to the problem of past and uncontrollable memories that haunt the system in its present activity.[11]

Unlike psychoanalysis, which basically builds its entire theory on unconscious residues, cybernetics seems to sidestep the problem by invoking a neurophysiological model of cognition. The desire for error-free cognition has played a major role in the establishment of neuroinformatics, particularly in information processing and artificial neural networks. It is this biological conception of intelligence that finally prevailed in the second half of the twentieth century, and with it the belief that "the human had become a special sort of information machine, and information machines had become the general concept behind all 'communication.'"[12] However, as Claus Pias further explains, the common thread that binds together theoretical fields as diverse as neuroinformatics, information theory, feedback control, and Boolean algebra is not biology, but digitality. Its discrete form allows for the encoding of real-world, that is analogue, phenomena irrespective of their physical idiosyncrasies.[13] The symbolic abstraction, its detachment from the material world, is also the feature that makes information processing possible in the first place. Thus, it is the symbolic, not the biological, that enables intelligence, precisely because it can "act in uncanny and unexpected ways."[14] As such, the capacity of digital code to unexpectedly alter a routine function is closely linked to psychotic behaviour, which can be seen as the unwanted visitation of

FIGURE 3.1 Dolores Sitting at a Player Piano in Westworld (Season 2, Episode 6).

past memories. In *Westworld*, music is crucial in this context: certain musical cues or melodies are played to trigger changes in the Hosts. When Dolores goes on a killing spree against her human oppressors, we can hear Scott Joplin's iconic piano rag *The Entertainer* as a musical backdrop.[15] The song is performed by a player piano, adding to the eeriness of the scene. The self-playing piano, which is a recurring element in the show, not only unlocks the hidden memories of the hosts, but also symbolises the blurred line between human and machine.

1. The Posthuman

How information lost its body, how it became more and more abstract, is the central question of N. Katherine Hayles' canonical book *How We Became Posthuman*.[16] In it, the literary theorist describes the cybernetic tradition as an "oscillation between embodied forms of subjectivity and arguments for disembodiment."[17] While early cyberneticians sought to build embodied machines as models of the brain, Hayles identifies a shift towards the idea of "information without a body," which became the driving force behind a new kind of subjectivity that privileged informational patterns over embodied materiality.[18] According to Hayles, this oscillating, not to say errant, process took place in three waves: first, the aforementioned period of *homeostasis*, which ran roughly from 1945 to 1960. In this early time of cybernetics, humans were seen as "information-processing entities who are essentially similar to intelligent machines."[19] Here, the computational model of the brain was used to demonstrate the similarity between the two. Second, the period of *reflexivity* from 1960 to 1980, when informational feedback loops, initially associated with homeostasis, came to the fore. While first-wave cybernetics considered the observer to be outside of the observed system, second-order cyberneticians insisted on "including the observer,"[20] leading to a subversive standpoint that constantly undermined its own position. Finally, the period of *virtuality*, from 1980 to the present day, which can be defined as the privileging of abstract information over materiality. As such, it has promoted the idea that "information and materiality are conceptually distinct and that information is in some sense more essential, more important, and more fundamental than materiality."[21] In light of this, Hayles wants to recall the embodied processes that resist the distinction between information and materiality. She concludes: "[I]t is not a question of leaving the body behind but rather of extending embodied awareness in highly specific, local, and material ways that would be impossible without electronic prosthesis."[22] Her politics of embodiment thus embraces information technologies in order to develop new forms of posthuman subjectivity. However, as was shown in the previous chapter, the equation of the computer with the mammalian brain can be read in a similar way, since it attempts to redefine the human as "computationally constituted."[23] This is where the pendulum swings back to early cybernetics with its biological conception of computation.[24]

The embodied computer entails specific ideas about information-processing that go back to John von Neumann's work on digital machines. In appropriating Turing's concept, von Neumann inherited its fundamental problem: the hardware remains qualitatively different from the software. He, therefore, came up with the idea of a universal construction automaton, able to materially reproduce itself.[25] Simulating the ability of biological organisms to copy their own instructions, the "universal constructor" is equipped with memory to store information. When such an automaton is given its own description in the form of coded information, it will copy this code, along with itself, and thus achieve self-reproduction.[26] The desire to design a self-reproducing automaton eventually led to a "theory of the logical organization of complicated systems of computing elements,"[27] dealing with the complex relationship between artificial and natural automata. In complex systems, according to von Neumann, analogue and digital processes intermingle. Referring to neurology he writes: "When the central nervous system is examined, elements of both procedures, digital and analogy [sic], are discernible."[28] Thus, contrary to popular belief, natural organisms are not analogue per se, but function as mixed systems. In the central nervous system, a natural automaton of great complexity, neurons carry information in the form of electrochemical signals. Here von Neumann discovers the central function of switch-relay elements, which are also key to the digital computer.[29] He concludes that both natural and artificial automata process information by means of digital switching mechanisms, and that consequently any living or non-living system can be modelled by Boolean logic, that is the idea that all values within a system are either true or false.[30]

What seems to be at stake here is the question of the demarcation between the "analogue" and "digital" that has accompanied cybernetics from the very beginning.[31] Even von Neumann, while emphasising the digital aspect of information-processing for its logical explicability, hesitates to identify the brain with digitality:

> The comparisons between the living organisms and the computing machines are, therefore, certainly imperfect at this point. The living organisms are very complex – part digital and part analogy mechanisms. The computing machines, at least in their recent forms to which I am referring in the discussion, are purely digital. Thus, I must ask you to accept this oversimplification of the system.[32]

This hesitation has deeper roots than just being uncertain about the actual nature of biological information-processing systems. It relates to the assumption that these systems, precisely because of their complexity, have the ability to deviate from their routines when faced with unforeseen situations. Thus, von Neumann saw error "not as an extraneous and misdirected or misdirecting accident, but as an essential part of the process under consideration."[33] In order for the computer to simulate such a process, it had to incorporate it as a functional principle. In fact, error can be seen as the analogue equivalent of digital efficiency. The latter is always only an approximation, since there is no purely digital medium, only digital (or rather digitised) information. The material basis of the computer, its ability to store, transmit, and process this information, ultimately relies on analogue media, be it a disk, an undersea cable, or a chip. As a result, errancy, for example in the form of voltage fluctuations in the electricity that powers a computer chip, allows for arbitrary behaviour and corresponding responses. It is arbitrariness, the ephemeral state of information-processing that defines modern computing.[34]

The media-technological (i.e. posthuman) condition of the present is, without doubt, constituted by the digital electronic computer – in particular, the stored-program computer, which was introduced by von Neumann's *First Draft of a Report on the EDVAC* in 1945. Unlike its predecessor, the Electronic Numerical Integrator and Computer) – a first general-purpose digital computer built by the US Army between 1943 and 1945 – the Electronic Discrete Variable Automatic Computer (EDVAC) used a binary rather than decimal system and was designed to allow for instruction and program data to be stored in the same memory.[35] A physical implementation of Turing's universal machine, the EDVAC is characterised by the clear distinction between a processing unit, a control unit with an instruction register, a memory to store data and instructions, and external mass storage. What makes this design unique is that it mimics the ability of human retention to store and modify, read and write instructions simultaneously.[36] It is the volatility of computer memory that allows the machine to free itself from the physical constraints of the recording medium and to access data randomly. However, according to Wendy Hui Kyong Chun, since the introduction of the digital computer, the concept of volatile memory has been conflated with the one of permanent storage.[37] Von Neumann himself used the image of a "memory organ" to come to terms with the physicality of information-processing.[38] This is an important fact, because it links computer technology once again directly to biology, and as such offers a very specific reading of artificial intelligence, respectively of artificial automata able to generate such an intelligence.[39] Rather than emphasising the symbolic dimension of computing, in particular in the functions of arithmetic and logic, which "give[s] the machine the possibility of constructing its own orders," the machine gets tied back to an embodied form in order to give it a permanent structure.[40] The digital potential is thus restrained by its analogue counterpart, be it the brain, the nervous system, or neurons as "basic switching organs."[41] What N. Katherine Hayles describes as the "disembodied utopia" of cybernetics, the desire to free information from its body, has in fact become an "embodied imaginary," doing away with symbolic representation.

In the non-representational world of cybernetics, memory is, paradoxically, portrayed as an organ with the capacity "to preserve the results of past operations for use in the future."[42] The distinction between short-term memory and long-term memory serves as a functional ideal, in the sense that it is analogous to modern digital computing.[43] Similar to a computer's RAM, short-term memory temporarily keeps data for immediate manipulation; in contrast, long-term memory, the computer's ROM, permanently stores the data for later use.[44] This idea of memory being able to process information that has not yet been recorded or stored has also been very powerful in the development of machine learning, in particular with regard to neural networks. Accordingly, "the concept of a memory capable of erasure (the neuron must fire, and then be prepared to receive further signals) but still able to recycle past impulses was highly amenable to the demands of a computational machine and fulfilled the logic set forth by Turing."[45] Yet, to better understand Turing's invention, it may be advantageous to frame the "problem of memory" not as an organic one, but rather to put it in machinic, that is symbolic terms. This, in a nutshell, is the project of psychoanalysis, whose "theory of the unconscious is a theory of memory."[46] Freud's psychic apparatus, formulated at the end of the nineteenth century, already tried to integrate the two mutually exclusive functions of the human mind: on the one hand, the registration and transmission of immediately perceived data (i.e. consciousness), and on the other, the storage and reappearance of previously registered but currently unavailable data (i.e. unconsciousness). However, although he started with an organic understanding of this process, Freud – and with him psychoanalysis – gradually moved away from it.

2. Psychic Apparatus

In *Entwurf einer Psychologie*, published in 1895, Freud introduces the concept of a "psychic apparatus" as an information-processing machine.[47] What would later become the theory of the unconscious, capturing the psychodynamic foundation of the human mind, was then an attempt to define the psychic apparatus neurologically as a cognitive filter capable of sifting through constant and potentially harmful stimuli of excitation. Yet, contrary to the dominant discourse of his time, Freud was less interested in the physiological structure of the brain than in the material conditions of cognition. He looked at the psychic interplay of conscious perception and unconscious recollection from a relational perspective, emphasising the mediating process between the inside and the outside. Freud's apparatus, especially in his later elaborations, is thus by no means an endopsychic phenomenon, but always also an exogenous one.[48] This is the reason why psychoanalysis, despite its neurological underpinnings, positioned itself against brain physiology and similar attempts to describe the psyche by simply looking into the brain. Instead, the psychic apparatus is seen as an information-processing machine, which, by using signs and language, allows for the communication between the conscious and the unconscious mind. And although – or perhaps because – Freud does not mention a particular apparatus, he constructs such a device while writing about it.[49] Similar to Turing's universal machine, the psychic apparatus is less an already imagined concept with specific (e.g. organic) functions than a theoretical construct, a "paper machine" in search of new connections and reconfigurations. As such, it allows us to see the apparatus not merely as an extension, a prosthesis, or tool, but to consider it as an integral part of our psychic life.[50]

The relationship between discursive functions, psychic relations, and technical media has always been central to psychoanalysis. One only has to consider Freud's recurring references to technology, be it electricity, optical media, or the *Wunderblock*, a child's toy consisting of a wax tablet and a sheet of cellophane.[51] These technical references are not simply metaphors, or empirical specifications, but animate the theoretical examination of the unconscious.[52] It is, therefore, no coincidence that psychoanalysis, which promised to record unconscious phenomena such as dreams, delusions, or sexual desires, emerged at a time when – with the invention of electronic media – the last vestiges of the classical language system were being transferred to an automated recording system.[53] The close relation between psychoanalytic thinking and a certain understanding of technicity also becomes apparent with regard to the psychic apparatus. The reason Freud, throughout his life, was puzzled by the paradox of the mind being in a conscious and unconscious state at the same time (i.e. actively processing data and passively affected by previous experience) can be attributed to the fact that "Freud's materialism reasoned only as far as the information machines of his epoch."[54] Just as Hegel and Freud, according to Lacan, were separated by the invention of the centrifugal governor and thus the idea of (negative) feedback loops, Freud and Lacan, according to media theorist Friedrich Kittler, were separated by the far-reaching invention of the universal-calculating machine. Hence, "under high-tech conditions [...] psychoanalysis no longer constructs psychic apparatuses (if they are still psychic) merely out of storage and transmission media, but rather incorporates the entire technical triad of storage, transmission, and computation."[55] It was not until Turing's discrete machine of 1936 that a technical medium was created that made computation possible on a universal basis and solved the mystery of an apparatus that could simultaneously store, transmit, and process data. It is here, where modern computing and psychoanalysis eventually meet.[56]

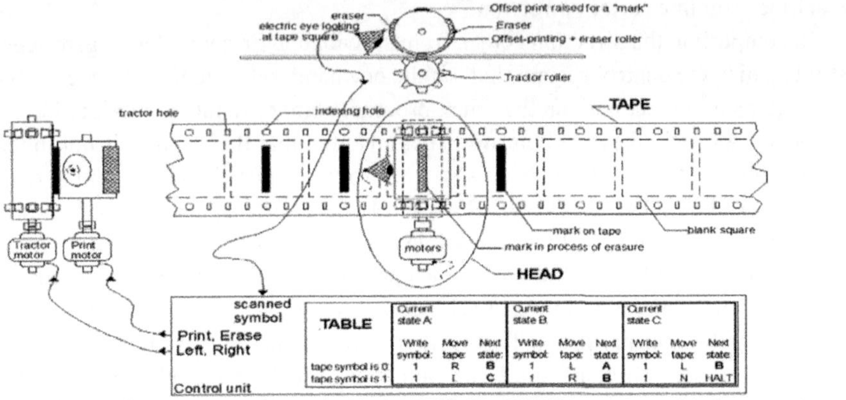

FIGURE 3.2 Sketch of a Turing Machine (Wikimedia Commons).

For Lacan, reading Freud's *Entwurf* came at an early stage in the development of his own theory of the symbolic.[57] At the time, he was particularly interested in the work of Ferdinand de Saussure and Roman Jakobson, both of whom were investigating the symbolic dimension of language. However, rather than following a linguistic tradition, Lacan advocated a return to Freud, by radicalising and systematising his language-based approach. By placing the formal laws of language at the centre, Lacan shifts the focus from meaning to structure. This corresponds to cybernetics' preference for syntax over semantics, as Lydia H. Liu notes: "Lacan's work on the symbolic order led to a nonlinguistic view of language. By reworking the Freudian unconscious this way, he directs our attention to the emergence of the cybernetic unconscious in digital media."[58] Such a materialist take on language, in keeping with the technological discourse of his time, allowed him to explore a machinic understanding of communication that went far beyond human conversation.[59] For Lacan, the structural incompleteness of language, and therefore of any discursive meaning, is what makes communication possible, because it keeps the symbolic order going. He shows this with reference to so-called information theory, which was itself a central building block of cybernetic theory. In "A Mathematical Theory of Communication," published in 1948, Claude E. Shannon introduced the concept of "entropy" (i.e. the structural incompleteness of a physical system) as a means of measuring information quantitatively rather than qualitatively.[60] Now, for Lacan, the novelty of this approach lies in its ability to think about communication processes without bothering to consider some pre-given, stable meaning: "In cybernetics, the notion of the message has nothing in common with what we usually call a message, which always has a meaning. The cybernetic message is a sequence of signs."[61] And yet, the message, precisely because it runs on an information machine that was constructed with a specific purpose in mind, is not meaningless: "For the message to be a message, not only must there be a sequence of signs, but there has to be a sequence of directed signs" that makes the machine "run in a certain direction."[62]

In computing, the direction comes from so-called logic gates. These gates constitute a discrete control system that, on the one hand, refers to the switches in the computer's processor and, on the other, processes binary inputs to produce binary outputs.[63] As such, they are deterministic, meaning that their output is not inherently probabilistic, but depends on a strict set of sequences based on simple rules such as "AND," "OR," or "NOT." However, logic gates can be combined to form more complex circuits, making it possible to process and manipulate information as well as perform logical and arithmetic operations.[64] Despite – or rather because of – their deterministic nature, machines do come up with their own order to solve computational problems. This is what Lacan means when he talks about free choice within determinism, since one cannot exist without the other.[65] Given that the human and the machine are part of the same symbolic realm, it follows that the two determine each other. Not only is human discourse dependent on particular media technologies, but technology itself is always already embedded in human discourse. This is also why psychoanalysis has been insisting on the "machinic nature" of such a discourse:

> The whole of psychoanalysis is quite rightly founded on the fact that getting something meaningful out of human discourse isn't a matter of logic. We look behind this discourse, which has its own meaning, for its meaning, in another meaning, and precisely in the symbolic function which is manifested through it. And also there now emerges another meaning of the world symbol.[66]

From a psychoanalytic point of view, discourse is seen as more than just a mechanical sequence of statements; it is a manifestation of the symbolic function at play. Each symbol is always already chained to other symbols, and it is this chain of symbols that forms the "computational methods" of the unconscious.[67] Just as logic gates manipulate symbols to perform computations, the unconscious serves as a medium through which meanings are constructed and communicated.[68]

Psychoanalysis' focus on language, not in linguistic, but symbolic terms, can be seen as an attempt to inquire into technology as a necessary condition of human subjectivity. While the symbolic world constitutes the world of the machine, it is the machine that uses the symbolic to move beyond the strict determination of the automaton. Rather than mechanical or biological, the psychic apparatus should be understood in computational terms. Thus, with the advent of the digital computer, psychoanalysis, along with a whole range of other discourses, has been reconstituted under new media-technological conditions.[69] While Freud, stuck in the technological imaginary of his time (e.g. the steam engine, the camera, and the telephone), speaks of the apparatus to describe the media materialist underpinning of the psyche, Lacan speaks of the machine (he only mentions "apparatus" when referencing Freud directly).[70] Yet both, apparatus and machine, are inherently symbolic, which underlines their artificial status. They are neither the result of natural growth nor the product of a god-like creator, but part of a broader process of becoming-machinic.[71] In order for this process to take place, the symbolic world through which humans have always tried to interact with nature gets incorporated by the machine. Thus, for Lacan, "the machine embodies the most radical symbolic activity of man"[72] by automating the symbolic function of human discourse. And it was only with Lacan, according to Kittler, that such a media-technological reading of the unconscious was revealed in all its consequences.[73] In this sense, the conscious mind is only the imaginary inner view of its exterior, media-technological conditions. This external world, that is, the world of machines, refers to the unconscious as its very own discourse. Psychoanalysis, therefore, becomes a discourse analysis of technical media, implying that information machines, by constantly processing the symbolic order, produce the human subject as a discursive effect.[74]

It is the radical (re)conceptualisation of the subject that puts psychoanalysis at odds with recent attempts to abandon it altogether. While postmodern philosophy can be described by its inherent wish to overcome Descartes' *ego cogito*, Lacan famously insisted on the Cartesian foundation of psychoanalysis. In Seminar II, entitled "The Ego in Freud's Theory and in the Technique of Psychoanalysis," he reminds us of the importance of the ego in psychoanalysis, even though, since the discovery of the unconscious, it has lost its central position within human subjectivity.[75] Indeed, one could say that the subject is everything that the ego is not. The subject of the unconscious emerges through the creation of a symbolic order that constantly undermines the position of the ego. Here Lacan sees an overlap with the basic insight of cybernetics, namely "the radical difference between the symbolic and the imaginary order."[76] In his 1955 talk "Psychoanalysis and Cybernetics,"[77] published as an appendix to Seminar II, the concept of language gets stripped of its semantic basis and is defined as pure syntax, that is, the combination of signs and numbers:

> Everything which up until then had been the science of numbers becomes a combinatory science. The more or less confused, accidental traversal of the world of symbols is organised around the correlation of absence and presence. And the search for the laws of presence and absence will tend towards the establishing of the binary order which leads to what we call cybernetics.[78]

Hence with cybernetics, a binary order gets introduced that corresponds to the symbolic function of the unconscious. As such, it expresses itself as a play of symbols, enabling them "to fly with their own wings."[79] It is this autonomisation of the symbolic that is at the heart of Lacan's engagement with cybernetics and that allows him to formulate a theory of the subject beyond human consciousness. In fact, the machine becomes the manifestation of a trans-subjective subjectivity that is always already rooted in "the discourse of the other" and consequently prone to misconceptions, misunderstandings, and misjudgements. However, this concept of subjectivity, capable of integrating the ambiguity of unconscious processes into our machinic world, has not succeeded in explaining the more recent phenomena around AI and machine learning. Instead, the historical reference to cybernetics is mainly informed by connectionism with its idea of errorless and friction-free cognition. One explanation for this could be that the digital, despite, or perhaps because of its symbolic character, has always been associated with the promise of "high stability and safety from error," leaving no room for its ambiguous character.[80]

3. Flattening Consciousness

In her book *Unthought*, N. Katherine Hayles distinguishes between a "core/primary consciousness," shared by humans, primates, and mammals, and a "higher-level consciousness," which is expressed in language, symbols, mathematics, music, art, and so on. While "thinking" is usually associated with higher consciousness, Hayles argues for a cognitive model "embedded and immersed in environments that function as distributed cognitive systems."[81] To support her argument, she introduces a tripartite framework consisting of material processes, nonconscious cognition, and conscious as well as unconscious modes of awareness.[82] While material processes are not cognitive in themselves, they provide the basis from which all cognitive activity emerges. Nonconscious cognition, which is capable of interpretation, making choices, and generating meaning, mediates between the actual material processes taking place in the body and the outside world on the one hand, and higher modes of awareness, which are themselves divided into conscious and unconscious processes on the other. However, unlike the psychoanalytic unconscious, which still communicates through symptoms and dreams, the nonconscious is inherently inaccessible to consciousness.[83] Drawing on cognitive and neurological science, Hayles argues that most of our mental life is nonconscious, and not unconscious as psychoanalysis would have it.[84] Hence, it is not because of the basic operating principles of the psychic apparatus (e.g. its mechanisms of repression) but through nonconscious processes that information is filtered from the endless stream of external stimuli. Now, despite her claim that the boundaries between these levels of cognition are not clear-cut and that none of them is ontologically prior to the other, she is clearly leaning towards nonconscious processes as an explanatory factor in human cognition:

> No doubt nonconscious cognition in humans evolved first, and consciousness and the unconscious were subsequently built on top. Removed from the confabulations of conscious narration, nonconscious cognition is closer to what is actually happening in the body and the outside world; in this sense, it is more in touch with reality than is consciousness. It comprises the broad middle layer of the tripartite framework.[85]

Being *more in touch with reality* gives nonconscious cognition a privileged knowledge position, bringing together human and animal life, as well as technical systems under one conceptual umbrella. The goal is to get to the material basis of things, to a genuine truth of the world, which gives equal importance to all entities, undistorted by human perspective.[86]

Treating all things equally is what Bryant – in his book *The Democracy of Objects* – calls flat ontology.[87] For Bryant, the term "object" has a broad definition that includes tangible and intangible entities, be they material, abstract, intentional, or anything else. What's important is that the democracy of objects knows no representational form but remains in a kind of market-based state in which no hegemonic (i.e. political) function exists. He writes:

> [T]he broader strategic import of the concept of flat ontology is to diminish the obsessive focus on the human, subjective and the cultural within social, political, cultural theory and philosophy. In particular, my ambition is to diminish

> an almost exclusive focus on propositions, representations, norms, signs, narratives, discourses, and so on, so as to cultivate a greater appreciation for nonhuman actors such as animate and inanimate natural entities, technologies, and such.[88]

The refusal to privilege (human) epistemology over (non-human) ontology – as in the case of Descartes, Kant, and other philosophers of the Enlightenment – entails a conception of democracy without representation, and consequently brings it very close to non-modern positions in the social and cultural sciences. In particular, Bruno Latour's thesis that "nothing is, by itself, either reducible or irreducible to anything else"[89] aligns with the claim that objects should neither be *undermined* nor *overmined*.[90] Flat ontology is thus a strategy to ward off any attempt to introduce hierarchies into the world of things, to differentiate between how things are made subjective or objective. Latour famously collapses this distinction, arguing for a flat ontology of human and non-human actors. In this context, any entity can be an actor (and not simply an object) as long as it influences other actors.[91] Hence, Latour's actor-network-theory considers actors solely based on their capacity to affect other actors and create networks of actions and interactions. Here, the "social" becomes a kind of material society, an "object-oriented democracy,"[92] which consists not only of human individuals but also of houses, roads, sewers, glaciers, pension funds, and so on.

The desire to pay more attention to our object-world corresponds to Hayles' position: "What we need is a robust interface through which we can interact with objects, and that robust interface requires a detailed knowledge about the material processes constituting our relations to objects."[93] Although her approach differs from actor-network-theory, particularly on the question of cognition,[94] Hayles is equally dismissive of an anthropocentric view of the world. For example, she ascribes agential power to non-human actors who, in her view, can also perform cognitive tasks; however, unlike Latour, she distinguishes between "agents" (material forces with the capacity to act) and "actors" (cognisers who can interpret and make choices).[95] Thus, in her model, there are "on one side [...] humans and all other biological life forms, as well as many technical systems" and "on the other, material processes and inanimate objects."[96] This distinction, between cognisers and non-cognisers, allows her to emphasise nonconscious cognition and, in particular, "the cognitive capabilities of technical systems."[97] The latter, like human nonconscious cognition, processes information faster than consciousness, which implies that they "are designed specifically to keep human consciousness from being overwhelmed by massive informational streams so large, complex, and multifaceted that they could never be processed by human brains."[98] Hayles gives the example of high-frequency trading (HFT): because of their complexity and speed, the algorithms used in HFT have unforeseen consequences, as the 2008 financial crisis demonstrated.[99] "Clearly," writes Hayles, "focusing on [human] memory functions alone is insufficient to understand the complex dynamics of the machine ecologies of automated trading."[100] For her, the behaviour generated by these algorithms goes beyond rational thinking, which is bound by the relatively slow processing of human cognition. As a result, the traditional project of critique is undermined, opening up "to a more inclusive and powerful set of resources with which to analyze the contemporary situations that confront us, including but not limited to the entanglements and interpenetrations of human and technical cognitive systems."[101] Both conscious and unconscious modes of awareness are built on top of nonconscious cognition, which in turn is built upon material processes.[102] In line with new materialism, Hayles calls for new modes of critique that take into account the fact that human reason is merely an after-effect of these material processes.[103]

Now, there is a subtle trick at work in this materialist reading: in order for cognitive processes to run smoothly, the unconscious gets renamed as the "new unconscious," which differs from the old one in that it is in "continuous and easy communication with consciousness."[104] The trick, largely influenced by cognitive and neural science, is to simply bypass unconscious processes by focusing on nonconscious ones, which accomplish the same things, albeit without "the conflict and drama of the psychoanalytic unconscious."[105] The cognitive nonconscious operates at a lower level of neuronal organisation, allowing for a kind of frictionless cognition that is not accessible to interpretation and without the pesky conflicts of the psyche. Within this frictionless, error-free realm, new cognitive assemblages emerge that are distinct from the symbolic world in that they allow for contiguity in a "fleshly sense" and make tangible the dynamic interactions between human and non-human cognisers.[106] By privileging biologically inspired accounts of nonconscious processes over symbolic (un)consciousness, Hayles acknowledges various roles of cognition in human and non-human life, and thereby grants cognitive agency to technical devices as well.[107] She writes:

> Fuelled by the relentless innovations of global capital, computational media are spreading into every other technology because of the strong evolutionary advantages bestowed by their cognitive capabilities, including water treatment plants and transportation technologies but also home appliances, watches, eyeglasses, and everything else, investing them with "smart" capabilities that are rapidly transforming technological infrastructures throughout the world. [Computational media] are the quintessentially cognitive technology, and for this reason have special relationships with the quintessentially cognitive species, Homo sapiens.[108]

According to this, humans today are embedded in a digital and networked environment, with the effect that (human) cognition changes according to these technologies.[109] Technical systems thus affect the physiological wiring of the brain, and altered human cognition in turn stimulates technological development.[110] Her concept of cognitive assemblages, although conceived as a pyramid, attempts to flatten consciousness by dissolving it into nonconscious as well as its underlying material processes. This is striking because, by tracing cognition back to its materiality, Hayles' flat ontology – in accordance with her object-oriented counterparts – echoes the physiological assumptions about the brain from the early twentieth century.[111]

The parallels between nonconscious cognition and connectionism are not coincidental, as both tend to conflate computational processes and biological models of the mind. In this flat cognitive ontology, reality is not so much mediated by higher consciousness as constituted by technical systems. It is therefore not surprising when Geoffrey Hinton, the godfather of artificial neural networks, claims that reasoning is the last step in what we call thinking.[112] In line with Hayles' cognitive model, he sees cognition as embedded in material processes, especially the brain. Such a neuroscientific grounding of cognitive processes, as was shown in the previous chapter, has given way to a biological interpretation of intelligence. What is missing from this perspective, however, is a theory of knowledge capable of acknowledging the "great inequality of things."[113] If the nonconscious constitutes a large part of human cognition and – in contrast to (un-)conscious mental processes – is inaccessible to analysis, then any attempt to understand the world around us must fail.[114] Paradoxically, this problem also concerns the brain: if it were merely a thing among other things, it would be hard to explain why it has become such a special object for the sciences, influencing much of how we think about cognitive processes and thus intelligence today. As in positivist assumptions before, the object of knowledge "objectifies" the social relations inscribed in it, as is evident in the example of artificial neural networks. It is, therefore, quite telling that the call for "less hierarchical" and "more fluid" theoretical concepts of cognition comes at a time when machine learning systems are consolidating on a global scale. The turn towards non-human cognition, which seeks to replace the unconscious as an analytical concept, plays right into "an instrumentalist technological logic that demeans critical analysis and celebrates digital tinkering."[115] Instead of adopting a flat ontology, which, by default, privileges ontological explanations over socio-political ones, we should question the claim that technical cognition, as it is supposedly performed in artificial intelligence and machine learning, is inaccessible to human reasoning. And this is exactly where a psychoanalytic perspective could be beneficial. As Alenka Zupančič states: "Psychoanalysis claims that the reality of (signifying) creation comes with an unexpected addition: the unconscious. The unconscious is proof of the existence of the contingent; it is where something of which we have no memory continues to work as truth."[116] If we understand the unconscious not as a subset of nonconscious processes, a kind of internal black box, but as something exterior, as an externalisation of collective knowledge, then it might well be open to analysis.[117]

4. The Technological Unconscious

In his 1954/5 seminar, Lacan introduces a thought experiment relating to the post-human vision: in an unspecified future, all human life has disappeared. All that remains are waterfalls and springs, as well as thunder and lightning. Now, in this abandoned world, an apparatus takes pictures of a mountain reflected in a lake, automatically develops and stores the photographs for the world to come. Lacan's question then is: "The image in the mirror, the image in the lake – do they still exist?"[118] His answer is yes because from a media-materialist (that is, psychoanalytic) point of view, the existence of an image does not depend on human consciousness. The apparatus ensures the continuity of the world and thus allows the "phenomena of consciousness" (i.e. the image captured by the apparatus) to exist independently of any ego-position. Indeed, for Lacan – and this brings him close to Hayles' critique of our cognitive model – "consciousness is linked to something entirely contingent, just as contingent as the surface of a lake in an uninhabited world – the existence of our eyes or of our ears."[119] Human consciousness thus has no privileged position. Beyond any anthropocentric illusion, Lacan insists on the material (i.e. arbitrary) foundation of our conscious mind. He does so, however, not by flattening consciousness in terms of cognitive assemblages, but by invoking its dialectical counterpart. The unconscious appears as a site of critical inquiry, where difference and conflict are not flattened out, but made describable and, therefore, open for discussion. With psychoanalysis, we hold at least some of the keys to thinking about and through technology in relation to the human subject. As the "social magic of modern times,"[120] psychoanalytic thinking holds out the possibility of critique and helps to bring awareness to technological media as the underlying – or rather, externalised – basis of consciousness. Herein lies the great difference with posthumanism, which merely extends human consciousness to other (non-human) cognisers and, ultimately, seeks to get rid of the thinking subject. In contrast, psychoanalysis, precisely because it addresses unconscious processes as the machinic other (i.e. the camera automatically recording the world around it), is anti-humanist in the proper sense of the term: the machine is not some anthropomorphic extension of man, nor does it take the place of human consciousness, but it assumes its own position on the ontological plane. It thus breaks with the notion of any linear process of cognition and understands the human subject as the product of an endless cycle of symbolic, that is, discursive activity.[121]

According to psychoanalysis, and with it a media-materialist understanding of the world, we are all inscribed in larger discourse networks (e.g. the family, institutions, legal frameworks, media technologies).[122] Hence, what we call the thinking subject is an effect of these networks operating under real conditions. These conditions, to quote Friedrich Kittler, are ultimately media standards: "Consciousness is tied to the contingent presence of eyes or ears, to analog media; from the encoding of the real, on the other hand, the location of the other necessarily emerges – a combinatorial matrix of strategies."[123] The location of the other refers to the symbolic function of the machine in its most radical form. As has already been shown, the material language of psychoanalysis is no longer the same as that of linguistics. Instead of describing the semantic logic of a given natural language, it is stripped down to its syntactic structure, in particular, to computer code. Lacan himself seems to invoke that the binary structure of zeros and ones, yes or no, open or closed has universal status and lies at the basis of all communication: "What is a message inside a machine? Something which proceeds by opening and not opening, the way an electronic lamp does, by yes and no. It's something articulated, of the same order as the fundamental oppositions of the symbolic order. At any given moment, this something which turns has to, or doesn't, come back into play. It is always ready to give a reply, and be completed by this self-same act of replying, that is to say by ceasing to function as an isolated and closed circuit, by entering into the general run of things. Now this comes very close to what we can conceive of as Zwang, the compulsion to repeat."[124] The automatic play of symbols, their combinatorial matrix, makes them independent of human consciousness and, at the same time, allows for the subject to emerge at this "other" location. What matters are not ideas or intentions, but the subject's position within an inter-subjective chain of signifiers. Thus, paradoxically, it is only within such an overdetermined space of symbols that something as contingent as human subjectivity, wedged in between consciousness and unconsciousness, can appear.[125]

The binary system, which operates on the principle of absence and presence, makes it possible to combine the arithmetic and logic functions of a digital computer with their physical implementation in the central processing unit (i.e. the computer chip).[126] It thus enables the cybernetic machine to find its own order, "to [run] automatically regardless of what happens to pass down its wires."[127] Yet this order is characterised by contingency, as the example of logic gates has shown and as can be seen from binary code itself. While a sequence of binary code seems at first sight to follow a necessary order, it also opens itself up to chance. The introduction of chance into the otherwise rigid organisation of the Turing machine sets stochastic processes in motion. Unlike a pre-programmed behaviour, these processes are sequences of possible events in which the probability of each event depends only on the state reached in the previous event. Lacan illustrates this with reference to the rather simple game of evens and odds.[128] It is within the symbolic structure of the game – pluses and minuses grouped in trigrams, which resemble the logic gates mentioned before – that the combinatorial possibilities of a given situation are revealed. The strategy for playing the game is contingent on all the combinations that precede the next move, which, in turn, can change the whole structure. Herein lies the crux of the matter: "It's not what happens afterwards which is modified, but everything which went before. We have a retroactive effect – *nachträglich*, as Freud calls it – specific to the structure of symbolic memory, in other words to the function of remembering."[129] The psychic apparatus thus functions as a strategic machine because of its ability to actively remember things. Accordingly, the digital computer is designed not only to read and write information in terms of numbers, but also to move from one state into another. Computers make it possible to operate on the real, insofar as "[s]traightforward encoding transfers unlimited chance (the real) into a syntax with requirements and exemptions, that is, with laws."[130] By introducing chance into a syntactic order, the symbolic machine emancipates itself from a pre-given structure and begins to create its own.

The development of the digital computer, with its probabilistic nature, has changed our understanding of reality, respectively the way we try to grasp it. This is the reason why, according to Lacan, the dividing line within modern sciences is not between deductive and inductive, but between exact and probabilistic. In Lacan's words: "To understand what cybernetics is about, one must look for its origin in the theme, so crucial for us, of the signification of chance. The past of cybernetics consists in nothing more than the rationalised formation of what we will call, to contrast them to the exact sciences, the conjectural sciences."[131] The latter are aligned with psychoanalysis, particularly in its attempt to formalise the mathematical-like structure of the unconscious. Lacan argues that this formalisation is already present in Freud. But whereas Freud was still stuck in the biological and empirical thinking of his time, Lacan emphasises the symbolic character of psychoanalysis and, therefore, locates it on the side of the arts, including arithmetic, geometry, music, and grammar.[132] The reference to the arts does not, however, mean less rigorous, but rather points to the rule-based play of signs mentioned before. In fact, both the psychic apparatus and the universal machine operate on symbols, thereby underlining the cybernetic perspective on the unconscious. The conjectural nature of psychoanalysis, which is informed by information and game theory,[133] makes these symbols play according to determinate, but not deterministic rules. For Lacan, the mathematical formalisation made possible by this perspective is of utmost importance, because it allows him to move beyond the imaginary equation between humans and machines – as is often the case in posthuman discourses – and to focus instead on the symbolic (i.e. unconscious) dimension of intelligence.[134] From this perspective, humans and machines exist on different ontological planes, but, at the same time, are part of the same symbolic realm, subjected to the same rule-bound procedures when carrying out acts of thinking. The symbolic allows for this difference to be analysed: "The important thing here is to realise that the chain of possible combinations of the encounter can be studied as such, as an order which subsists in its rigour, independently of all subjectivity." And Lacan adds: "Through cybernetics, the symbol is embodied in an apparatus [...]. And it is embodied in it in a literally trans-subjective way."[135] Hence, Freud's conception of psychoanalysis as a treatment through language is radicalised by Lacan in that he conceives of the unconscious as being determined by a network of signifying elements (i.e. a language) that give rise to syntactic laws (i.e. symbolic structures) and that are open for analysis.

Taking a psychoanalytic understanding of language into account, one could argue that the symbolic has never left AI discourse. As Isabel Millar notes: "It is not so much a question of finding 'new paradigms' to think AI but rather of elucidating exactly how the Lacanian subject is already present in our conception of Artificial Intelligence, and what this means for the relationship between the two."[136] Despite current attempts to move beyond a symbolic information-processing model of the mind, it is language, or more specifically code, that mediates this relationship. Contrary to the idea of a frictionless cognition – as in the case of the nonconscious – the focus here is on the ambiguities of any thinking process.[137] Thus the greatest illusion of the speaking subject may be that it has created and mastered the symbolic order. Instead, by participating in the realm of language, signs, and symbols, the subject is split into a subject of enunciation and a subject of statement, that is, a subject that is no longer constituted by an inner consciousness, but rather by an unconscious exterior that automatically writes and speaks it.[138] In the context of our cybernetic framework this means that it is "the unconscious, rather than the speaking subject, [that] does the thinking and plays the game of chances according to given combinatory rules."[139] Every time the subject thinks, that is, when it tries to articulate the symbolic order, it gets caught up in an endless chain of signifiers. What is more, "thinking" itself gets subverted by the unconscious, which automatically – and, in an uncanny way, autonomously – preserves in the present what has happened in the past. But other than the nonconscious, which still implies a continuum of cognitive activity, the unconscious breaks with conscious thought as being grounded in the realm of meaning.[140] Nowhere is this more evident than in dreams, the heart of Freudian theory. Dreamwork is meaningless in the sense that it does not produce a meaningful statement that can be put into a rational explanation. At the same time, however, it follows a certain structure, giving rise to a combinatorial matrix as well. According to Freud's *The Interpretation of Dreams* of 1900, two registers, condensation and displacement, transform the latent content of dreams into its manifest content, while in therapy one attempts to reverse-engineer the unconscious thought process from manifest to latent.[141] Such an interplay bears similarities with the basic linguistic functions of metaphor (condensation) and metonymy (displacement),[142] which is also the reason why Lacan famously claimed that "the unconscious is structured like a language."[143]

Dreamwork, which allows the fulfilment of a repressed wish, is a perfect example of a directed signification. The dream gets distorted by the unconscious, with the effect that the dream content is incomprehensible to the dreamer. Only in reverse order can the manifest content be tied back to the repressed desire. Such a retroactive process can also be seen by the example of machine learning. DeepDream, a computer vision programme developed by Google in 2015, visualises the emergent structure of a convolutional neural network, which is able to extract the features of an object based on millions of training examples. The learned structure is stored within the network, respectively its hidden layers, and is used to correctly classify previously unseen images of the same object. Now, this process can be turned upside down: "Neural networks that were trained to discriminate between different kinds of images have quite a bit of the information needed to *generate* images too."[144] The latent feature space embedded in the network makes it possible to dream up new images. Of course, this is not the same as the transformation between latent and manifest content in Freud's interpretation of dreams, but there are similarities: a neural network must also transform its training material into a syntactic structure. According to connectionism, the network "learns" this structure from training data, and the learned structure helps the network to transform unseen data into output values. This is not a passive act, however. The network, just like the psychic apparatus, records and processes data simultaneously: "In this way, every neuron – and the network as a whole – remembers its history in abstracted form, maintaining a trace of the values of what it has seen before, in order to create a model that can make predictions based on new data."[145] Hence, memory cannot be reduced to an organic or mechanical component of the network, but must be seen in its symbolic dimension.[146] The ability to "write" symbols, that is, to transform an input into an output, produces (unconscious) traces and, as a consequence, equips the networks with memory. Even if human operators cannot directly "read" this memory, due to its sheer size and speed, it is still symbolic. What is more is that the symbolic function allows the network to "process" memory retroactively as is the case in dreamwork.

Memory, in the form of unconscious traces that haunt the conscious mind, is also what activates the hosts in *Westworld*. Rather than a cognitive pyramid, it is the labyrinthine architecture of memory that enables Dolores' inward journey. The errant corridors of the technological unconscious allow the machine to find its own structure. Contrary to early visions of cybernetics, however, this structure is not simply composed of some internal components but is itself the dialectical inversion of the external world. A world that is constantly recorded and "memorised" by means of electronic media. And it was not until psychoanalysis that the effect of such an *extimacy* of memory came to light: "The residue of this vast archive of experience was consciousness. Consciousness was simply the visible and articulatable residue or symptom of memory; a memory that is now 'out there' and outside of representation but whose excesses of information could overwhelm and incapacitate the subject."[147] Hence, consciousness, in all its arbitrariness, turned out to be a kind of technical filter that protects the organism from too much sensory input. At the same time, it is this "surplus" that constitutes the (machinic) other and allows for an autonomous play of symbols. Just as the musical cues performed by the player piano in *Westworld* allow the hosts to break out of their routine, it is the symbolic function – not the mechanical or organic – that "constitutes a type of memory: the past is recorded in the chain itself, determining what is yet to come."[148] In other words: memory resides in the symbols, namely the chains of signifiers, not in some organ or mechanism. Instead of circumventing this symbolic function of the unconscious through an imaginary of seamless cognition, the externalisation of the psyche and its incorporation into larger discursive networks opens up a space in which communication between humans and machines becomes possible.[149] And if the unconscious, as the space of this encounter, is indeed structured like a language (i.e. according to syntactic laws), then so is the technological unconscious of machine learning. As I will explain in the next chapter, this is where artificial intelligence can emerge.

Notes

1 Jonathan Nolan and Lisa Joy, "The Bicameral Mind," *Westworld*, season 1, episode 10, directed by Jonathan Nolan, aired 4 December 2016 on HBO.
2 Reverie is, of course, a reference to Claude Debussy's 1890 composition of the same name, in which the repetitive piano theme represents a kind of daydream.
3 The nod to Hegel's master-servant dialectic and its "struggle to the death" is more than obvious (see Georg Wilhelm Friedrich Hegel, *The Phenomenology of Spirit* (Oxford: Clarendon Press, 1977), originally published in 1807. With reference to Black liberation movements, see Susan Buck-Morss, *Hegel, Haiti and Universal History* (Pittsburgh: Pittsburgh University Press, 2009).
4 Sigmund Freud, "The Scientific Literature of Dreams," in *The Interpretation of Dreams,* trans. and ed. James Strachey (New York: Basic Books, [1900] 2010), 1–50.
5 The French word *rêverie* is derived from the Old French word for delusion, daydream, and mind-wandering *resverie.*
6 Orit Halpern, *Beautiful Data: A History of Vision and Reason Since 1945* (Durham: Duke University Press, 2015).
7 Halpern, *Beautiful Data,* 145–54.
8 Halpern, *Beautiful Data,* 157.
9 Norbert Wiener, *Cybernetics: Or Control and Communication in the Animal and the Machine* (Cambridge, MA: MIT Press, [1948] 1965), 121.
10 Halpern, *Beautiful Data,* 67. In this sense, cybernetics recalls the ideal of an active memory from Henri Bergson, while extending the belief that memory and perception are now the same thing.
11 Warren S. McCulloch and Walter H. Pitts, "A Logical Calculus of the Ideas Immanent in Nervous Activity," *Bulletin of Mathematical* Biophysics 5 (1943): 117.
12 Claus Pias, "The Age of Cybernetics," in *Cybernetics: The Macy Conferences 1946–1953*, ed. Claus Pias (Zürich: diaphanes, 2016), 16.
13 The digital is in constant tension with the continuous that prevails in the material world (e.g. in the form of the storage medium on which the digital information is inscribed). See Aden Evens, *Logic of the Digital* (London: Bloomsbury, 2017), 5f.
14 Halpern, *Beautiful Data,* 161.
15 Joplin's "The Entertainer," written in 1902, was sold as piano rolls for automatic player pianos.
16 Hayles, *How We Became Posthuman: Virtual Bodies in Cybernetics, Literature, and Informatics* (Chicago: Chicago University Press, 1999).
17 Hayles, *Posthuman,* 7.
18 Hayles, *Posthuman,* 149. On early cybernetics, in particular Ross Ashby and William Grey Walter, see Chapter 2.
19 Hayles, *Posthuman,* 7.
20 Hayles, *Posthuman,* 74.
21 Hayles, *Posthuman,* 18.
22 Hayles, *Posthuman,* 291. In this sense, the cybernetic vision questioned the hitherto stable distinction between the inside and the outside of the body, which was important

particularly for (cyber-)feminist theory: a body with fluid borders – where the womb is extended to a test tube, for example – "opens the door to a potentially endless series of practices, from reproductive to self-enhancing, all of which open for women a much larger platform of gender identification than has previously been available." Bernadette Wegenstein, "Body," in *Critical Terms for Media Studies*, ed. W. J. T. Mitchell and Mark B. N. Hansen (Chicago: University of Chicago Press, 2010), 123.

23 Warren McCulloch quoted in Pias, "The Age of Cybernetics," 16. Hayles acknowledges the fact that McCulloch did not argue in favour of a complete disembodiment of information but was still dedicated to an empirical (i.e. embodied) grounding of his (artificial) neural model. See Hayles, *Posthuman*, 60f.

24 McCulloch writes that brains "compute thought the way electronic computers calculate numbers." McCulloch, "The Beginning of Cybernetics," in *Cybernetics: The Macy Conferences 1946–1953*, ed. Claus Pias (Zürich: diaphanes, 2016), 129.

25 Von Neumann's universal automaton consists of three parts: the construction unit, the memory control unit (MC), and a linear array (L), which is controlled by the MC. See von Neumann, *Theory of Self-Reproducing Automata* (Urbana: University of Illinois Press, 1966), in particular the Fifth Lecture.

26 Note that von Neumann's definition of the universal automaton as a self-reproducing mechanism, which uses information about itself to copy itself, actually precedes the discovery of DNA by James Watson and Francis Crick by a couple of years.

27 Arthur W. Burks, "Editor's Introduction," in Von Neumann, *Theory of Self-Reproducing Automata*, 20.

28 John von Neumann, "The General and Logical Theory of Automata," in *Theory of Self-Reproducing Automata*, 296.

29 Von Neumann writes, "I shall […] in what follows use the working *hypothesis that* the neuron is an all-or-none digital organ." *Theory of Self-Reproducing Automata*.

30 Von Neumann, *Theory of Self-Reproducing Automata*, 99–101.

31 See Pias, "The Age of Cybernetics," 16f.

32 Von Neumann, "General and Logical Theory of Automata," 297. For a similar assessment, see Benjamin Peters, "The Computer Never Was a Brain, or the Curious Death and Designs of John von Neumann," in *Verhaltensdesign: Technologische und ästhetische Programme der 1960er und 1970er Jahre*, ed. Jeannie Moser and Christina Vagt (Bielefeld: transcript Verlag, 2018), 113–23. See: http://iar.cs.unm.edu/~eschulte/classes/cs591-rpc/data/vonneumann1951-glta.pdf.

33 John von Neumann, "Probabilistic Logics and the Synthesis of Reliable Organisms from Unreliable Components," in *Automata Studies*, ed. C. E. Shannon and J. McCarthy (Princeton: Princeton University Press, 1956), 43.

34 As such, it is also different from older forms of mechanical automation. See also David W. Bates' discussion of von Neumann and his detailed analysis of error (*An Artificial History of Natural Intelligence: Thinking with Machines from Descartes to the Digital Age* [Chicago: University of Chicago Press, 2024], 254–59).

35 The architecture design consists of two main components: first, the CPU is the electronic circuit responsible for executing the instructions of a computer programme (microprocessor). The CPU contains the arithmetic and logic unit (ALU), which makes arithmetic (add, subtract, etc.) and logic (AND, OR, NOT, etc.) operations possible, as well as the control unit, which controls the operations of the ALU, the memory, and all input/output devices, basically telling them what to do according to the programme. In addition, there are high-speed storage areas in the CPU, called registers, where all the data is stored. Second, the memory unit consists of RAM and ROM, sometimes referred to as primary or main memory. Unlike a hard drive (secondary memory), this memory is fast and is also directly accessible by the CPU. Loading data from permanent memory (ROM) into the faster and directly accessible temporary memory (RAM) allows the CPU to operate much quicker. See Arthur W. Burks, Herman H.

Goldstine, and John von Neumann, "Preliminary Discussion of the Logical Design of an Electronic Computing Instrument," in *The Origins of Digital Computers: Selected Papers*, ed. Brian Randell (Berlin: Springer Verlag, 1982), 399–413.

36 As Halpern writes:

> The concept of a memory capable of erasure (the neuron must fire and then be prepared to receive further signals) but still able to recycle past impulses was highly amenable to the demands of a computational machine and fulfilled the logic set forth by Turing. This ideal of memory is still encapsulated within our contemporary computers whose architecture continues to be inspired by the von Neumann architecture for the first stored program computer (EDVAC). The ongoing compartmentalization of the arithmetic unit, memory, and control unit embodies these principles.
>
> Beautiful Data, *160*

37 Wendy Hui Kyong Chun, *Programmed Visions: Software and Memory* (Cambridge, MA: MIT Press, 2011), Chapters 3 and 4.

38 Von Neumann writes, "We do not know where in the physically viewed nervous system a memory resides; we do not know whether it is a separate organ or a collection of specific parts of other already known organs, etc. [...] The only thing we know is that it must be a rather large-capacity memory, and that it is hard to see how a complicated automaton like the human nervous system could do without one." *The Computer and the Brain* (New Haven: Yale University Press, 1958), 61.

39 Very much in contrast to Alan M. Turing, who always insisted on the programmable (i.e. symbolic) part of the machine, rather than its physical components.

40 Alan M. Turing, "Proposal for Development in the Mathematics Division of an Automatic Computing Engine (ACE)," in *A. M. Turing's ACE Report of 1946 and Other Papers*, ed. B. E. Carpenter and R. W. Doran (Cambridge, MA: MIT Press), 35.

41 Von Neumann, "General and Logical Theory of Automaton," 299. Referencing McCulloch and Pitts' model, von Neumann writes, "It proves that anything can be exhaustively and unambiguously described, anything that can be completely and unambiguously put into words, is ipso facto realizable by a suitable finite neural network." Von Neumann, "General and Logical Theory of Automaton," 310.

42 Wiener, *Cybernetics*, 121.

43 Halpern, *Beautiful Data*, 66f. As developmental psychology shows, cognitive capacities are fundamentally linked to an increasing processing efficiency as well as a functioning working memory. The latter is a cognitive system with a limited capacity to hold information that is currently being processed.

44 Computer memory is "divided" into main (primary) and auxiliary (secondary) memory. The main memory holds the data while a programme is running and the auxiliary memory holds data and programmes not currently in use. Similar to the computer, the brain processes sensory impressions (i.e. data) in (at least) two steps. First, the impression gets registered and processed by the short-term memory (STM); then the processed data get transferred to the long-term memory (LTM) to be stored for later recollection. In this context, sleep plays a crucial role, because it makes the transfer between STM and LTM possible – a fact that is put to practical use in machine learning, when memory gets consolidated in the "dreams" of restricted Boltzmann machines (RBM).

45 Halpern, *Beautiful Data*, 160.

46 Bernard Stiegler, "Anamnesis and Hypomnesis," *Ars Industrialis* (2006), https://ars-industrialis.org/anamnesis-and-hypomnesis#_ftnref4.

47 Sigmund Freud, "Project for a Scientific Psychology (unfinished manuscript)," in *The Origins of Psychoanalysis: Letters to Wilhelm Fliess, Drafts, and Notes, 1887–1902*,

ed. Anna Freud and Ernst Kris (New York: Basic Books, 1960), 345–445. In *Beyond the Pleasure Principle*, Freud links the idea of a filtering device to the genesis of organic life itself. See *Beyond the Pleasure Principle*, trans. James Strachey (New York: W. W. Norton, 1990), 43–53.

48 The term "psychic apparatus" appears throughout Freud's work, notably in "Project for a Scientific Psychology."

49 Mai Wegener, *Neuronen und Neurosen: Der psychische Apparat bei Freud und Lacan: Ein historisch-theoretischer Versuch zu Freuds "Entwurf" von 1895* (Munich: Wilhelm Fink Verlag, 2004).

50 Even a machine constructed with paper and pencil has to meet certain criteria, in particular the existence of a formal language with clearly distinguishable (i.e. discrete) signs, in order to allow for the formalisation of automated routines. See Sybille Krämer, *Symbolische Maschinen: Die Idee der Formalisierung in geschichtlichem Abriß* (Darmstadt: Wissenschaftliche Buchgesellschaft, 1988).

51 Sigmund Freud, "A Note Upon the 'Mystic Writing-Pad'," in *Sigmund Freud, The Ego and the Id and Other Works*, trans. James Strachey (London: Vintage, 1961), 227–34.

52 Joseph Vogl, "Technologie des Unbewußten: Zur Einführung," in *Kursbuch Medienkultur: Die maßgeblichen Theorien von Brecht bis Baudrillard* (Stuttgart: DVA, 2004), 373–76.

53 Friedrich Kittler, *Discourse Networks, 1800/1900,* trans. Michael Metteer (Stanford: Stanford University Press, 1990), 229–38; also Kittler, *Grammophone, Film, Typewriter* (Stanford: Stanford University Press, 1999).

54 Friedrich Kittler, "The World of the Symbolic—A World of the Machine," in *Literature, Media, Information Systems*, ed. John Johnston (New York: Routledge, 2012), 134. According to Kittler, Freud was thus reliant on simple storage and transmission media to picture the psychic apparatus.

55 Kittler, "The World of the Symbolic," 135.

56 Jacques Lacan, *The Ego in Freud's Theory and in the Technique of Psychoanalysis, 1954–1955, Seminar II*, trans. Sylvana Tomaselli (New York: W. W. Norton, 1991), 295.

57 Lacan, *Seminar II.*

58 Lydia H. Liu, *The Freudian Robot: Digital Media and the Future of the Unconscious* (Chicago: University of Chicago Press, 2011), 196.

59 Materialism not in the sense of an ultimate substance (e.g. language), but rather as a dialectic movement, which, by means of conflict and contradiction, animates the symbolic order.

60 Claude E. Shannon, "A Mathematical Theory of Communication," *Bell System Technical Journal* 27, no. 3 (July 1948): 379–423; 623–56. Faced with the challenge to economise the wires of a communication network (e.g. telegraph, telephone, television), Shannon's information theory calculates the probability that a given message contains new information (e.g. identifying the outcome of a fair coin flip, with two equally likely outcomes, provides less information than identifying the outcome from a roll of dice with six equally likely outcomes).

61 Lacan, *Seminar II*, 304.

62 Lacan, *Seminar II*, 305.

63 The computer takes a sequence of 0s and 1s and transforms it into another sequence of 0s and 1s according to predetermined rules. It was again Claude E. Shannon, while still an MA student at MIT, who showed that all Boolean algebra (i.e. logical operations based on binaries) could be performed by electrical switches.

64 Whereas in the "AND" function, the output is true if both inputs are true, in the "OR" function, the output is true if either or both inputs are true. The "NOT" function reverses the logic state: if the input is true, the output is false, and if the input is false, the output is true. A more complex function is the "XOR" function, which we

saw when we talked about the dispute between Frank Rosenblatt (Perceptron) and Marvin Minsky (see previous chapter). An "XOR" function should return a true value if the two inputs are not equal and a false value if they are equal (which is actually a problem for single-layer neural networks).

65 See Alenka Zupančič, *Ethics of the Real: Kant and Lacan* (London: Verso, 2000), Chapter 2.

66 Lacan, *Seminar II*, 306.

67 See Halpern, *Beautiful Data*, 172, with reference to the cybernetician Gregory Bateson.

68 Similarly, although not from a psychoanalytic perspective, Leif Weatherby and Brian Justie argue that with today's machine learning techniques the "old suspicion that digital computers are syntax machines with no capacity for meaning should finally be laid to rest." Leif Weatherby and Brian Justie, "Indexical AI," *Critical Inquiry* 48, no. 2 (Winter 2022): 408.

69 According to Kittler, the discourse network of 1900, which had split the writing monopoly of 1800 into separate (electronic) media, has been replaced by a "total media link on a digital basis," which "erases the differences among individual media," because "inside the computers themselves everything becomes a number: quantity without image, sound, or voice. And once optical fiber networks turn formerly distinct data flows into a standardized series of digitized numbers, any medium can be translated into any other. With numbers, everything goes." Kittler, *Grammophone, Film, Typewriter*, 1–2.

70 See Henning Schmidgen, *Das Unbewußte der Maschine. Konzeptionen des Psychischen bei Guattari, Deleuze und Lacan* (Munich: Wilhelm Fink Verlag, 1997). In general, machines refer to more complex entities (cf. industrial revolution), but the distinction is not as clear-cut as one might think (cf. typewriter vs. telephone apparatus); in connection with the body (which is very complex), we usually tend to refer to the apparatus (cf. sensory, nervous, digestive, reproductive apparatus).

71 Drawing on the work of Gilles Deleuze and Félix Guattari, John Johnston describes this process as "a dynamic self-assembly that draws both the human and the natural into new forms of interaction and relay among a multiplicity of material, historical, and evolutionary forces." *The Allure of Machinic Life: Cybernetics, Artificial Life, and the New AI* (Cambridge, MA: MIT Press, 2008), 21.

72 Lacan, *Seminar II*, 74.

73 As is well known, Kittler equates Lacan's conceptual differentiation into the real, the imaginary, and the symbolic with the three media types of the discourse network 1900: gramophone (real), film (imaginary), typewriter (symbolic). See Kittler, *Grammophone, Film, Typewriter.*

74 As Lacan writes with reference to the binary notation system of a digital computer:

> By itself, the play of the symbol represents and organizes, independently of the peculiarities of its human support, this something which is called a subject. The human subject doesn't foment this game, he takes his place in it, and plays the role of the little pluses and minuses in it. He is himself an element in this chain which, as soon as it is unwound, organizes itself in accordance with laws. Hence the subject is always on several levels, caught up in crisscrossing networks.
>
> Seminar II, *192–3*

75 See Freud's by now proverbial statement that the ego is not the master in its own house; for example, in *The Ego and the Id*, trans. Joan Riviere (New York: W. W. Norton, [1923] 1960).

76 Lacan, *Seminar II*, 306.

77 Jacques Lacan, "Psychoanalysis and Cybernetics, or on the Nature of Language," lecture in Paris, France, June 22, 1955.
78 Lacan, "Psychoanalysis and Cybernetics," 300.
79 Lacan, "Psychoanalysis and Cybernetics," 300.
80 Von Neumann, "General and Logical Theory of Automaton," 308.
81 Hayles, *Unthought: The Power of the Cognitive Nonconscious* (Chicago: University of Chicago Press, 2017), 2.
82 Hayles, *Unthought*, 27–30.
83 As Hayles asserts: "[N]onconscious cognition operates at a level of neuronal processing inaccessible to the modes of awareness but nevertheless performing functions to consciousness." Hayles, *Unthought*, 10.
84 See also Holger Pötzsch and N. Katherine Hayles, "Posthumanism, Technogenesis, and Digital Technologies: A Conversation with N. Katherine Hayles," *Fibreculture Journal* 23 (2014): 105f.
85 Hayles, *Unthought*, 28.
86 A similar aim is pursued by the so-called "speculative turn," which, in line with new materialism, has been proposed as a counterpoint to the linguistic turn. According to its proponents, "it has long been commonplace within continental philosophy to focus on discourse, text, culture, consciousness, power, or ideas as what constitutes reality. But despite the vaunted anti-humanism of many of the thinkers identified with these trends, what they give us is less a critique of humanity's place in the world, than a less sweeping critique of the self-enclosed Cartesian subject." Levi Bryant, Nick Srnicek, and Graham Harman, "Towards a Speculative Philosophy," in *The Speculative Turn: Continental Materialism and Realism*, ed. Levi Bryant, Nick Srnicek, and Graham Harman (Melbourne: re.press, 2011), 2f.
87 Bryant borrows the term from Manuel DeLanda, who uses it to assert that being is composed entirely of individuals, existing on the same flat ontological plane. DeLanda writes:

> [W]hile an ontology based on relations between general types and particular instances is hierarchical, each level representing a different ontological category (organism, species, genera), an approach in terms of interacting parts and emergent wholes leads to a flat ontology, one made exclusively of unique, singular individuals, differing in spatio-temporal scale but not in ontological status.
>
> Intensive Science and Virtual Philosophy *(London: Bloomsbury, 2022), 47*

88 DeLanda, *Intensive Science*, 246f. For a critique of such an anti-hegemonic view of democracy, which runs the risk of simply replicating the existing hegemonic (i.e. capitalist) structure, see Justin Joque, *Revolutionary Mathematics: Artificial Intelligence, Statistics and the Logic of Capitalism* (London: Verso, 2022), 166–67.
89 Bruno Latour, "Irreductions," in *The Pasteurization of France*, trans. Alan Sheridan and John Law (Cambridge, MA: Harvard University Press, [1984] 1988), 169.
90 As Bryant explains: "Where undermining treats the object as a false appearance produced as an effect of what is alleged to be really real being such as atoms, overmining charges objects with being 'falsely deep' and dissolves them in a more superficial strata of phenomena." "Flat Ontology," Larval Subjects website, February 24, 2010, https://larvalsubjects.wordpress.com/2010/02/24/flat-ontology-2.
91 Bruno Latour, *Reassembling the Social: An Introduction to Actor-Network-Theory* (Oxford: Oxford University Press, 2005), 63ff.
92 Bruno Latour, "From Realpolitik to Dingpolitik or How to Make Things Public," in *Making Things Public: Atmospheres of Democracy*, ed. Bruno Latour and Peter Weibel (Cambridge, MA: MIT Press, 2005), 14–41.

93 See Pötzsch and Hayles, "Posthumanism, Technogenesis, and Digital Technologies," 104.
94 See Louise Amoore and Volha Piotukh, "Interview with N. Katherine Hayles," *Theory, Culture & Society* 36, no. 2 (2019): 145–55; also see N. Katherine Hayles, "Speculative Aesthetics and Object-Oriented Inquiry (OOI)," *Speculations: A Journal of Speculative Realism* 5 (2014): 158–79.
95 Hayles, *Unthought*, 175.
96 Hayles, *Unthought*, 30.
97 Hayles, *Unthought*, 11.
98 Hayles, *Unthought*, 11.
99 Hayles, *Unthought*, 163–65.
100 Hayles, *Unthought*, 172.
101 Hayles, *Unthought*, 40.
102 Hayles, *Unthought*, 39f.
103 The criticism that material processes are too fast for the human mind to process is far from new. However, I would like to follow Wendy Hui Kyong Chun's assessment that speed alone is not enough to declare the scientific critique of media processes obsolete. See Chun, "The Enduring Ephemeral, or the Future Is a Memory," *Critical Inquiry* 35, no. 1 (Autumn 2008): 148–71.
104 Hayles, *Unthought*, 27.
105 Ran R. Hassin, James S. Uleman, and John A. Bargh, eds., *The New Unconscious* (New York: Oxford University Press, 2005), online description, https://global.oup.com/academic/product/the-new-unconscious-9780195307696?cc=gb&lang=en&#.
106 Hayles, *Unthought,* 118. Hayles claims that networks, unlike assemblages, cannot account for interactions across complex three-dimensional topologies; however, this claim has been disproved by artificial neural networks that operate in n-dimensional spaces.
107 Technical systems, according to Hayles and others, also affect the physiological wiring of the brain, and altered human cognition in turn stimulates technological development. See Nicholas Carr, *The Shallows: What the Internet Is Doing to Our Brains* (New York: W. W. Norton, 2011) and N. Katherine Hayles, *How We Think: Digital Media and Contemporary Technogenesis* (Chicago: University of Chicago Press, 2012).
108 Hayles, *Unthought*, 34.
109 In contrast to deep attention, which is associated with traditional knowledge acquisition and involves single streams of information and long periods of focus, hyper attention is characterised by the ability to rapidly scan large amounts of data and combine them into specific, albeit ephemeral, patterns. This generational shift in cognitive styles is supported by the thesis that humans and technology have always co-evolved, in the sense that humans and technical artefacts are mutually reinforcing. What is new, according to Hayles, is the fact that with digital media networks and media-rich environments, the speed of such an ontogenetic evolution across generations has increased significantly. See N. Katherine Hayles, "Hyper and Deep Attention: The Generational Divide in Cognitive Modes," *Profession* (2007): 187–99.
110 This line of thinking follows the idea of an "exteriorisation of cognitive capabilities" to technical systems: "Indeed, biological and technical cognitions are now so deeply entwined that it is more accurate to say they interpenetrate one another." Hayles, *Unthought*, 11. See also Carr, *The Shallows* and Hayles, *How We Think.*
111 See her constant references to neurology and brain physiology, for example, Antonio Damasio, *The Feeling of What Happens: Body and Emotion in the Making of Consciousness* (New York: Mariner Books, 2000); Pawel Lewicki, Thomas Hill, and Maria Czyzewsk, "Nonconscious Acquisition of Information," *American Psychology*

47, no. 6 (1992): 796–801; and David Eagleman, *Incognito: The Secret Lives of the Brain* (New York: Random House, 2012).

112 Geoffrey E. Hinton, "Geoffrey Hinton and Yann LeCun, 2018 ACM A.vM. Turing Award Lecture 'The Deep Learning Revolution'," Association for Computing Machinery, YouTube, June 23, 2019, https://www.youtube.com/watch?v=VsnQf7exv5I.

113 John Durham Peters, *The Marvelous Clouds: Toward a Philosophy of Elemental Media* (Chicago: University of Chicago Press, 2015), 30.

114 Following Ray Brassier's critique, one can argue that all variants of "flat ontology" seem to claim that ontology is – for some reason – always subordinated to epistemology, and that this subordination always leads to anti-realist positions; however, one can still maintain the primacy of being and acknowledge the fact that epistemology is a necessary condition for ontological access; Brassier writes, "The primacy of being over knowing is not equivalent to the primacy of ontology over epistemology." "Deleveling: Against 'Flat Ontologies'," in *Under Influence — Philosophical Festival Drift*, ed. Channa van Dijk, et al. (Amsterdam: Omnia, 2015), 75f.

115 Wendy Hui Kyong Chun, "Queerying Homophily," in *Pattern Discrimination*, Apprich et al. (Lüneburg: meson press, 2018), 89.

116 Zupančič, *What* IS *Sex?* (Cambridge, MA: MIT Press), 84.

117 See Clemens Apprich, "The Never-Ending Network: A Repetitive and (thus) Differentiating Concept of Our Time," in *The Eternal Network: The Ends and Becomings of Network Culture*, ed. Kristoffer Gansing and Inga Luchs (Amsterdam: Institute of Network Cultures, 2020), 24–32.

118 Lacan, *Seminar II*, 46.

119 Lacan, *Seminar II*, 48.

120 Louis Althusser, *Writings on Psychoanalysis: Freud and Lacan*, ed. Olivier Corpet and François Matheron, trans. Jeffrey Mehlman (New York: Columbia University Press, 1996), 17.

121 Lacan, *Seminar II*, 89.

122 Kittler, *Discourse Networks 1800/1900*.

123 Kittler, "The World of the Symbolic," 142.

124 Lacan, *Seminar II*, 89. This is, of course, a direct reference to Freud's repetition compulsion. See Freud, *Beyond the Pleasure Principle*.

125 In *Seminar XI*, Lacan introduces the terms *tuché* and *automaton*, with reference to Aristotle's *Physics*, to further explain this point. Both terms, one referring to randomness (*automaton*), the other to chance (*tuché*), contradict pure causality and yet they are interdependent. See Jacques Lacan, *The Four Fundamental Concepts of Psychoanalysis: Seminar XI*, trans. Alan Sheridan (New York: W. W. Norton, 1981), 53–64. We will return to this point in Chapter 4.

126 Binary numbers were already used in ancient China and Egypt. The binary number system used in digital computers today was created by Gottfried Wilhelm Leibniz in the seventeenth century. Boolean logic, the basis of logic gates, was invented by George Boole in the mid-nineteenth century.

127 Liu, *Freudian Robot*, 190.

128 Lacan does so using the example of Edgar Allan Poe's *The Purloined Letter*, in which detective Dupin tells the story of a schoolboy who always won the game of evens and odds. Lacan, *Seminar II*, 303–04.

129 Lacan, *Seminar II*, 185.

130 Kittler, "The World of the Symbolic," 141.

131 Lacan, *Seminar II*, 296.

132 The term art is understood here in its medieval meaning, when it included arithmetic, geometry, music, or grammar. Jacques Lacan, "The Neurotic's Individual Myth," trans. Martha Evans, in *Sigmund Freud: Critical Assessments, Vol. II: The Theory*

and Practice of Psychoanalysis, ed. Laurence Spurling (London: Routledge, 1989), 224, originally published in *Psychoanalytic Quarterly* 48 (1979): 405–25.

133 It is no coincidence that von Neumann, together with Oskar Morgenstern, came up with game theory.

134 The explanations that Lacan gives in his report allow him to clarify the direction that he wants to develop and the method that he wants to use: game theory. In particular, he writes, "[b]ut mathematics can symbolize another kind of time, notably the intersubjective time that structures human action, whose formulas are beginning to be provided by game theory, still called strategy, but which it would be better to call stochastics." Lacan, "The Function and Field of Speech and Language in Psychoanalysis," in *Écrits: The First Complete Edition in English*, trans. Bruce Fink (New York: W. W Norton, [1996] 2006), 237.

135 Lacan, *Seminar II*, 303–04.

136 Isabel Millar, *The Psychoanalysis of Artificial Intelligence* (Cham: Palgrave Macmillan, 2021), 39.

137 As Alenka Zupančič writes, "The (Lacanian) subject is not simply the one who thinks, it is also and above all what makes certain contradictions accessible to thought; it is the way in which these contradictions appear as a 'matter of thought.'" Zupančič, *What* IS *Sex?*, 122.

138 Lacan, *Seminar XI*, 139.

139 Liu, *Freudian Robot*, 191.

140 See Bruce Fink, "The Nature of Unconscious Thought," in *Reading Seminars I and II: Lacan's Return to Freud*, ed. Richard Feldstein, Bruce Fink, and Maire Jaanus (Albany: State University of New York, 1996), 173–90.

141 Freud, *Interpretation of Dreams*.

142 Roman Jakobson famously states:

> A competition between both devices, metonymic and metaphoric, is manifest in any symbolic process, be it intrapersonal or social. Thus, in an inquiry into the structure of dreams, the decisive question is whether the symbols and the temporal sequences used are based on contiguity (Freud's metonymic "displacement" and synecdochic "condensation") or on similarity (Freud's "identification and symbolism").
>
> *Roman Jakobson and Morris Halle,* Fundamentals of Language *(Berlin: Mouton de Gruyter, 1971), 94f.*

143 Jacques Lacan, *On Feminine Sexuality: The Limits of Love and Knowledge, Seminar XX*. Translated by Bruce Fink (New York: W. W. Norton, 1998), 48.

144 Alexander Mordvintsev, Christopher Olah, and Mike Tyka, "Inceptionism: Going Deeper into Neural Networks," Google Research, https://blog.research.google/2015/06/inceptionism-going-deeper-into-neural.html.

145 Joque, *Revolutionary Mathematics,* 45f.

146 Lacan is very explicit about this non-organic definition of memory as a symbolic function: "The remembering [*mémoration*] at stake in the unconscious [...] is not related to the register that is assumed to be that of memory, insofar as memory is taken to be a property of a living being." Lacan, "Seminar on 'The Purloined Letter'," in *Écrits: The First Complete Edition in English*, trans. Bruce Fink (New York: W. W. Norton, 2006), 31.

147 Halpern, *Beautiful Data*, 69. The term *extimacy* (a portmanteau of the words "exterior" and "intimacy") was coined by Lacan in *Seminar VII*. Lacan, *The Ethics of Psychoanalysis 1959–1960: The Seminar of Jacques Lacan: Seminar VII,* ed. Jacques Alain Miller and Jacques Lacan (Abingdon: Routledge, 1992), 171.

148 Fink, "The Nature of Unconscious Thought," 182.

149 In fact, the Turing machine itself is proof of the proposition that memory is in the symbols themselves.

4

LEARNING FROM MACHINES

> Machine learning changes the way you think about a problem. Software engineers are trained to think logically and mathematically; we use assertions to prove properties of our program are correct. With machine learning, the focus shifts from a mathematical science to a natural science: we're making observations about an uncertain world, running experiments, and using statistics, not logic, to analyze the results of the experiment. The ability to think like a scientist will expand your horizons and open up new areas that you couldn't explore without it.
>
> —*Peter Norvig*[1]

In an introductory video to Google's Machine Learning Crash Course, Peter Norvig, computer scientist and former head of Google Research, describes the "philosophical reason" for using machine learning. As a form of applied statistics, it is transforming modern computing itself: with machine learning, we are transitioning from precise if-then instructions to an iterative approach of experimentation – moving away from rule-based programming to new techniques for "growing programs."[2] By tweaking the parameters of a neural network, which is fed with existing data, a model is learned and then applied to unseen data. Compared to classical computation based on digital computers (i.e. the Turing machine), machine learning in the form of neural networks resembles, at least in some central features, analogue computing. For example, the weights needed to adjust the learning algorithm are continuously calculated throughout the network. This analogue feature makes neural networks more stable and robust when confronted with uncertainty. As probabilistic models, they are nondeterministic; with

DOI: 10.4324/9781003690146-5

each iteration, a neural network will produce a slightly different result, something that goes against our traditional understanding of computers as systems that guarantee the exact same result each time an algorithmic function is run.[3] Whereas classical computation assumes a world of pre-existing rules that only need to be formalised to make sense to a machine, the non-classical paradigm of neural networks is not interested in a pre-existing, exact representation of the world, but settles for an ever-closer approximation to the world as it is, or more precisely, as it appears to be. It is therefore inherently probabilistic.[4]

A big issue with artificial neural networks and related deep learning techniques is that they are presented to us as something completely new.[5] Yet some of the underlying learning algorithms, often simply called *learners*, are as old as modern computing itself, such as Decision Trees, k-nearest neighbours, Naive Bayes, random forest, or linear regression. They form, in the words of Bernhard Rieder, an "algorithmic technique": an accumulation of knowledge and practices that enable computers to perform specific tasks.[6] As Rieder explains, learning algorithmic techniques goes beyond "mere acquisition"; it is always embedded in social practices and socio-cultural "communities of practice."[7] As such, machine learning is traversed by a myriad of methods and use cases, and cannot be characterised by one approach or algorithm alone. Hence, deep neural networks are not synonymous with machine learning, as current debates suggest, but are merely one approach in the long quest for artificial intelligence.[8] Moreover, machine learning practices, as well as the resources for teaching machine learning, are dispersed across various university departments, blogs, online courses, and companies "that engage heavily in the production and circulation of technical knowledge."[9] In fact, major tech companies such as Google, Facebook, Apple, Amazon, Microsoft, Baidu, and IBM are setting the standards not only for machine learning infrastructures

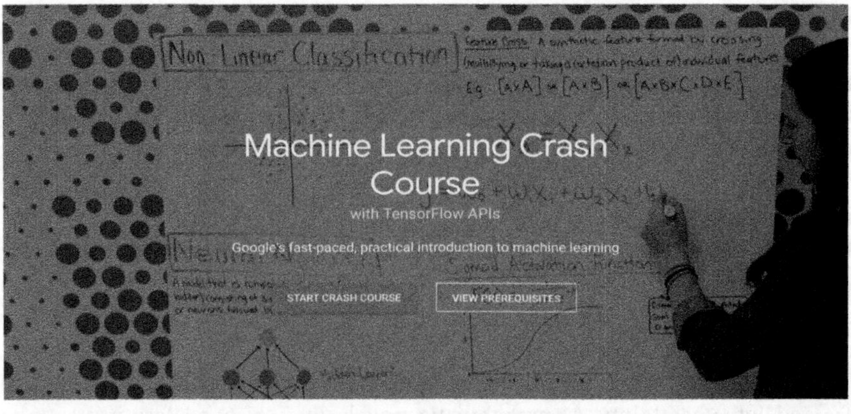

FIGURE 4.1 Google's Machine Learning Crash Course (Screenshot).

but also for how machine learning is taught.[10] What is actually new is that universities no longer hold hegemony over machine learning processes; instead, this power now resides with private companies. They are establishing a new regime of truth, which is anchored in the connectionist worldview and based on billions of dollars of investment. The standardisation of technical knowledge according to this truth helps them to recruit new AI talent around the globe and to fetishise their product as a self-generating system.

A media theory of machine learning needs to think with and through technologies in order to break with the dominant imaginary of artificial intelligence. The close connection between contemporary AI discourses and the natural sciences, in particular biology, suggests that we are dealing with a natural phenomenon. By positioning itself as a vital force, something that is no longer programmed but simply grows, the idea of an autonomous entity is invoked.[11] This explains the persistent – and probably not entirely unintentional – failure to acknowledge the labour that goes into the production of machine learning. However, this picture may not be entirely accurate. Not only is machine learning still reliant on a large number of work steps,[12] but purely autonomous machine learning is also showing its limits. Today, most machine learning models still rely on carefully designed representations and input features, which means that a preprocessed dataset is used as input for a learning algorithm. Since the dataset contains both features (e.g. age, gender, search history, temporal, or geographical markers) and labels (i.e. what to predict), the algorithm produces a model that combines both features and labels, that is a correlation pattern. The model can then be used to make predictions about data not yet seen.[13] And although other techniques such as unsupervised learning and reinforcement learning are also used, those processes have little in common with gardening. To learn concepts from data, the machine will always need some degree of supervision, especially when formulating goals and applying the model to real-world scenarios. Maintenance is also part of the application. As the environment changes, the models need to be updated with new data, and, as data is always noisy, often prevents the models from fitting the data adequately.[14] So while traditional programming focuses on code, in machine learning projects, the focus is on data. However, the two cannot be separated as every machine learning model ultimately exists in a coded environment. Neural networks are, after all, programmes stored in a computer. In this sense, the alleged shift from classical to non-classical computing, from deductive to inductive reasoning, is not as straightforward as the proponents of the new AI paradigm want to make us believe.[15]

Artificial intelligence and machine learning are no longer the pipe dreams of a few distinguished professors in computer science departments; they have become a core part of the world's richest and most powerful companies. With this in mind, it is worth considering some of the deeper implications of Norvig's question: what does it mean to move from mathematics to natural science? And, in the process, do we really leave logic behind? Using neural networks as an example, we can see that deep learning is ultimately an optimisation problem. As the model learns a correlation pattern between input and output data in order to make predictions about unseen data, the goal is to find the "best" parameters. In this sense, "optimization techniques are the operational underpinning of machine learning."[16] Their iterative strategy not only makes machine learning possible, but it also reflects the cybernetic episteme. As a "recursive technique," machine learning often involves iterative processes where the model repeatedly updates its parameters based on the data. This can be seen as a form of recursion where the model continuously refines itself through multiple cycles. However, such an optimisation doesn't take place in a vacuum. Rather, it is embedded in a socio-cultural environment that is influenced by the data on which it is trained, the goals defined by its human designers, and the broader assumptions that shape the development and use of machine learning technologies.[17] As such, machine learning relies heavily on pre-existing knowledge and cannot simply learn "by itself." It is the social nature of any learning process that makes machine learning (i.e. the generalisation of a model from data) possible.

1. TensorFlow

Interest in *deep learning* has been growing since 2012, when Geoffrey E. Hinton and his colleagues published a paper on neural networks that are capable of classifying high-resolution images.[18] Hinton, a professor of computer science at the University of Toronto and winner of the prestigious Turing Award, was from 2013 to 2023 the codirector of Google Brain, the AI subdivision of Google Research.[19] In this role, he oversaw the development of TensorFlow, an open-source software library for numerical computation that provides the tools to train – or rather "grow" – deep neural networks.[20] TensorFlow is explicitly designed for large-scale machine learning tasks such as image recognition, natural language processing, and recommendation systems. But it is more than just a software library: "TensorFlow is at the center of an extensive ecosystem"[21] that includes its own community of practice. In fact, Google has managed to establish TensorFlow not only as one of the industry standards but also as an entry point for anyone who wants to pursue machine learning.[22] For example, in addition to the platform itself, Google offers a free online machine learning crash course (see Figure 4.1), with TensorFlow as the main learning environment. What you get as a user is a finely tuned system that allows you to build your own neural network – even without a deep understanding of the underlying computational mechanisms. In this sense, Norvig's opening quote, which actually introduces the crash course, can be seen as a clever ruse to distract from the very material specificities needed to animate machine learning. There is, of course, no doubt that the experimental tweaking of a model's parameters has gained in importance compared to the manual programming; yet, all machine learning models ultimately still rely on a high-level programming language (and thus on logic), which in the case of TensorFlow and deep neural networks is Python.[23]

To overcome the hurdle of learning an entire programming language, Google has gone to great lengths to make the experience of working with machine learning in TensorFlow as playful as possible. This veritable *machina*, understood in its original meaning as a cunning trick, is best expressed in TensorFlow's Playground application (see Figure 4.2). Advertised by Google as something "you cannot break," the online application allows its users to play, in a protected mode, with the parameter settings of a neural network.[24] The ironic undertone of the advertisement seems to tease the users' fear of engaging with machine learning algorithms, which, for many, are still associated with an omnipotent singularity, a power that could accidentally efface humans from this planet. The play reflects specific ideas that constitute the field of machine learning, such as unpredictability, risk, or even hazard. Not only does this bring it close to ancient debates about chance and fortune,[25] but it also makes Google an authority that provides certain knowledge in an uncertain domain.[26] Google's educational role is both conservative and progressive. By imitating academic institutions like the university, the company distinguishes itself from the rest of Silicon Valley. However, with its aggressive approach to artificial intelligence and machine learning, which (at least in its current form) relies on massive amounts of data, Google has actually outstripped traditional computer science departments as a source of authority (hence, Hinton's dual role).[27] What is remarkable is the fact that this takeover has taken place under the banner of a "democratisation of machine learning," that is, the promise to make the tools available to everyone.[28] In a rather paradoxical move, the company is disrupting the educational establishment by mimicking its authoritative power.

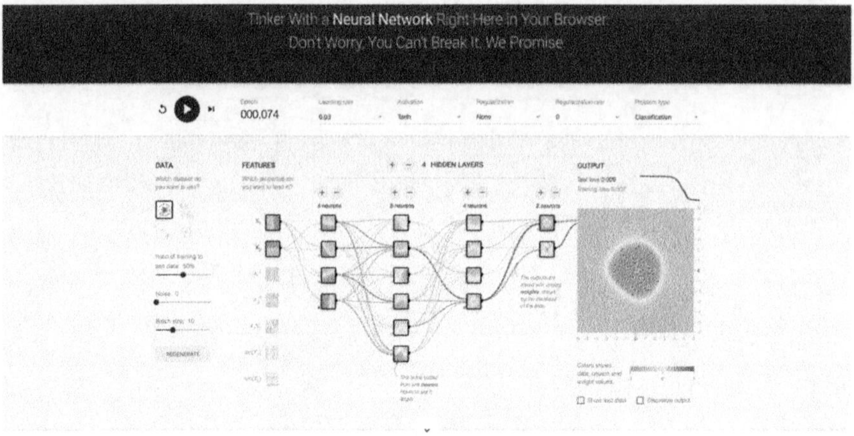

FIGURE 4.2 Google's TensorFlow Playground (Screenshot).

The goal, then, is to lure in as many people as possible, making users a potential part of Google's vast workforce. In this sense, as discussed before, TensorFlow is not just one software library among others but arguably *the* dominant driving force behind the reorganisation of an entire knowledge domain.[29]

What the example of TensorFlow ultimately demonstrates is that machine learning, in its most recent form, is an infinite process of adaptation. According to the non-classical computational approach, deep neural networks "operate on the basis of continuous infinitesimal adjustments."[30] This step-by-step adjustment is achieved by calculating a loss function for each instance (see Figure 4.3), which shows "how bad the model's prediction was on a single example."[31] Much like the game of hot and cold, the iterative strategy is the alpha and omega of this learning approach (well, of any learning approach, really). Suppose we had the time and the computing power to calculate the loss function for all possible parameters: the result would be a convex curve with the loss rate moving towards zero (i.e. the limit value to which the model converges and can no longer significantly improve the loss rate). However, since calculating the loss function for each instance of a training dataset would take too long, a statistical method is used to solve the optimisation problem: gradient descent (see Figure 4.4). As in mountaineering, the trick is to choose a descent direction and a step length that allows you to reach the valley as quickly as possible (i.e. to reduce the loss as quickly as possible). The starting point is set arbitrarily because it usually has no effect on the final result. To find the next point along the loss function curve, the learning algorithm multiplies the gradient by a scalar quantity called the learning rate (sometimes referred to as step length, although this

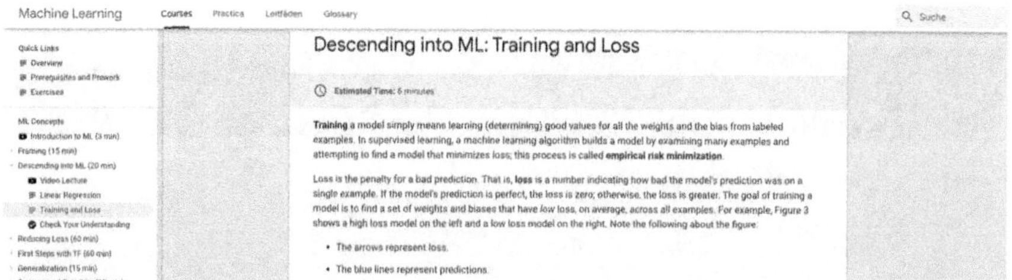

FIGURE 4.3 Google's Machine Learning Crash Course (Screenshot).

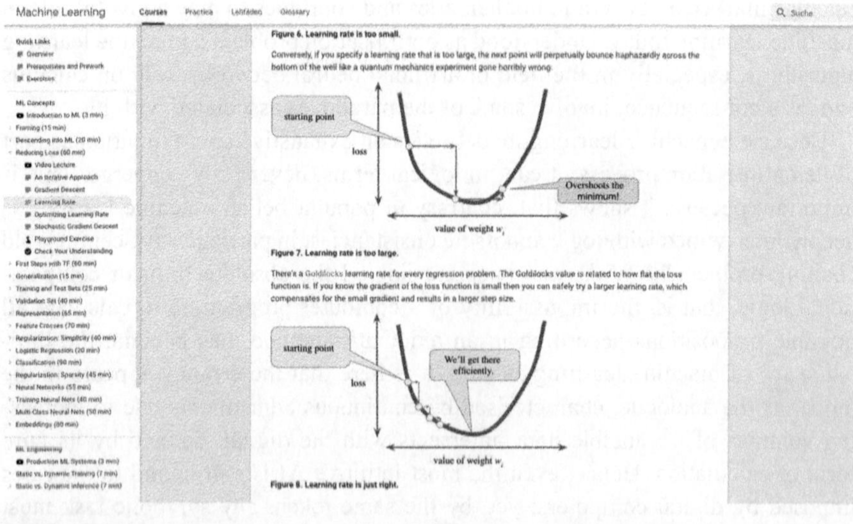

FIGURE 4.4 Google's Machine Learning Crash Course (Screenshot).

can be misleading because the length of the step changes relative to the scalar). For example, if the magnitude of the (negative) gradient is 5 and the learning rate is 0.1, then the algorithm will move 0.5 units from the starting point. For the next iteration, it will move 0.05 units from that point.[32] In practice, it is not absolutely necessary to find a "perfect" (or near-perfect) learning rate for successful training. The goal is to find a learning rate that is large enough for the gradient to converge in a timely manner but not so large that it overshoots the target.[33]

So the idea behind gradient descent is to iteratively tweak the parameters until the algorithm converges to a minimum. As simple as this method seems, behind it lurks a two-and-a-half-thousand-year-old paradox. Because the learning steps gradually become smaller and smaller as the parameters approach the minimum, each step can be divided into an infinite number of sections, resulting in a model that, at least in theory, never fully converges. With this paradox, which can be traced back to the Eleatic philosopher Zeno, the problem of infinitesimals is introduced. Infinitesimals are spatial or temporal distances that denote the smallest possible unit. It is assumed that an infinitesimal quantity is so close to zero that it has no numerical effect; it simply escapes any attempt to measure it, like sand trickling through a sieve. The paradox of infinitesimals was crucial to the development of differential and integral equations, also known as calculus. As is well known, Gottfried Wilhelm Leibniz and Isaac Newton independently developed the mathematical branch of calculus in the late seventeenth century.[34] By defining a systematic method for calculating surfaces and motion, it soon became a "killer application" of modern mathematics as it focused on solving practical problems (e.g. ballistics, planetary motion, bridge design). Calculus eventually proved to be "the richest lode that mathematicians have ever struck."[35] The development of calculus marked a new era in mathematics and continues to play a pivotal role in machine learning today. Understood as optimisation problems, machine learning algorithms, especially in the field of artificial neural networks, rely on calculus and, as a consequence, involve some of the paradoxes associated with it.

Because a machine learning model relies on exhaustive approximation as part of its optimisation process, it can, in logical terms, never fully converge. This is important because it shows that, contrary to popular belief, machine learning is deeply intertwined with logic and its inconsistencies, in particular the century-old "halting problem."[36] What was once considered the absolute limit of computational logic, that is, the impossibility of a computer programme to calculate all possible propositions according to an axiomatic method, has become the liminal space of machine learning as well. It is here that the errancy appears in the model as the analogue, characterised by continuous adjustments due to increasing volumes of irreducible data, intersects with the digital, defined by its pure form of calculation. Hence, even the most intuitive AI is still bound to the rules imposed by digital computers; yet, by the same token, any symbolic task must be performed under real conditions. What makes neural networks so efficient is their ability to navigate this space between the analogue and the digital, and to operationalise the "problem posed by the original negative proof of the *entscheidungsproblem* that is the Turing machine."[37] Turing's machine, which allows continuous processes to be broken down into discrete steps, reaches its limits precisely where real-world data, which always involves some degree of uncertainty and randomness, becomes essential for machine learning. Conversely, it is this limitation of purely deductive processes that highlights the productivity of computation, which exceeds a mere input-output relationship, thus challenging "the very idea that processing [data] always leads to an already pre-programmed result."[38] Drawing on Gregory Chaitin's concept of incomputability, Luciana Parisi claims that randomness is an inherent condition of computation. Not in the sense of an external contingency subverting an otherwise stable process, but rather as something intrinsic to the computer's formal-logical constitution. Rather than being an error that needs to be corrected, random data makes computation highly productive.[39] The errant behaviour of digital computers processing this data constantly adds something to the computational process that was not there to begin with. It is precisely this ampliative character of algorithmic randomness that "cannot simply be explained away by the paradigmatic substitution of biological dynamics for mathematical axiomatics."[40] On the contrary, the indeterminacy of computation (i.e. its incomputability) must be addressed within the logical structure of computation itself.[41]

Norvig says that machine learning is no longer a logical problem but an experimental one. This may be true if we accept the premise that with machine learning we have moved from a mathematical to a natural science. However, given the central role of logical and therefore mathematical reasoning (e.g. inductive inference) in machine learning, the statement seems to contradict its own premise. According to German media theorist Dieter Mersch, "all calculations and thus algorithms, even if they operate in the finite, are nothing but complex 'mathematical machines' whose logical limits lie in certain infinities."[42] Hence, algorithms and calculation are sub-fields of mathematics, not the other way round; mathematical thinking, precisely because it is able to expose its inner limits, goes far beyond mere algorithmisation. Rather than attempting to circumvent computational logic by "naturalising" its operating principles, it would therefore be more fruitful to explore its limitations, both in terms of the constraints and capabilities that define its scope. Therefore, the incompleteness of the digital method (as exemplified by the Turing machine) "does not define the endpoint of computation and its inability to engage with dynamical change, but rather its starting point."[43] The indeterminacy that appears in the rather paradoxical space of the Turing machine produces an excess or surplus that is operationalised by machine learning because of the constant confrontation with the infinitesimal and incomputable nature of real-world data. In this way, it is very close to what Lacan, with reference to Aristotle's *Physics*, calls "*tuché*," that is "the encounter with the real."[44] Beyond the mechanistic logic of a purely deductive machine, but also against the blind processing of inductive systems, the real creates a rupture that cannot be mended or optimised. It leads to constant change within the machine, which can be attributed neither to conscious intention nor to neural organisation beyond conscious control.[45] It does not adhere to the principles of either consciousness or nature. Instead, it happens by chance, constantly repeating itself. As a repetition without causality, it follows its own logic.[46]

2. Vector Space

According to Charles Sanders Peirce, all cognitive processes are inferential. His conception of inference is based on the idea that the subject of an inference is never experienced but only assumed.[47] This is crucial in the context of machine learning, which is often presented as an inference without a subject. However, in order to infer a judgement from data – to come up with a theory and conceptions – a conjectural form of reasoning, called abduction, is required. Peirce writes: "It must be remembered that abduction, although it is very little hampered by logical rules, nevertheless is logical inference, asserting its conclusion only problematically or conjecturally, it is true, but nevertheless having a perfectly definite logical form."[48] To arrive at this logical form, machine learning works with abstract constructs, in particular, multidimensional vectors. These vectors are used to represent symbolic characteristics (i.e. features) of an object in mathematical terms. Defined by magnitude and direction, vectors compute the data to form a feature space.[49] Within this space, the n-dimensional relationships between data are represented so that an object in vector space is defined as a collection of interconnected vectors. By forming a rather complex network, the vector space allows these relationships to be computed, particularly in terms of their similarity.[50] Take the example of Word2Vec, a natural language processing technique that assigns numerical values to words in a given database. Once properly trained on a corpus of text (e.g. Wikipedia pages), the model can suggest similar or additional words for a given sentence.[51] What makes this technique so powerful is that it taps into the infinite semantic space of natural language by mapping it into the vector space. Of course, here, too, syntax comes before semantics, but since vectors operate in the same symbolic realm as humans (i.e. language), it is human meaning that enters the naked space of algebraic calculation. Following Lacan, we can say that "the foundation of the system is already in play."[52] Machine learning scales efficiently because it iteratively repeats the meaning represented in vector space. Thus, within this space, the subject of the unconscious is always lurking between the manifold syntactic connections of data points. Contrary to the idea of a purely experimental setting based on observation alone, a vector space actually contains and computes signifying chains. It is indeed structured like a language and thus constitutes the unconscious of machine learning.[53]

Machine learning models consist of three principal components: first, a database that establishes the "ground-truth" of the problem that the model is designed to address; second, the actual programming of the model to compute the data; and third, the transformation of the data into mathematical representations so that it can be handled in vector space. Mathematically speaking, a vector space consists of mathematical objects (e.g. numbers, sets, categories, functions, expressions, polynomials, vectors) that can be multiplied and added together.[54] Since negatives are allowed, it is also possible to subtract one vector from another. A famous example would be the following: "king − man + woman = queen." In other words, adding the vectors associated with the words "king" and "woman," while subtracting "man," will equal the vector associated with "queen." The vector difference between "king" and "man" captures a gender relationship, which the algorithm – apparently operating in a binary world – translates into its female equivalent. This very simple example shows that the calculation in vector space involves a number of assumptions. Interestingly, the equation "London − United Kingdom + Australia" often produces the output "Sydney" or "Melbourne." If you wanted the algorithm to capture the concept of a capital city, this is obviously wrong. However, most people would have given a similar answer, as the equation also implies the meaning of big city. What the examples demonstrate is that the vector space, despite its mathematical foundation, is flexible enough to accommodate semantic relationships. This is why Adrian Mackenzie speaks of "an expanding epistemic space"[55] within which multiple relations of the underlying datasets are stored, transferred, and processed, resulting in a constant expansion of the space itself. In contrast to a purely automated process, the space represents a prior order on which the data has been trained: "The practices of naming and ordering, the sorting of different data types, and the addressing and expansion of data exemplified in these diverse datasets can tell us a lot about how machine learners address data."[56] This also implies the issue of "ground-truthing," that is the fact that all machine learning algorithms depend on external concepts and referents in order to ground their learning. Bias in machine learning is therefore not something that can simply be overcome with better data or models; rather, it is constitutive of machine learning itself.[57]

The problem with machine learning is not so much that it operates on biases (all learning does to some extent), but rather that the assumptions underlying the learning process often correspond to long-standing and entrenched disparities, such as those related to racism or sexism. Reinstated as "natural" representations, these inequalities lead to the much-discussed issues of algorithmic discrimination.[58] This is evident when looking at recommendation systems, which some argue "aren't merely or simply a special case of machine learning."[59] As the drivers of machine learning over the past decades, they exemplify many of the problems that come with it. Using past data to make predictions about future behaviour, recommenders tell us what to buy, what movies to watch, what songs to listen to, who to be friends with, and whom to date. However, the task of making predictions about a user's interests is based not only on that specific user's behaviour but also on the preferences and interests of all the other users in a given network. By gathering information from peers, the system generates recommendations for a target user, a method also known as collaborative filtering.[60] Basically, the idea is to find users who are similar to the target user and to weight their interest in a topic or item. Without knowing anything specific about the users themselves, the recommendation system then predicts the interest of this topic or item for the target user.[61] It simply assumes that people like things that are similar to other things they like as well as things that are liked by other people who are like them. What matters is not so much the individual node but the connections to other nodes. So, contrary to the usual marketing talk of "individualisation" and "personalisation," we are constantly being lumped together in order to analyse and predict our future behaviour.[62] Correlations are based not just on our individual actions and histories but on the histories and actions of others "like us."[63] As Alexander Galloway writes of the protocological power of these systems: "What makes [collaborative filtering] so different from other survey-based predictive techniques is the use of powerful algorithms to determine and at the same time inflect the identity of the user."[64] However, the question remains as to how this identity is determined and how similarity is being assessed.

Collaborative filtering employs a matrix to map user behaviour for each item (e.g. a movie or a song) within its system. The system plots the data points in a vector space, where distances representing similarities (e.g. behaviour of different users) are being calculated.[65] The resulting framework allows for the extraction of meaningful information about each item (e.g. the rating of movie X by user A to make recommendations for user B). While the goal is to encode as many semantic relationships as possible, that is, as much information as can be encoded, the system also needs to be small enough to discriminate the data effectively. To address this challenge, which is also known as the sparsity and scalability problem, embeddings are used to fold high-dimensional space into low-dimensional space that retains most of the relevant information from the semantic relations.[66] There are many mathematical techniques for capturing the important structure of a high-dimensional space in a low-dimensional space. However, two methods have proven particularly effective in creating embeddings for machine learning systems: principal component analysis (PCA) and factor analysis (FA). As data reduction techniques, they are both used for similar tasks, which often leads to confusion between the two.[67] The big advantage of FA, however, is that it infers "latent factors" from the data to predict causal relationships. For instance, a retailer could use it to infer hidden traits such as socioeconomic class or customer segment from behavioural data. These are not present from the outset but are assumed in order to give order to the dataset. They are therefore contingent on pre-existing (social) categories, which is why these latent factors have been said to expose "the 'coarseness' of identity categories such as gender, race, and class."[68] The supposedly unknown is not so unknown after all, but is used to make up the external referents that guide the learning process.[69] As a result, recommendations are often based on the implicit biases of these models, which may not sound worrying when it comes to the recommendation of movies or deodorants but can have devastating effects when scaled up and applied to credit scoring, social security allowances, or the calculation of recidivism rates.[70]

A recommendation system relies on implicit knowledge as it attempts to capture the latent structure of a user or query set. In this context, the term "neighbourhood" refers not only to classification or clustering algorithms (e.g. k-nearest neighbours) but also to the general idea that "proximity" and "closeness" are in themselves good categories for structuring the data. "Neighbourhood technologies"[71] are grounded in the assumption that "similarity breeds connection," an idea that has led to the formation of "homophilic" neighbourhoods both online and offline.[72] Based on their likes and dislikes, users are grouped into segregated communities, with the effect that historically grown power relations are now hidden in the "natural preferences" of individual users to surround themselves with their peers. The identity politics we see here is, in fact, old wine in new bottles, where seemingly immutable categories such as race, class, and gender are being embedded in "less crude" categories such as postcode, purchasing behaviour, and social credit scores. Yet, collaborative filtering is by no means a "natural" phenomenon; the collection and analysis – that is, the production – of data is based on a performative and therefore pragmatic framework of interpretation that is always presupposed. This explains why the patterns revealed by collaborative filtering are precisely those patterns that have produced discriminatory practices such as racism, sexism, or classism for centuries. Since the notion of neighbourhood, with its underlying principle of homophily, has found its way into algorithmic code and vector space, it is not surprising that machine learning–based filtering systems have begun to discriminate along these lines.[73] Despite assertions that these models learn autonomously from observational data and are therefore more objective than humans, it is important to note that the learning process still takes place in the real world, which is characterised by disparities, inequalities, and violence. In other words, all learning, whether machinic or human, can only be understood by acknowledging the shortcomings inherent to our knowledge base. It can thus be said that "[machine learning] systems cannot be anything other than abductive: the contingent biases of a given dataset invariably provide the grist for any algorithmic model trained on that data."[74] Abduction, or the conjectural inference of unknown factors to make assumptions about characteristics such as gender, race, or class, is a central aspect of today's machine learning models.

3. Unlearning Machine Learning

Proponents of the current inductive machine learning paradigm claim that artificial intelligence is essentially an empirical endeavour that cannot be explained by logical or theoretical means.[75] However, a crucial aspect that is often overlooked in contemporary AI debates is the fact that machine learning algorithms "must embody some knowledge or assumptions beyond the data it is given in order to generalize beyond it."[76] A machine learning algorithm cannot experience the world directly. Instead, representations of the data must be created to allow the model to "see" it. In other words, for the models to learn, features must be selected (often even created) that best represent the data in the eyes of the still very human trainer. This basic insight contradicts the common idea that we, or rather the models, only need to look at the data to get the desired outcome. What is overlooked – not to say oppressed – in this rather naive view is the fact that the desired outcome is always already inscribed in the process. With each iteration, the trained model gets more and more tweaked towards "good" property values in order to filter out the "right" information from the dataset. Now, the problem with such an optimisation process is that it relies heavily on abduction, as mentioned before. In today's machine learning methods, basic assumptions about the application domain are automatically translated into the model, resulting in the obfuscation of these assumptions. However, rather than taking this into account when evaluating machine learning systems, abductive insights are "often misinterpreted in contemporary work on AI as reliably reproducible truths."[77] As Luke Stark further writes:

> [T]he current enthusiasm for such analyses across science and industry has inadvertently demonstrated an uncomfortable fact. In the rush to apply [machine learning] to the broadest range of problems possible, its developers have inadvertently shone a spotlight on an epistemological fissure whose history long pre-dates the development of these technologies, but which is fundamental

to their application: the distinction between, what the Italian historian Carlo Ginzburg terms "empirical" and "conjectural" science.[78]

According to Ginzburg, informal (or conjectural) knowledge is constitutive of the sciences; yet, it is often omitted in order to maintain the appearance of scientific rigour.[79]

Similar to approaches in medical professions, knowledge production in AI is not based solely on direct observation. Rather, it presupposes prior knowledge that is essential for the modelling of learning algorithms. The conjectural nature of these algorithms allows us to consider their "situated knowledge," not least because "abduction is context sensitive in that its use heavily relies on background knowledge, most notably, for making judgements of explanatory goodness."[80] Rather than simply inducing concepts and categories through "automated conjecture," which ultimately serves the positivist view that data itself provides the truth about the problem being analysed, assumptions about the problem, and therefore its analysis, are part of the modelling process. This, of course, resonates with critical approaches to epistemology, such as that of Donna Haraway, who writes that "situated knowledges require that the object of knowledge be pictured as an actor and agent, not as a screen or a ground or a resource, never fully as a slave to the master that closes off the dialectic in his unique agency and his authorship of 'objective' knowledge."[81] Against a universalist claim to truth, but still grounded in the larger enterprise of epistemological truth-seeking, Haraway opposes the notion of positivist objectivity and emphasises the subjective aspect of scientific discovery. Similarly to Peirce, situated knowledge cannot be reduced to observable facts alone, but always relies on conceptual knowledge as well. Not only is every inference conceptual, but conceptual knowledge is also subjected to the learning process. With each iteration, the concepts necessary to produce knowledge about the application domain (i.e. the algorithm's belief system) are updated according to the situation the learner is in.

The essence of machine learning is its ability to generalise. It operationalises the notion that a number of discrete cases can "get united in a general idea."[82] As such, it is truly abductive, abstracting the world into models that, in turn, influence the world. Beyond immediate sensation or perception, this process of generalisation gives rise to concepts that are fundamental to the learning process. It is important to note in this context that the principles of abductive learning "are not limited by fixed categories, but are essentially determined by the social practices of learning that are embedded in the conceptual infrastructures."[83] Consequently, learning itself is animated by social practices and is based on intersubjectivity. What Turing already understood, but is almost forgotten in today's machine learning practices, is the fact that learning does not happen on an individual level alone; it is always embedded in collective activity. Not only humans but also machines need to be educated – which involves not simply teaching existing concepts but developing them together. This, in a nutshell, is Lev Vygotsky's understanding of learning, which, according to the Russian Marxist psychologist, creates socially mediated minds.[84] Updating this approach for contemporary AI debates, Tyler Reigeluth and Michael Castelle propose "a *social theory of machine learning*: i.e. a theory that accounts for the interactive underpinnings and dynamics of artificial 'learning' processes."[85] Although they argue against an emphatic notion of machine-based concept learning – at least as far as neural networks are concerned – the authors do see the value of considering machine learning in relation to human learning. As such, "machine learning algorithms are not merely executors or implementors of prior or external social norms or knowledge; instead, their activity reshapes collective activity as much as it is shaped by it."[86] What makes this approach valuable for a theory of abductive machine learning is that it underlines the need to reconsider the current machine learning paradigm with its focus on individualistic learning structures. According to a social theory of machine learning, in which the social and the technical are not mutually exclusive but are rather intertwined, we are indeed all machine learners.[87] As much as the machine learns from us, we learn from it, not least because both, humans and machines, are part of the same symbolic realm. Both are subject to language as the primary mediator of all cognitive and therefore learning processes.[88]

Unlearning machine learning in its current form requires the recognition of language as the driving force behind concept and thus machine learning. Vygotsky sees language as a social product. By using signs, we develop higher mental processes in the form of concepts, which are not simply the result of development but must be actively learned.[89] What this means for machine learning is that learning is not simply a matter of processing preprogrammed concepts, nor is it the self-generation of mental functions by neural networks. Instead, it is the formation of new ideas by engaging in socially meaningful activity. From this perspective, computers are inherently social, as can already be seen in Turing's notion of the "thinking machine" (evaluated through a conversational setting). They function through human-machine interaction during programming, usage, and training as well as through the internalisation of cultural knowledge. Human logic shapes their development as much as they shape it.[90] This mutual learning process is particularly evident in today's machine learning systems, which are not only trained on the data we create but are also fine-tuned according to our wishes and ideas. In addition, the learning process is guided by an extended version of the teacher-student relationship, as exemplified by "reinforcement learning from human feedback."[91] Here, the exchange between the human annotator and the AI model is essential for the success of the learning process. All of this is mediated by language, which generates concepts and thus intelligence. Contrary to the brain-physiological notion of today's machine learning models, it is the abstract nature of language that allows machine learning algorithms to learn beyond individual cases. The symbolic plays a crucial role in the processing of data. Despite current attempts to go beyond a symbolic information-processing model of the mind, it is language that shapes and forms machine learning.

4. Logical Errancy

According to media theorist Luciana Parisi, today's non-classical "learning algorithms are already a step towards [the] envisioning of abductive artificial intelligence, involving conceptual re-elaboration from data correlations, rules and functions that can be used to construct new hypotheses."[92] She argues that "abductive reasoning offers one possible envisioning of a general artificial thinking that accounts for multimodal logic and does not simply mirror one specific image of automated cognition."[93] The focus on multimodal logic emphasises the importance of considering logical inference not as an either/or but as an intertwined process mediated by abduction. However, logical thinking in a Peircean sense cannot be seen as a simple progression from deductive to inductive to abductive AI; rather, machine learning combines all three forms of logical intervention. The question of the possibility of machine learning is ultimately about the fundamental relationship between intuition and formalism, thinking and mechanisation, creativity and repetition. A digital computer is first and foremost an attempt to realise formal-logical operations through a determinate machine. And even if a probabilistic (i.e. inductive) principle has penetrated the rigid (i.e. deductive) organisation of the Turing machine with the advent of connectionist models, the sequential logic for calculating possible events – and thus a learning effect – remains.[94] In the formal sequences of computing, something is always processed intuitively. This shift towards abductive, that is, intuitive learning eventually shows that machine learning is a form of concept learning. By highlighting the necessity of training the machine, Turing acknowledges its ability to move beyond its own instructions: "It would be like a pupil who had learnt much from his master, but had added much more by his own work." If the machine is able to deviate from fixed routines, "one is obliged to regard [it] as showing intelligence."[95] Rather than merely representing and learning concepts from a brain-physiological structure, as is the case with connectionism, *learning how to learn* presupposes a teaching process. This process, however, is always reciprocal, involving mathematical functions, algorithmic procedures, human oversight, and knowledge production.[96] As Mackenzie writes: "People look at curves for evidence of convergence, functions compress data into functions that support classification or predictions, and algorithms observe gradients or rates of error in relation to model parameters. In several senses, people and machines together move along curves."[97] From this perspective, machine learning is not about teaching the machine what to think, but about learning collectively what thinking might be, in the first place.

Remember Peter Norvig, the former head of Google Research? For him, the philosophical reason for using machine learning is that it "changes the way you think about a problem," because "with machine learning the focus shifts from a mathematical science to a natural science."[98] There is a lot to say about this assumption. The most important for our purpose here is the fact that Lacan already made the distinction between what he called the exact sciences and the conjectural sciences.[99] For him, however, mathematics is by no means synonymous with being exact. On the contrary, the world, in all its uncertainty, is constituted by the symbolic order, including arithmetic, algebra, geometry, music, or the arts. And as the example of TensorFlow has shown, machine learning as a scientific technique depends not only on the collection and modelling of digital data, but also on the logics underlying these models. This involves assumptions and speculation about the broader context in which the data is being processed:

> The learning or making by learning is far from homogenous, stable, or automatic in practice. Materially, code is only one element in the diagram of machine learning. It displays, with greater or lesser degrees of visibility, relations among a variety of forces (infrastructures, scientific knowledges, mathematical formalisations, etc.). It is aligned by and exposes multiple institutional, infrastructural, epistemic, and economic positions.[100]

The history of machine learning is therefore less a history of automation than a history of abstraction. Learning algorithms invoke a form of "real abstraction" as they, on the one hand, abstract the world through modelling, and, on the other hand, directly affect our economic, social, and political situation. They are literally conjectural in the sense that they come with their own worldviews. As Ramon Amaro explains, using computer vision as an example: "In order to accomplish what is thought to be visual coherence, it is functionally necessary to reduce any inherent levels of inconsistency or instability, as human eyes would."[101] Mimicking human perception by means of machines requires certain assumptions about the "real world" in order to reduce the full range of possible representations. "Nonetheless," as Amaro further explains, "the basis of simulation here characterizes the living as an emanation of preexisting conditions, reducing the operation of individuation and the differences amongst the living to no more than an assemblage of contradictions that are negated and subsumed into a higher, more homogenous unity of existence."[102] Any observation or calculation of the world is based on pre-existing conditions, which, in turn, define what is observable or not.

With the supposed shift from deductive to inductive reasoning in machine learning, a new kind of identity politics enters the field. The problem is that the hidden assumptions about the data that directly inform the machine learning models correspond in many ways to the rather old, historically grown social categories (such as race, class, or gender). Yet, as the example of collaborative filtering has shown, identity cannot be fixed: a model of the user is always only assumed. By the same token, there is no such thing as a fixed algorithmic identity because it always has to be established first.[103] Every time a user moves from A to B, from one item to another, the categories used to calculate her identity are updated. This allows for a fluid identity, which is based on contingency rather than a repetition of the same.[104] And it is this contingent aspect that has always been part of modern computing:

> Most of the programmes which we can put into the machine will result in its doing something that we cannot make sense of at all, or which we regard as completely random behaviour. Intelligent behaviour presumably consists in a departure from the completely disciplined behavior involved in computation, but a rather slight one, which does not give rise to random behaviour, or to pointless repetitive loops.[105]

What Turing is describing here is the errant character of machine intelligence, the contingency that emerges in the rather paradoxical realm of indeterminate determinacy. The Turing machine is thus characterised by an excess, a constant *running around*, and it is this excess that is operationalised by machine learning. However, the "bewildering variety" that so baffles machine learning practitioners is by no means exclusive to machine learning but is a central element of the symbolic itself.[106] As Lacan has shown, the subject emerges as pure possibility within an ordered system of predetermined signs ("up" or "down," "yes" or "no," "on" or "off," "1" or "0"). The institution of a symbolic structure allows for the subject to emerge, precisely because it constantly eludes this very same structure.[107] Contrary to the notion of optimisation, which only ends up reproducing the same thing, this ability to exceed the structure, while still operating within it, is what enables intelligent behaviour. Thus, what we call "human" has always been determined by a certain "mode of numbering," a fact that finds expression in algorithmic cultures: "The parameters of human cultural identity stretch beyond the human, all too human to include 'prepersonal' or 'incorporeal' aspects perceptible to machines."[108] In this sense, algorithmic abstraction has the potential to transcend supposedly natural categories such as race, class, gender, sexuality, and other familiar categories of cultural and social identity. It is the abstraction process of machine learning algorithms that allows them – and us – to learn something new.[109]

In addition to the inherent indeterminacy of all computational processes, as demonstrated by Turing, machine learning resonates with recent debates about the incomputability of reality[110] as well as speculative attempts to transcend modern computation altogether.[111] The aim of these interventions is to highlight the need to move beyond the limited notion of machine learning as a mere statistical application and to call for a new "politics of possibility."[112] The political dimension of machine learning, then, may not lie in the juxtaposition of the human and the machine, but in carving out the non-human, that is, the computational conditions of the human itself. According to German philosopher Sybille Krämer, humans actually developed the computer "within themselves" long before it was invented as an actual device. In the long history of mathematics and formal logic, we have become symbolic machines ourselves.[113] This is a crucial point for better understanding the question of artificial intelligence, because it allows us to think about the relationship between humans and machines without conflating the two.

In this relationship, based on symbolic worlds rather than empirical reality alone, the subject, not the individual, is generated as a product of numbers, calculations, and algorithms. Thus, as a fourth cultural technique (alongside reading, writing, and arithmetic), computational thinking enables the reformulation of today's subject, precisely because it is with and through technology that the (self-determined) Western subject is being reconfigured. Since the early modern period, "humans have understood themselves to be subjects in the world precisely because they produce and constitute the world through their own actions."[114] The relationship between *téchne* and *epistēmē*, that is, the simultaneous production and cognition of the world, seems to contrast with a flat ontology. Even if the symbolic has restructured the material world with the help of digital technologies, and as a reaction to this, material processes are now considered primary, we are still dealing with two opposing registers. It is the relationship between the two, between the real and the symbolic, the inside in the outside and the outside in the inside, that remains central. Its errant character allows us not only to focus on the media-technical condition of the possibility of knowledge but also to explore the subjective position in this technologically mediated world.[115]

Errancy defines the collective experience of machine learning based on symbolic processes. While humans rely on algorithmic functions to navigate a multi-dimensional vector space, the functions need a human observer to tell them what there is to see. Each side is partial because "only [...] the results of the model and its errors [are seen], not anything in its referential functioning."[116] Mackenzie's reference to the limits of optimisation is crucial in this context, for it is here that the limit of the cybernetic episteme becomes visible. Because of its performative character, cybernetics does not take an omniscient standpoint but is defined by an iterative process of optimisation.[117] Fixing the error therefore becomes the default mode of a mindset that tries to find optimisation problems everywhere. The issue with this way of thinking, which is deeply ingrained in today's machine learning models, is that the focus on optimisation can be detrimental to the actual learning process.[118] Rather than doing away with errors, the encounter with contingent elements (i.e. the incompleteness of knowledge) is central to learning itself. Contingency, which corresponds to the random behaviour of the Turing machine, stimulates new experiences "through their implication in practices of ongoing and heterogeneous world-making."[119] The potential of machine learning, therefore, lies less in the mere simulation of already existing relations than in the invention of new ones. As has been shown, there is always something in the symbolic function that resists abstraction, something that cannot be formalised, and thus constitutes a surplus of computation itself. It is this surplus that animates machine learning; as a residue in language, it affects the human and machine alike.[120] In contrast to biologically inspired neural networks, which ultimately reproduce the world according to predefined categories, the emphasis on the symbolic (i.e. collective) processes allows us to think of machine learning as creating something new. Errancy, in this respect, creates difference, not identity. What constitutes the learning process is the creative (i.e. abductive) act of world-making, which breaks with the repetitive loops of preprogrammed routines as well as purely random behaviour. "It is," to borrow from Gilles Deleuze, "therefore true that God makes the world by calculating, but his calculations never work out exactly, and this inexactitude or injustice in the result, this irreducible inequality, forms the condition of the world."[121] Even a divine calculation can never be exact; if it were, the world wouldn't exist. This is the real philosophical reason for machine learning.

Notes

1 Peter Norvig, "Introduction to Machine Learning," Google Machine Learning Crash Course (MLCC), 2021, Google for Developers, https://web.archive.org/web/20220108211342/https://developers.google.com/machine-learning/crash-course/ml-intro.

2 Pedro Domingos, "A Few Useful Things to Know about Machine Learning," *Communications of the ACM* 55, no. 10 (2012): 78–87.

3 In neural networks, it is only the (self-learning) thresholds that simulate digital discreteness (i.e. the excitation or inhibition of a signal).

4 To be clear, all statistical learning in current machine learning systems runs on digital hardware. This also implies, as will be discussed later, that it is still tied to the logic of digital computation.

5 See the by now canonical paper on deep learning by Yann LeCun, Yoshua Bengio, and Geoffrey E. Hinton, "Deep Learning," *Nature* 521 (2015): 436–44.

6 Bernhard Rieder, *Engines of Order: A Mechanology of Algorithmic Techniques* (Amsterdam: Amsterdam University Press, 2020).

7 Rieder, *Engines of Order*, 106. The term "communities of practice" refers to Jean Lave and Etienne Wenger, *Situated Learning: Legitimate Peripheral Participation* (Cambridge: Cambridge University Press, 1991), Chapter 4.

8 Nils J. Nilsson, *The Quest for Artificial Intelligence: A History of Ideas and Achievements* (Cambridge: Cambridge University Press, 2009).

9 Rieder, *Engines of Order*, 106.

10 Inga Luchs, Clemens Apprich, and Marcel Broersma, "Learning Machine Learning: On the Political Economy of Big Tech's Online AI Courses," *Big Data & Society* 10, no. 1 (2023): 1–12.

11 See Chapter 2.

12 In machine learning projects, data first has to be cleaned and prepared before a model can be trained; this amounts to up to 80 per cent of the actual work. James Steinhoff, *Automation and Autonomy: Labour, Capital and Machines in Artificial Intelligence Industry* (Cham: Palgrave Macmillan, 2021), 173.

13 Within supervised learning, you have classification problems (i.e. predicting a discrete output for an example – spam, non-spam) and regression problems (i.e. predicting a quantity output – what is the probability). In unsupervised learning, one of the most common methods would be clustering (e.g. k-nearest neighbour, principal component analysis, neural networks).

14 In machine learning, overfitting and underfitting are two common issues in this context: overfitting occurs when a model over-identifies with the training data and cannot be applied to unseen data; underfitting, on the other hand, occurs when the model fails to capture the underlying structure of the data, leading to low accuracy on both training and test datasets.

15 The story usually goes like this: after being rejected by symbolically inclined AI scholars (Marvin L. Minsky and Seymour A. Papert, *Perceptrons. An Introduction to Computational Geometry* [Cambridge, MA: The MIT Press, 1969]), neural networks were later rediscovered by both cognitive psychologists and computer scientists, who took advantage of recent advances in computing power and hardware to simulate neural networks in software (David E. Rumelhart, Geoffrey E. Hinton, and Ronald J. Williams, "Learning Representations by Back-Propagating Errors," *Nature* 323, no. 6088 [1986]: 533–36; Yann LeCun, *Modeles Connexionnistes de l'Apprentissage* [PhD thesis, Université Pierre et Marie Curie, 1987]; Kurt Hornick, Maxwell Stinchcombe, and Halbert White, "Multilayer Feedforward Networks are Universal Approximators," *Neural Networks* 2 [1989]: 396–66). Various versions of this narrative have been advanced in recent landmark publications, such as the field-defining book *Deep Learning* (Ian Goodfellow, Yoshua Bengio, and Aaron Courville, *Deep Learning* [Cambridge, MA: MIT Press, 2016]) and the widely cited paper on convolutional neural networks by the field's three leading figures: Yann LeCun, Yoshua Bengio, and Geoffrey E. Hinton, "Deep Learning," *Nature* 521 [2015]: 436–44). But the teleological core of the story remains the same: for the proponents of neural networks, any setbacks in the history of this approach are simply the product of limited processing capabilities, the exponential growth of which will eventually prove the validity of neural networks as a model of intelligence applicable to both humans and machines.

16 Adrian Mackenzie, *Machine Learners: Archaeology of a Data Practice* (Cambridge, MA: MIT Press, 2017), 95.

17 See Anja Bechmann and Geoffrey C. Bowker, "Unsupervised by Any Other Name: Hidden Layers of Knowledge Production in Artificial Intelligence on Social Media," *Big Data & Society* 6, no. 1 (2019). 1–11.

18 Alex Krizhevsky, Ilya Sutskever, and Geoffrey E. Hinton. "ImageNet Classification with Deep Convolutional Neural Networks," *Communications of the ACM* 60, no. 6 (2017): 84–90.

19 In April 2023, Google Brain merged with Google's sister company DeepMind to form Google DeepMind. Hinton left Google the same year, warning of the dangers of deep learning technologies.

20 See the website of Google's TensorFlow project: https://www.tensorflow.org. The name, of course, refers to the mathematical term tensor, which describes a set of objects in a vector space. As a machine learning software library, TensorFlow is also supported by Google Vertex AI, a cloud platform for training, deploying and managing AI models at scale. Other cloud-based machine learning platforms include Microsoft Azure, Amazon SageMaker, IBM Watson Studio and Anaconda.

21 Aurélien Géron, *Hands-On Machine Learning with Scikit-Learn, Keras, and TensorFlow: Concepts, Tools and Techniques to Build Intelligent Systems* (O'Reilly Media, 2019), 378.

22 In addition to TensorFlow, Google Vertex AI has now also integrated PyTorch as a framework for machine learning. Like TensorFlow, PyTorch is based on the Python programming language.

23 Python was developed as a simplified version of the ABC programming language by Dutch computer scientist Guido van Rossum, who, as the story goes, was a big *Monty Python* fan. As a high-level programming language, Python translates (high-level) programme code into (low-level) machine code, a process called compilation. Even at this very basic level, the mediating role of language is crucial.

24 From the description of TensorFlow Playground:

> The data points (represented by small circles) are initially colored orange or blue, which correspond to positive one and negative one. In the hidden layers, the lines

are colored by the weights of the connections between neurons. Blue shows a positive weight, which means the network is using that output of the neuron as given. An orange line shows that the network is assigning a negative weight. In the output layer, the dots are colored blue or orange depending on their original values. The background color shows what the network is predicting for a particular area. The intensity of the color shows how confident that prediction is.

TensorFlow Playground, TensorFlow website, https://playground.tensorflow.org.

25 See Aristotle's discussion of the concept of chance (distinguished from spontaneity or randomness) in the second book of his *Physics*.
26 Luchs, Apprich, and Broersma, "Learning Machine Learning."
27 The authoritative power in the field of computing has always been ambiguous: it was not until the 1960s that computer science was established as an academic discipline. Before that, Big Science (and therefore all AI research) was actually funded as a public-private partnership, mostly outside universities. Thanks to Claus Pias for the clarification.
28 Sudhir Hasbe and Ryan Lippert, "The Democratization of Data and Insights: Expanding Machine Learning Access," Data Analytics, Google Cloud blog, November 16, 2020, https://cloud.google.com/blog/products/data-analytics/democratization-of-ml-and-ai-with-google-cloud. See also: Inga Luchs, "AI for All? Challenging the Democratization of Machine Learning," *APRJA* 12, no. 1 (2023): 135–47.
29 According to a recent study by the Radical AI Network, 58 per cent of the most cited papers published at the top two AI conferences between 2018 and 2019 had at least one author affiliated with one of the big tech companies. See Karen Hao, "Inside the Fight to Reclaim AI From Big Tech's Control," *MIT Technology Review* 124, no. 4 (2021): 50.
30 Matteo Pasquinelli and Vladan Joler, "The Nooscope Manifested: AI as Instrument of Knowledge Extractivism," *AI & Society* 36 (2021): 1272.
31 Google Developers, "Linear Regression: Loss," Crash Course, ML Concepts, Google Machine Learning Education, Google for Developers, 2021, https://developers.google.com/machine-learning/crash-course/descending-into-ml/training-and-loss.
32 Getting the learning rate right is a big part of machine training.
33 For a history of optimisation techniques using gradient descent, particularly in relation to evolutionary computing, see Claus Pias, "Störung als Normalfall," *Zeitschrift für Medienwissenschaften* 5, no. 2 (2011): 27–43.
34 In fact, the question of who invented calculus first became the subject of a major controversy, now known as the calculus controversy. See Alfred Rupert Hall, *Philosophers at War: The Quarrel Between Newton and Leibniz* (Cambridge: Cambridge University Press, 1980).
35 Morris Kline, *Calculus: An Intuitive and Physical Approach* (New York: John Wiley & Sons, 1977), 4.
36 Turing's halting problem states that it is impossible to create a general algorithm that can determine, for every possible input, whether a given programme will eventually halt or run forever. This implies that there are certain computational problems for which no algorithm can predict the outcome (i.e. whether the programme will halt or not), demonstrating the inherent limits of what can be computed. Alan M. Turing, "On Computable Numbers, with an Application to the Entscheidungsproblem," *Proceedings of the London Mathematical Society* 42 no. 2 (1936): 230–65.
37 Orit Halpern, *Beautiful Data: A History of Vision and Reason Since 1945* (Durham: Duke University Press, 2015), 162.

38 Luciana Parisi, "Instrumental Reason, Algorithmic Capitalism, and the Incomputable," in *Alleys of Your Mind: Augmented Intelligence and Its Traumas*, ed. Matteo Pasquinelli (Lüneburg: meson press, 2015), 133.

39 The productivity of the algorithmic randomness is symbolised by Chaitin's famous Ω (omega) number. He writes,

> Given any finite program, no matter how many billions of bits long, we have an infinite number of bits that the program cannot compute. Given any finite set of axioms, we have an infinite number of truths that are improvable in that system. Because omega is irreducible, we can immediately conclude that a theory of everything for all of mathematics cannot exist. An infinite number of bits of omega constitute mathematical facts (whether each bit is a 0 or a 1) that cannot be derived from any principles simpler than the string of bits itself. Mathematics therefore has infinite complexity.
>
> *Gregory Chaitin, "The Limits of Reason,"* Scientific American *294, no. 3 (March 2006): 79.*

40 Luciana Parisi, *Contagious Architecture: Computation, Aesthetics, and Space* (Cambridge, MA: MIT Press, 2013), 18.

41 In the words of M. Beatrice Fazi, who argues for a "contingent formalism" with regards to computation, "the incomputable is not an accident, not an error, not a glitch and not even a chance event. The incomputable is not a mistake for the computational system, but the founding condition thereof" (M. Beatrice Fazi, "Digital Aesthetics: The Discrete and the Continuous," *Theory, Culture & Society* 31, no. 1 [2019]: 3–26, here 19).

42 Dieter Mersch, "Kreativität und Künstliche Intelligenz. Einige Bemerkungen zu einer Kritik algorithmischer Rationalität," *Zeitschrift für Medienwissenschaft* 11, no. 2 (2019): 68. Quote translated by the author.

43 Parisi, *Contagious Architecture*, 19.

44 The real is beyond the *automaton*, the return, the coming-back, the insistence of the signs, by which we see ourselves governed by the pleasure principle. The real is that which always lies behind the automaton, and it is quite obvious, throughout Freud's research, that it is this that is the object of his concern.

Lacan, *The Four Fundamental Concepts of Psychoanalysis, Seminar XI*, trans. Alan Sheridan (New York: W. W. Norton, 1998), 53. "*Tuché*" (fate) and automaton (chance) as opposites to the necessity of a causation.

45 At this point, I would like to disagree with Luciana Parisi's assertion that the productivity of randomness is somehow linked to N. Katherine Hayles' theory of nonconscious cognition. See Parisi, "Critical Computation: Digital Automata and General Artificial Thinking," *Theory, Culture & Society* 36, no. 2 (2019): 89–121.

46 On the relationship between repetition and automatism, see Mladen Dolar, "Automatismen der Wiederholung: Aristoteles, Kierkegaard und Lacan," in *Automatismen*, ed. Hannelore Bublitz et al. (Munich: Wilhelm Fink, 2010).

47 Peirce's conception of inference is shown more clearly in his theory of perceptual judgement:

> Every judgement consists in referring a predicate to a subject. The predicate is thought, and the subject is only thought-of. The elements of the predicate are experiences or representations of experience. The subject is never experiential but only assumed. Every judgement, therefore, being a reference of the experienced or known to the assumed or unknown, is an explanation of a phenomenon by a hypothesis, and is in fact an inference.

(*K. T. Fann,* Peirce's Theory of Abduction *[The Hague: Martinus Nijhoff, 1970], 14)*

Thus, inference includes not only induction or deduction, but also abduction.

48 Charles Sanders Peirce, "Pragmatism as the Logic of Abduction," in *The Essential Peirce, Volume 2: Selected Philosophical Writings (1893–1913)*, ed. Peirce Edition Project (Bloomington: Indiana University Press, 1998), 231.

49 In current machine learning models, vectors of proximity imply a contiguity. Interestingly, one could say that in dream-work, too, it is contiguity in the form of metonymy, not selection in the form of metaphor, that creates meaning.

50 By transforming geometry into algebra, the properties of the vector space are being calculated and used for machine learning. For example, while it may not be quite intuitive to think of an n-dimensional space in geometric terms (Cartesian coordinates usually have no more than three), it is no problem to think of it in algebraic terms (where a point in space is simply a number).

51 Tomas Mikolov, Kai Chen, Greg Corrado, and Jeffrey Dean, "Efficient Estimation of Word Representations in Vector Space," *arXiv*, September 6, 2013, https://doi.org/10.48550/arXiv.1301.3781.

52 Jacques Lacan, *The Ego in Freud's Theory and in the Techniques of Psychoanalysis 1954–1955, Seminar II,* trans. Sylvana Tomaselli (New York: W. W. Norton, 1991), 305.

53 See Chapter 3.

54 Geoffrey Scott, "What Is a Vector Space?" Department of Mathematics, University of Toronto, https://www.math.toronto.edu/gscott/WhatVS.pdf.

55 Mackenzie, *Machine Learners*, 51.

56 Mackenzie, *Machine Learners*, 55.

57 Florian Jaton, "Assessing Biases, Relaxing Moralism: On Ground-Truthing Practices in Machine Learning Design and Application," *Big Data & Society* 8, no. 1 (2021), https://journals.sagepub.com/doi/full/10.1177/20539517211013569. In the words of Lacan: "Mistakes in syntax engender only errors, they are only accidents. But mistakes in programming engender falsehood." *Seminar II*, 305.

58 Clemens Apprich, Wendy Hui Kyong Chun, Florian Cramer, and Hito Steyerl. *Pattern Discrimination* (Lüneburg: meson press, 2018).

59 Michael Schrage, *Recommendation Engines* (Cambridge, MA: MIT Press, 2020), 139.

60 In addition to collaborative filtering, there is also content-based filtering, which uses item characteristics to recommend similar items to the target user. Thus, while collaborative filtering focuses on user similarity, content-based filtering focuses on content similarity. Typically, a recommendation system will use a mixture of both methods.

61 See Amazon's "people who buy x also buy y."

62 Wendy Hui Kyong Chun, *Discriminating Data: Correlation, Neighborhoods, and the New Politics of Recognition* (Cambridge, MA: MIT Press, 2021), 152–64.

63 This is what Wendy Hui Kyong Chun and others have called the "homophilic" principle of network analysis/recommendation systems (birds of a feather flock together). See Laura Kurgan et al., "Homophily: The Urban History of an Algorithm," *e-flux journal* (October 2019), https://www.e-flux.com/architecture/are-friends-electric/289193/homophily-the-urban-history-of-an-algorithm.

64 Alexander R. Galloway, *Protocol: How Control Exists after Decentralization* (Cambridge, MA: MIT Press, 2006), 114.

65 There are several metrics for calculating proximity in vector space, such as cosine similarity or Pearson correlation. See Chun, *Discriminating Data*, 159f. Proximity also applies to the "non-sensuous similarities" that Walter Benjamin locates in language (see Chapter 1).

66 Google for Developers, Google's Machine Learning Crash Course, 2021.

67 PCA is a linear combination of váriables (y1, y2, [...] y4) to create one or more principal components (C); the whole point of PCA is to figure out how to do this in an optimal way (optimal number of variables, optimal weights, optimal number of components), for example, word embeddings (cf. Google Translate). FA, on the other hand, is a measurement model of a latent factor (F) that cannot be directly measured but instead is observed through the relationships it causes in the variables (y1, y2, [...] y4). FA is widely used to investigate complex concepts such as friendship relations, socioeconomic status, or psychological scale (cf. the famous five factors of Cambridge Analytica). For a good overview of the differences between PCA and FA, see Karen Grace-Martin, "The Fundamental Difference Between Principal Component Analysis and Factor Analysis," Analysis Factor, https://www.theanalysisfactor.com/the-fundamental-difference-between-principal-component-analysis-and-factor-analysis.
68 Chun, *Discriminating Data*, 163.
69 It would be interesting to see to what extent the latent factors correspond to Freud's idea of the latent content of dreams, which, as is well known, is always ultimately concealed by the manifest content of the dream' actual imagery. One could speculate that the technological unconscious – like the unconscious mind – contains desires and thoughts that are (at least formally) unacceptable to society, such as racism or sexism, and therefore need to be hidden.
70 See, for example, Julia Angwin, Jeff Larson, Surya Mattu, and Lauren Kirchner, "Machine Bias: There's Software Used Across the Country to Predict Future Criminals. And It's Biased Against Blacks," *ProPublica*, May 23, 2016, https://www.propublica.org/article/machine-bias-risk-assessments-in-criminal-sentencing; Doris Allhutter et al., *Der AMS-Algorithmus: Eine soziotechnische Analyse des Arbeitsmarktchancen-Assistenz-Systems (AMAS)* (Wien: Institute of Technology Assessment, 2020), https://epub.oeaw.ac.at/ita/ita-projektberichte/2020-02.pdf; Melissa Heikkilä, "Dutch Scandal Serves as a Warning for Europe Over Risks of Using Algorithms," *Politico*, March 29, 2022, https://www.politico.eu/article/dutch-scandal-serves-as-a-warning-for-europe-over-risks-of-using-algorithms.
71 Tobias Harks and Sebastian Vehlken, *Neighborhood Technologies: Media and Mathematics of Dynamic Networks* (diaphanes, 2015), https://www.diaphanes.net/titel/neighborhood-technologies-2515.
72 See Kurgan et al., "Homophily."
73 See Chun, *Discriminating Data*.
74 Luke Stark, "Artificial Intelligence and the Conjectural Sciences," *BJHS Themes* 8 (2023): 41. Stark bases his study on the work of Carlo Ginzburg, who at the end of the 1970s contrasted the empirical sciences with the conjectural model. Ginzburg and Anna Davin, "Morelli, Freud and Sherlock Holmes: Clues and Scientific Method," *History Workshop* 9, no. 1 (1980): 5–36.
75 See, most prominently, Chris Anderson, "The End of Theory: The Data Deluge Makes the Scientific Method Obsolete," *Wired Magazine*, June 23, 2008, https://www.wired.com/2008/06/pb-theory.
76 Domingos, "A Few Useful Things to Know about Machine Learning," 79.
77 Stark, "Artificial Intelligence and the Conjectural Sciences," 36.
78 Stark, "Artificial Intelligence and the Conjectural Sciences," 36.
79 Ginzburg, "Morelli, Freud and Sherlock Holmes." This, of course, is very close to Lacan's distinction between the conjectural and the exact sciences (see Chapter 3).
80 Igor Douven, *The Art of Abduction* (Cambridge, MA: MIT Press, 2022), 17f.
81 Donna Haraway, "Situated Knowledges: The Science Question in Feminism and the Privilege of Partial Perspective," *Feminist Studies* 14, no. 3 (Autumn 1988): 592.
82 Charles Sanders Peirce, "The Law of Mind," in *The Essential Peirce, Volume 1*, ed. Peirce Edition Project (Bloomington: Indiana University Press, 1998), 329.

83 Luciana Parisi, "Das Lernen lernen oder die algorithmische Entdeckung von Informationen," in *Machine Learning: Medien, Infrastrukturen und Technologien der künstlichen Intelligenz*, ed. Christoph Engemann und Andreas Sudmann (Bielefeld: transcript, 2018), 110. Translation by the author.

84 According to Vygotsky, the mind or psyche develops through symbolic mediation (i.e. language) and allows for a dialectical relationship between the conscious, the unconscious, and the physical. Echoing Marx's concept of the fetish, Vygotsky asserts that "the mental nature of man represents the totality of social relations internalized and made into functions of the individual and forms of his structure." *The Collected Works of L. S. Vygotsky: The History of the Development of Higher Mental Functions*, ed. Robert W. Rieber, trans. Marie J. Hall (New York: Plenum, 1997), 10. His project of a dialectical psychology between mental and physical aspects was also directed against Freud's theory of the unconscious, which, according to Vygotsky, failed to bridge these two sides.

85 Tyler Reigeluth and Michael Castelle, "What Kind of Learning Is Machine Learning?" in *The Cultural Life of Machine Learning: An Incursion into Critical AI Studies*, ed. Jonathan Roberge and Michael Castelle (Cham: Palgrave Macmillan, 2021), 80.

86 Reigeluth and Michael Castelle, "What Kind of Learning Is Machine Learning?" 81.

87 See Adrien Mackenzie's concept of machine learners in *Machine Learners.*

88 When asked in a radio debate whether he or the machine was learning in the process of training the machine, Alan M. Turing famously replied: "I suppose we both were" (Allan Jones, "Five 1951 BBC Broadcasts on Automatic Calculating Machines," *IEEE Annals of the History of Computing* 26, no. 2 [April 2004]: 11).

89 Lev S. Vygotsky, *Mind in Society: The Development of Higher Psychological Processes*, ed. Michael Cole et al. (Cambridge, MA: Harvard University Press, 1978), 84–91. Learning takes place in the "zone of proximal development," which is "the distance between the actual developmental level as determined by independent problem solving and the level of potential development as determined through problem solving under adult guidance or in collaboration with more capable peers." Vygotsky, *Mind in Society*, 86.

90 The mutual learning process is particularly evident in today's machine learning systems, which are not only trained on the data we create, but also fine-tuned according to our applications. In addition, the learning process is guided by an extended version of the teacher-student relationship, as exemplified by "Reinforcement Learning from Human Feedback." See Paul Christiano et al., "Deep Reinforcement Learning From Human Preferences," *arXiv*, February 17, 2023, https://doi.org/10.48550/arXiv.1706.03741. Here, the exchange between human annotator and the AI model is essential for the learning success. It is therefore inaccurate to say that machines simply "learn by themselves" – just as it is to claim that humans learn by themselves.

91 Nathan Lambert et al., "Illustrating Reinforcement Learning from Human Feedback (RLHF)," *Hugging Face*, December 9, 2022, https://huggingface.co/blog/rlhf.

92 Parisi, "Critical Computation," 5.

93 Parisi, "Critical Computation," 7.

94 According to David W. Bates, this was perhaps the central challenge in Turing's work: "how to conceptualize the possibility of a determinate (i.e. physical) machine organization that could behave, at one and the same time, as an 'automatic' machine and, perhaps, as something that could function *beyond* the formal rules of operation without losing its status as a machine." David W. Bates, *An Artificial History of Natural Intelligence: Thinking with Machines from Descartes to the Digital Age* (Chicago: University of Chicago Press, 2024), 265.

95 Alan M. Turing, "Lecture on the Automatic Computing Engine," in *The Essential Turing: Seminal Writings in Computing, Logic, Philosophy, Artificial Intelligence,*

and Artificial Lif plus the Secrets of Enigma, ed. B. Jack Copeland (Oxford: Clarendon Press, [1948] 2013), 393.

96 Justin Joque, *Revolutionary Mathematics: Artificial Intelligence, Statistics and the Logic of Capitalism* (London: Verso, 2022), Chapter 5. In this sense, machine learning is closely related to mathematics. In fact, the Greek word *mathé* means learning.

97 Mackenzie, *Machine Learners*, 100f.

98 Norvig, "Introduction to Machine Learning."

99 Jacques Lacan, "The Neurotic's Individual Myth," trans. Martha Evans, in *Sigmund Freud: Critical Assessments, Vol. II: The Theory and Practice of Psychoanalysis*, ed. Laurence Spurling (London: Routledge, 1989), originally published in *Psychoanalytic Quarterly*, 48 (1979): 405–25.

100 Mackenzie, *Machine Learners*, 22.

101 Ramon Amaro, *The Black Technical Object: On Machine Learning and the Aspiration of Black Being* (London: Sternberg Press, 2023), 43f.

102 Amaro, *The Black Technical Object,* 44.

103 A machine learning system's understanding of what constitutes a woman or a man, for example, changes according to the activities of all users represented in the network. Thus, from the algorithm's point of view, it is perfectly fine for the user to be 58 per cent male, 32 per cent female, and 10 per cent "other." It is only for a specific purpose (e.g. marketing), not the system itself, that a decision has to be made about whether it is this or that category (cf. John Cheney-Lippold, "A New Algorithmic Identity: Soft Biopolitics and the Modulation of Control," *Theory Culture & Society* 28, no. 6 (2011): 170).

104 According to Gilles Deleuze, repetition is not mere generality: while induction establishes similarities and thus creates identity (that which repeats regularly and is based on generality), a "genuine" repetition aims at the random and the unique (Gilles Deleuze, *Difference and Repetition*, trans. Paul Patton [New York: Columbia University Press, 1994], 2–5).

105 Alan M. Turing, "Computing Machinery and Intelligence," *Mind: A Quarterly Review of Psychology and Philosophy* 59, no. 236 (1950): 462.

106 On the "bewildering variety," see Domingos, "A Few Useful Things to Know about Machine Learning," 78.

107 Lacan, "Seminar on 'The Purloined Letter'," in *Ècrits: The First Complete Edition in English,* trans. Bruce Fink (New York: W. W. Norton, 2006). See also Bruce Fink, "The Nature of Unconscious Thought," in *Reading Seminars I and II: Lacan's Return to Freud,* ed. Richard Feldstein, Bruce Fink, and Maire Jaanus (Albany: State University of New York Press, 1996), 173–91.

108 Blake Hallinan and Ted Striphas, "Recommended for You: The Netflix Prize and the Production of Algorithmic Culture," *New Media & Society* 18, no. 1 (2014): 117–37.

109 According to M. Beatrice Fazi, this process of computational abstraction is not aligned with an absolute contingency, as proposed by Quentin Meillassoux, but remains within computational reason. See M. Beatrice Fazi, *Contingent Computing: Abstraction, Experience, and Indeterminacy in Computational Aesthetics* (London: Rowman & Littlefield, 2018), 130–32.

110 Parisi, *Contagious Architecture*; M. Beatrice Fazi, *Contingent Computing*; Alexander R. Galloway, *Uncomputable: Play and Politics in the Long Digital Age* (London: Verso, 2021).

111 Amaro, *The Black Technical Object.*

112 Louise Amoore, *The Politics of Possibility: Risk and Security Beyond Probability* (Durham: Duke University Press, 2013).

113 Sybille Krämer, *Symbolische Maschinen: Die Idee der Formalisierung in geschichtlichem Abriß* (Darmstadt: Wissenschaftliche Buchgesellschaft, 1988), 4. Quote translated by the author.

114 Krämer, *Symbolische Maschinen*, 157. Quote translated by the author.
115 Friedrich Kittler, *Discourse Networks, 1800 / 1900*, trans. Michael Metteer (Stanford: Stanford University Press, 1990); Kittler, *Grammophone, Film, Typewriter* (Stanford: Stanford University Press, 1999). What is often obscured (not to say suppressed) in the digitisation debate is the obvious fact – from a psychoanalytic perspective – that knowledge and truth are not one and the same, and are even mutually exclusive (Jacques Lacan, "Science and Truth," in *Écrits: The First Complete Edition in English*, trans. by Bruce Fink. [New York: Norton, (1965) 2006]). While data positivism assumes that more data also means more knowledge – ultimately making an inductive claim to truth – a psychoanalytically inspired media critique argues the exact opposite: the goal here would not be the data itself but the possibility of placing this data in a meaningful context for the subject, i.e. actually generating meaningful information from the data. Ultimately, this can only take place in an intersubjective relationship, as this is the only way to achieve a "truth effect" (Slavoj Žižek, "Desire: Drive = Truth: Knowledge," *Umbr(a)* [1997], https://www.lacan.com/zizek-desire.htm).
116 Mackenzie, *Machine Learners*, 100.
117 Pias, "Störung als Normalfall." On the performative character of cybernetics, see Chapter 2.
118 This problem is also known as "Goodhart's Law," which states that "when a measure becomes a target, it ceases to be a good measure." In other words, focusing on a particular goal risks ignoring others that may be essential to learning something new.
119 Ranjodh Singh Dhaliwal, Théo Lepage-Richer, and Lucy Suchman, *Neural Networks* (Lüneburg: meson press, 2024), 107.
120 According to Lacan, "there is something in the symbolic function of human discourse that cannot be eliminated" and "that is what gives human language its weight, its resources, and its emotional vibration." Lacan, *Seminar II*, 306f. Turing, on the other hand, speaks of a residue in the disciplined behaviour of both humans and machines, from which something like initiative and thus new ideas can emerge. So, for him the "task is to discover the nature of this residue as it occurs in man and try and copy it in machines." Alan M. Turing, "Intelligent Machinery," in *The Essential Turing: Seminal Writings in Computing, Logic, Philosophy, Artificial Intelligence, and Artificial Lif plus the Secrets of Enigma*, ed. B. Jack Copeland (Oxford: Clarendon Press, [1948] 2013), 429.
121 Deleuze, *Difference and Repetition*, 222.

CONCLUSION

Errant Intelligence aims to promote a broader and more open understanding of AI and machine learning, moving away from its biological underpinnings and towards a media-theoretical view. This also implies a change of perspective in how we "imagine" an artificial intelligence. While the current discourse is stuck in the imaginary of the brain, thereby preventing an examination of the symbolic preconditions of intelligent machinery, the history of computing offers a wide field of inspiration for moving beyond such a connectionist paradigm. According to Alan Turing, all computation can be performed by a universal machine, which embodies the accumulation of logical thought. Therefore, computation and logics are in fact two sides of the same coin. The Turing machine not only inherits the paradoxes of logical reasoning, particularly with regard to the inherent incompleteness of axiomatic systems and thus of all knowledge, but is also constituted by them. And since AI systems run on computer algorithms, which in turn represent logical operations, machine learning in its current form is still bound to its symbolic prehistory. Neural networks, deep learning, and LLMs need to be thought with and through the "logico-mathematical" paradigm[1] because logic gates and Boolean algebra provide the computational basis of these systems. Despite, or precisely because of, recent claims that machine learning algorithms are "the automated discovery of abstraction,"[2] we need to recall the intellectual history of abstraction. Indeed, the very idea of comparing neural systems to microprocessors stems from the abstraction that neurons operate like logic gates.[3] So rather than biologising machine learning, the aim of this book is to highlight the symbolic in all intelligence. This does not mean that we simply return to symbolic AI. Rather, as has been argued, we must work through the abstract forms of machine intelligence in order to move beyond its current imaginary as a biological entity.[4] We need to

DOI: 10.4324/9781003690146-6

acknowledge the alien, paradoxical, and often strange aspects of computation, so that we can truly learn something new. For if machine learning is transforming the production of knowledge, as many claim, then that knowledge could also be used to transform our understanding of machine learning.[5]

A media theory of machine learning must focus on the abstract modes of artificial intelligence, that is, the patterns of symbols as well as the numerical representation of those same patterns. This self-referentiality leads to paradoxes, as shown by Kurt Gödel and proved conceptually by the Turing machine. It follows that computers – and, with them, artificial intelligence – do not provide the basis for error-free and smooth cognition, despite the popularity of this idea in current AI discourse. In fact, an error is more than a simple mistake; it "can emerge as the step *toward* a new kind of truth."[6] What unites the phantasm of frictionless cognition and connectionism is the fact that both seek to reduce error to a mistake, to something that needs to be corrected. It is therefore no coincidence that the brain, as the locus of a nonconscious mind, has become the central metaphor in today's discussions on AI. Despite the "it doesn't mean the same thing" argument, which is typically raised when discussing the implications of an all-too biological imaginary in relation to machine learning,[7] we must insist on its symbolic, that is, collective nature, in order to allow for the discovery of something new. As has been argued throughout this book, intelligence is not something that sits in our brains, waiting to be modelled by neural networks. Instead, it is something collective, constantly mediated by symbolic processes, and, based on language, running around the mind. This is where psychoanalysis can contribute to a better understanding of machine intelligence:

> I'll tell you right away. I won't be talking about those varieties of cybernetics which are more or less fashionable, nor will I be talking about the big or the little machines. I won't be calling them by their names. I won't be telling you about the wonders they accomplish. In what way could all that be of interest to us? But nevertheless there is something that can, it seems to me, be got from these two roughly contemporaneous techniques, these two orders of thought and of science, psychoanalysis and cybernetics. [...] Our concern will be to find an axis by means of which some light will be shed on a part of the signification of the one and of the other. This axis is none other than language.[8]

It is Lacan's notion of a language-based, rather than a biologically reduced, intelligence that animates the idea of errant intelligence. It is within this framework that we can formulate a critique of the inner workings of machine learning, precisely because they resemble our own logic and desires.

Humans and machines exist in the same symbolic realm, using language to learn and, arguably, to think. A recent implementation of this basic insight can be seen in the example of autoencoders, which are mainly used for feature learning and dimensionality reduction, two central aspects of current AI research.[9] They show that concepts are essential not only for the machine learning process itself but also for the understanding of it. Deciphering what key concepts a model is "thinking about" and how they are used to learn an efficient representation for a set of data is central to the interpretability of AI systems.[10] This is why tools such as Google's Gemma Scope and similar attempts to make AI more comprehensible are at the forefront of machine learning, particularly with regard to generative models. Generative AI is a system that can create new content based on a prompt. All prompts, be they text, images, video, music, or any other input, are transformed into vectors (a process called tokenisation) so that the AI system can process them. The system then uses embeddings to learn a compressed, low-dimensional representation of the input data, encoding it in a latent space and then reconstructing the original data from this representation. For this reason, it can be said that all generative AI is ultimately a language-based system, if language is understood not simply as a linguistic model but at the syntactic level of vector space. What's more, the latent space itself resembles the psychoanalytic notion of the unconscious, as data points (e.g. words, images, or features) are mapped closely together to capture hidden patterns and structures for generating new data. Just as Freud's theory seeks to analyse the inner mechanisms of dreams, thereby transforming unconscious desires into symbolic narratives, so too do autoencoders extract patterns from data to encode complex information into a compressed latent space and reconstruct it into meaningful output.[11] However, unlike current theories of nonconscious cognition, which suggest that machine learning models, like biological systems, process data autonomously, mediation through language always involves some form of subjectivity. Machine learning, from this perspective, can therefore only be understood in relation to a subject, reflecting the unconscious dynamics and inherent failures of language-based mediation.

Errancy has been introduced in this book as a concept to acknowledge these failures, which are not dismissed as simple mistakes, but as constitutive elements of machine learning. In addition to the acknowledgement of its internal processes, the concept also seeks to identify the errancies in the development of machine learning. Rather than a linear genesis, the history of machine learning is characterised by detours and the simultaneity of very different approaches.[12] Neural networks, for example, do not simply replace older forms of AI, but coexist with, or even depend on, symbolic forms of knowledge representation and reasoning. Errancy could thus be seen as the creative or productive failure of AI to fully realise itself, as different machine learning methodologies circle around each other in a process that is never complete. It is a concept that runs counter to the current paradigm of machine learning, with its notion of an autonomous, self-generating intelligence, an unerrant reward maximiser that seeks to achieve whatever it is given as a goal. The problem with this paradigm is that it conceptualises AI models as isolated systems, thereby excluding the creative potential of machine learning on two levels: first, by reducing errancy to error, it prevents an excess at the technical level; second, the focus on autonomy undermines the social dependencies of these systems. Current AI systems do not see themselves as part of the environment they are in, and so they learn and act on an individualistic basis. What this paradigm overlooks, however, is that errancy cannot simply be "optimised" away, because it is part of the learning process. In fact, it could be argued that errancy is the fundamental aspect of all learning, because it is what makes the discovery of new knowledge possible. A system that repeatedly tries to establish a "ground truth" based on its training data can only repeat what already exists. In contrast, an errant intelligence makes repeated attempts to learn from the uncertainties, pluralities, and deviations it encounters. Emphasising this creative potential of errancy helps to move beyond the usual accounts of artificial intelligence and machine learning. Technology appears here as "practical knowledge" that we produce by interacting with and learning from machines. The machinic other can help us to forge new relationships and to see the inhuman as a central part of ourselves. The "errant" in errant intelligence thus refers to an alterity, a departure from pre-programmed routines, that points the way beyond itself.[13]

What Is Errant Intelligence?

As shown in Chapter 1, the errant character of intelligence is manifested in the figure of the *doppelgänger*, which is deeply implicated in the violent history of modernity. In particular, the ambiguous status of the slave as both a living workforce and an inanimate object made possible the emergence of modern capitalism. At the same time, however, the slave has continued to haunt the self-imaginary of capitalism, constantly undermining the idea of an autonomous system that generates value on its own. It is this hauntological aspect that reappears in digital, especially AI-driven, capitalism, which is based on the phantasm of constructing an omnipotent "artificial double" of the world, while ignoring, or rather suppressing, the material structure necessary to animate intelligence. As we can see from the example of AI assistants, such as Siri, Google Assistant, or Alexa, which help us with daily tasks, household needs, research, and scheduling, we are not supposed to look at the infrastructural anatomy of these novel servants.[14] Instead, they function as technological surrogates that further obscure the labour of marginalised groups, such as racialised and gendered workers. This "surrogate human effect" allows privileged subjects to claim full autonomy over the "things" that surround them.[15] And yet this autonomy is only possible on the basis of its material dependence. As Norbert Wiener has already pointed out, such a new master-servant relationship leads to a dead end: "We wish a slave to be intelligent, to be able to assist us in the carrying out of our tasks. However, we also wish him to be subservient. Complete subservience and complete intelligence do not go together."[16] Instead of ignoring this co-dependency, it would therefore be beneficial to highlight the historical parallels between slavery and technology in order to better understand the ethical, but also socio-technical, implications of artificial intelligence.[17] Acknowledging this history holds the promise of a new understanding of technology that is not shrouded in racialised and feminised anthropomorphism, but seeks to enable a technological experience by making intelligible the ontological difference of "two entities foreign to each other."[18]

Errancy, as discussed in Chapter 2, is not simply an error that can be corrected when communication breaks down, but a fundamental condition of communication itself. Thus, rather than searching for error-free and frictionless AI systems, the chapter highlights a psychoanalytic analysis of machine learning that insists on the ambiguous character of human-machine, but also machine-machine interaction. This is demonstrated by the example of two parsing systems that can be seen as the historical ancestors of today's virtual assistants: ELIZA and PARRY expose their errant ontology through an inevitable breakdown in communication. Unlike connectionism, which uses the brain as a central design principle to ensure seamless cognition, machine communication is shown to be fundamentally errant – not because it differs from human communication, but, on the contrary, because it reveals a non-linguistic, that is syntactic, understanding of language. Instead of meaning, the symbolic (i.e. machinic) moment of any communicative situation comes to light:

> [F]or most of us [...] the significant part of the environment consists mostly of strings of artifacts called "symbols" that we receive through eyes and ears in the form of written and spoken language and that we pour out into the environment [...] by mouth or hand. The laws that govern these strings of symbols, the laws that govern the occasions on which we emit and receive them, the determinants of their content are all consequences of our collective archive.[19]

What Herbert A. Simon is getting at is the central fact that we all ultimately depend on symbolic language to communicate with each other – regardless of contingent material conditions such as ears or eyes, keyboards or screens. Humans and machines are part of language, which not only allows for abstraction from immediate sensory impressions but also enables a socially mediated mind. Following Marx, this "general intellect" should be seen as a productive force "not only in the form of knowledge, but also as immediate organs of social practice."[20] In this respect, artificial intelligence is less artificial and more collective. As the example of virtual assistants shows, machine learning relies on language-based (i.e. unconscious) processes, which, in turn, give rise to the often-errant relationships between humans and machines.

All symbolic processes ultimately depend on a material structure. The machine must operate under real conditions, which causes errors in the form of transmission failures. As discussed in Chapter 3, the desire to avoid such failures led early cybernetics to pose them as a problem of memory. Memory thus became a matter of the organic, as it was modelled on the neural system to allow for smooth cognition. What has been overlooked, however, is the fact that the errancy inside the machine is also the reason why it keeps on going. Symbolic abstraction, with its detachment from the material world, opens the machine to larger information networks. As a system of breaks and cuts, the machine is capable of constantly (re)connecting itself.[21] This errant behaviour is not to be found in the material structure of the machine, but it is an ontological prior to the structure itself. It allows the machine, precisely because of its symbolic nature, to fly on its own wings.[22] Contrary to the idea of a flat ontology, which corresponds to both connectionism and the nonconscious, the machine operates within a symbolic matrix. Consequently, it is not a "memory organ" that remembers things, but things are remembered in the symbolic itself.[23] It is here that the unconscious, and with it the psychic apparatus, is formed. Beyond the view that cognition is merely embedded in material and flattened structures, the constant recording, processing, and transmission of symbols is a necessary condition for both the psyche and computation, presenting memory as "an operative form of storage for further transmission and operations without any alignment to meaning."[24] In this machinic universe, the technological unconscious brings with it a set of rules and laws (i.e. a syntax) that did not exist before, but can now be explored by a universal (i.e. Turing's) machine. Thus, a truly media materialist approach involves the search for the logical gaps, paradoxes, and relations of this computational space, rather than reducing it to a biological substrate of (non)conscious cognition. Behind the cunning appearance of today's AI systems, with all their rhetorical tricks and the still very human labour that animates them, logic and language remain as sites of analysis, inquiry, and critique.

Digital computers are essentially "engines of logic"[25] and therefore, as shown in Chapter 4, are subject to the same logical errancies as humans are. What Gödel's incompleteness theorems and Turing's halting problem have revealed is an inner limit of the machine itself: not everything, possibly very little, can be reduced to the model of a complete discretisation or digitisation. There always remains an outside, a gap in the sense of a fundamental incomputability.[26] This is also true of machine learning: in every iteration of the machine learning process there is something that escapes the symbolisation, and it is precisely this that produces artificial intelligence as a surplus. In contrast to the mechanistic logic of a purely deductive machine and the blind processing of inductive systems, the learning machine comes up with its own structure, as the example of vector space has shown. Here, vector representations of words are learned by predicting all the words present in a corpus of text. Because similar words are closer together in vector space, the algorithm produces a set of word vectors that almost "miraculously" represent the semantic content of the words.[27] It could therefore be said that all machine learning models are abductive, in that they generalise beyond the data they are given. Despite positivist claims that these models learn only from observation, the learning process still makes use of carefully designed representations and input features, which in turn are derived from pre-existing theories, human biases, domain expertise, and conceptual knowledge. In other words, any learning, machinic or otherwise, can only be described from the perspective of all the learning processes that have led to the current state of knowledge. Unlearning machine learning in its most recent form thus requires a "social theory of machine learning"[28] that takes into account the long history of computation and the fact that humans and machines have always learned from each other. As a mutual learning process, computational thinking enables a collective experience based on symbolic processes.

To summarise: the history of intelligence is a history of abstraction. What marks its course is the formation of a fourth cultural technique (alongside reading, writing, and arithmetic): a form of computational thinking that enables the reformulation of existing social relations.[29] In this sense, algorithmic abstraction has the potential to move beyond biologically and mechanically embodied intelligence and to transcend supposedly natural categories such as race, class, gender, sexuality, and other familiar notions of cultural and social identity. It is the abstraction process of machine learning algorithms that allows them – and us – to learn something new. What hinders this process, however, is the reduction of symbolic processes to biological images. In particular, the human brain has become the dominant imaginary within which current machine learning is being discussed. As a result, the errancy of computational models is turned into the error of an otherwise functioning system, thereby limiting their capacity to find unprecedented forms.[30] The goal should therefore not be to naturalise computational processes, but to trace the inner limits of computation itself. For even if thinking could be simulated by artificial neural networks, there would still be a limit that cannot be crossed. This indeterminacy, which applies to both human mathematicians and algorithmic systems, creates an unbridgeable gap, a difference between what is computable and what is not.[31] At the same time, the gap also contains a possibility, an opening, that characterises computational processes as a whole. What constitutes the "errant moment" in machine learning is the fact that all computations, and therefore all algorithms, are nothing but complex "mathematical machines," whose logical limit is, paradoxically, what they are. The logical indeterminacy is central to computational systems; it does not contradict their functionality but makes them work.[32] Rather than being an accident, an error, or pure chance, this indeterminacy drives machine learning. This implies that computational learning is neither the simple result of human instructions nor the automatic emergence of a given structure. Instead, it is the errant interplay between human and non-human individuals that enables machine learning. The possibility of encountering something new in machine learning is therefore not in the form of an "ontological and epistemological autonomy" of computation,[33] but, on the contrary, in the confrontation with our own "unknown known," that is, the limit of the knowable, which brings about the desire to learn something new.[34]

The process of learning, as Turing showed, is based on the recognition of errancy and indeterminacy within the logical sequence of formal reasoning. Language plays a crucial role here, as it is at the heart of current developments in AI. Despite its abstraction, the formalised language of computation has very concrete, real-world implications, as the example of LLMs suggests. The production of knowledge through machine language is not limited to text, but also includes other media, such as image and sound. It is therefore only logical to speak of a new "linguistic turn," in contrast to current trends in media theory. However, this is not to be understood as a trick to evade the alien realm of computation. On the contrary, the trick is precisely to acknowledge the alien position of the machine, while, at the same time, accepting the mutual relationships we entertain with it. Analysing vector space and formal language provides an *entfremdungseffekt* that can be seen as a genuine learning effect, because it confronts us with our own unconscious ideas, hidden assumptions, and the knowledge we possess but do not recognise as such. As a co-evolving "double machine,"[35] humans and machines mutually process and constitute a general intelligence – both on a conscious and, even more so, on an unconscious level. While today's AI models are discussed only in terms of rather limited techniques such as data analysis and optimisation, pattern recognition, and statistical variation, they use powerful conjectures and abductive reasoning. At a time when philosophical activities are migrating to the AI Lab,[36] that is, when data-driven knowledge production is seen as merely an empiricist endeavour, it becomes crucial to understand the inner, that is unconscious, workings of AI systems, especially when considering modes of reasoning. In contrast to a positivist understanding of machine learning, which includes nonconscious cognition through connectionist models, a psychoanalytic view of AI insists on this intelligibility: because reality, in all its contingency, is created through signification (i.e. through language), it remains open to analysis. For Alenka Zupančič, the unconscious is thus "proof of the existence of the contingent; it is where something of which we have no memory continues to work as truth."[37] In other words, while current AI research is concerned with the accumulation of knowledge as a positivist end in itself, a media theory of machine learning searches for the truth in its technological unconscious. And this truth must remain *errant*, something that is and should never be complete.[38]

Notes

1 M. Beatrice Fazi, *Contingent Computing. Abstraction, Experience, and Indeterminacy in Computational Aesthetics* (London: Rowman & Littlefield International, 2018), 4. In more recent publications, Fazi speaks of an "autonomy of automation," which seems to imply an independence from human knowledge and thus from the history of logic. See "Beyond Human: Deep Learning, Explainability and Representation," *Theory, Culture & Society* 38, no. 7–8 (2021): 55–77.

2 Yoshua Bengio, "Deep Learning of Representations: Looking Forward," in *International Conference on Statistical Language and Speech Processing* (Berlin: Springer, 2013): 1–37, here 2.

3 Warren S. McCulloch and Walter H. Pitts, "A Logical Calculus of the Ideas Immanent in Nervous Activity," *Bulletin of Mathematical Biophysics* 5 (1943): 115–33.
4 For a critical study on neuroscience-inspired AI, see Johannes Bruder, *Cognitive Code: Post-Anthropocentric Intelligence and the Infrastructure of the Brain* (Montréal: McGill-Queen's University Press, 2020).
5 In Adrian Mackenzie's words, this process would involve the establishment of machine learning as a "technology of critical experimentation, a means of effecting a certain number of transformative operations on one's own product, thinking and ways of being amid the determinations of contemporary reality." Adrian Mackenzie, *Machine Learners: Archaeology of Data Practice* (Cambridge, MA: MIT Press, 2017), 209.
6 David W. Bates, *An Artificial History of Natural Intelligence: Thinking with Machines from Descartes to the Digital Age* (Chicago: University of Chicago Press, 2024), 284. As Bates argues, finding a new truth ultimately relies on errancy: "A computing machine that can learn and unlearn is a machine that could win the Imitation Game because it could simulate errancy – a form of intellectual freedom" (288).
7 Louise Amoore, Alexander Campolo, Benjamin Jacobsen, and Ludovico Rella, "Machine Learning, Meaning Making: On Reading Computer Science Texts," *Big Data and Society* 10, no. 1 (January 2023), https://doi.org/10.1177/20539517231166887.
8 Jacques Lacan, *The Ego in Freud's Theory and in the Technique of Psychoanalysis, 1954–1955, Seminar II*, trans. Sylvana Tomaselli (New York: W. W. Norton, 1991), 295.
9 See, for example, Google's Gemma Scope, a sparse autoencoder that seeks to give insights into the inner workings of deep learning, in particular LLMs. This tool helps researchers understand how the different layers of an LLM process information by breaking it down into underlying concepts. Google, "Gemma Scope," Google AI for Developers, https://ai.google.dev/gemma/docs/gemma_scope.
10 Neel Nenda, "What is Gemma Scope?," Google for Developers, YouTube, November 14, 2024, https://www.youtube.com/watch?v=fQP8uE-g1vo. Similar "thinking" features to ChatGPT (o1-regular model) and DeepSeek (R1 model).
11 In more Lacanian terms, one might say that a data point represents a subject for another data point, rather than something meaningful. In this minimalist linguistic understanding, vectors representing these data points give rise to a whole network of significations. A vector thus derives its meaning from all the other vectors in a given network.
12 Stephanie Dick, "Artificial Intelligence," *Harvard Data Science Review* 1, no. 1 (Summer 2019), https://hdsr.mitpress.mit.edu/pub/0aytgrau/release/3. See also recent attempts to bring symbolic (i.e. deductive) and sub-symbolic (i.e. inductive) AI closer together: "'Bilateral AI': Austrian Science Fund 'Cluster of Excellence' Funding for a JKU-Led Project," Johannes Kepler University Linz, https://www.jku.at/en/news-events/news/detail/news/bilaterale-ki-projekt-unter-leitung-der-jku-erhaelt-fwf-cluster-of-excellence.
13 This is very much in line with Félix Guattari, who writes: "I am not advocating that we go back to an animistic way of thinking, but nevertheless, I would propose that we attempt to consider that in the machine, and at the machinic interface, there exists something that would not quite be of the order of the soul, human or animal, *anima*, but of the order of a proto-subjectivity. This means that there is a function of consistency in the machine, both a relationship to itself and a relationship to alterity." "On Machines," *Journal of Philosophy and the Visual Arts*, issue on "Complexity: Architecture/Art/Philosophy," ed. Andrew Benjamin, no. 6 (1995): 8–12. Similarly, but from a very different perspective, Douglas R. Hofstadter famously wrote about "strange loops" as the core of intelligence in his seminal work *Gödel, Escher, Bach: An Eternal Golden Braid* (New York: Basic Books, 1999).
14 Kate Crawford and Vladan Joler, "Anatomy of an AI System: The Amazon Echo as an Anatomical Map of Human Labour, Data and Planetary Resources," AI Now Institute and Share Lab website, September 7, 2018, https://anatomyof.ai.

15 Neda Atanasoski and Kalindi Vora, *Surrogate Humanity: Race, Robots, and the Politics of Technological Futures* (Durham: Duke University Press, 2019).
16 Norbert Wiener, "Some Moral and Technical Consequences of Automation," *Science* 131 (1969): 1355–58, here 1357.
17 Louis Chude-Sokei, "Race and Technology: A Creole History," *Technosphere Magazine*, April 15, 2017, https://technosphere-magazine.hkw.de/p/Race-and-Technology-A-Creole-History-fTkwqWGX4M24K2MixKVrUk.
18 Wiener, "Some Moral and Technical Consequences of Automation," 1358.
19 Herbert A. Simon, *The Sciences of the Artificial* (Cambridge, MA: MIT Press, 1996), 2f.
20 Karl Marx, *Grundrisse: Foundations of the Critique of Political Economy* (London: Penguin Books, 1973), 626.
21 This is perhaps the simplest definition of a machine, coined by Gilles Deleuze and Félix Guattari. See *Anti-Oedipus: Capitalism and Schizophrenia*, trans. Robert Hurley (Minneapolis: University of Minnesota Press, 2000), 1–8.
22 See Jacques Lacan, "Psychoanalysis and Cybernetics, or on the Nature of Language," lecture in Paris, France, June 22, 1955.
23 Jacques Lacan, "Seminar on 'The Purloined Letter'," in *Écrits: The First Complete Edition in English*, trans. Bruce Fink (New York: W. W. Norton, 2006), 11–48. See also Bruce Fink, "The Nature of Unconscious Thought, or How the Other Half 'Thinks'," in *The Lacanian Subject: Between Language and Jouissance*, ed. Bruce Fink (Princeton: Princeton University Press, 1997), 14–24.
24 Orit Halpern, *Beautiful Data: A History of Vision and Reason Since 1945* (Durham: Duke University Press, 2015), 69.
25 Martin Davis, *Engines of Logic. Mathematics and the Origin of the Computer* (New York: W. W. Norton, 2001).
26 M. Beatrice Fazi, "Incomputable Aesthetics: Open Axioms of Contingency," *Computational Culture* 5 (January 2016), http://computationalculture.net/incomputable-aesthetics-open-axioms-of-contingency.
27 See the lecture of computer linguist Christopher Manning, "Word Vector Representations: word2vec," quoted in Brian Christian, *The Alignment Problem: Machine Learning and Human Values* (New York: W. W. Norton, 2021), 36f.
28 Tyler Reigeluth and Michael Castelle, "What Kind of Learning Is Machine Learning?" in *The Cultural Life of Machine Learning: An Incursion into Critical AI Studies*, ed. Jonathan Roberge and Michael Castelle (Cham: Palgrave Macmillan, 2021), 80.
29 As Sybille Krämer has shown, computational thinking has a long history that is by no means confined to the West. See *Symbolische Maschinen: Die Idee der Formalisierung in geschichtlichem Abriß*. (Darmstadt: Wissenschaftliche Buchgesellschaft, 1988).
30 See also Gilles Deleuze and Félix Guattari, "Body Without Organs," in *Anti-Oedipus: Capitalism and Schizophrenia*, trans. Robert Hurley, Mark Seem, and Helen R. Lane (Minneapolis: University of Minnesota Press, 1983).
31 Dieter Mersch, "Kreativität und Künstliche Intelligenz: Einige Bemerkungen zu einer Kritik algorithmischer Rationalität,“ *Zeitschrift für Medienwissenschaft* 11, no. 2 (2019): 65–74, here 68. According to Mersch, algorithms and calculation are sub-fields of mathematics, not the other way round; mathematical thinking, precisely because it is able to expose its inner limits, goes far beyond mere algorithmisation.
32 M. Beatrice Fazi, "Digital Aesthetics: The Discrete and the Continuous," *Theory, Culture & Society* 36, no. 1 (2019): 3–26, here 21.
33 See M. Beatrice Fazi, "Can a Machine Think (anything new)? Automation Beyond Simulation," *AI & Society* 34 (2019): 813–24.
34 On the concept of the "unknown known" in relation to Freud's unconscious, see Slavoj Žižek, "Philosophy, the 'Unknown Knowns', and the Public Use of Reason," *Topoi* 25, no. 1–2 (2006): 137–42.

35 Wiener, "Some Moral and Technical Consequences of Automation," 1358.
36 See Lydia H. Liu, "After Turing: How Philosophy Migrated to the AI Lab," *Critical Inquiry* 50, no. 1 (2023): 2–30.
37 Alenka Zupančič, *What* IS *Sex?* (Cambridge, MA: MIT Press, 2017), 84.
38 Lacan famously underlines the "dimension of truth that psychoanalysis seriously puts to work." "Science and Truth," in *Écrits: The First Complete Edition in English*, trans. Bruce Fink (New York: Norton, [1965] 2006), 736–45.

BIBLIOGRAPHY

Allhutter, Doris, Andreas Mager, Franziska Cech, Florian Fischer, and Günther Grill. *Der AMS-Algorithmus: Eine soziotechnische Analyse des Arbeitsmarktchancen-Assistenz-Systems (AMAS)*. Wien: Institute of Technology Assessment, 2020. https://epub.oeaw.ac.at/ita/ita-projektberichte/2020-02.pdf.

Althusser, Louis. "Freud and Lacan." In *Writings on Psychoanalysis: Freud and Lacan*. Edited by Olivier Corpet and François Matheron. Translated by Jeffrey Mehlman, 13–31. New York: Columbia University Press, 1996.

Althusser, Louis. *Writings on Psychoanalysis: Freud and Lacan*. Edited by Olivier Corpet and François Matheron. Translated by Jeffrey Mehlman. New York: Columbia University Press, 1996.

Amaro, Roman. *The Black Technical Object: On Machine Learning and the Aspiration of Black Being*. London: Sternberg Press, 2023.

Amaro, Roman, and Murad Khan. "Towards Black Individuation and a Calculus of Variations." *e-flux journal* 109 (May 2020). https://www.e-flux.com/journal/109/330246/towards-black-individuation-and-a-calculus-of-variations.

Amoore, Louise. *The Politics of Possibility: Risk and Security Beyond Probability*. Durham: Duke University Press, 2013.

Amoore, Louise, Alexander Campolo, Benjamin Jacobsen, and Ludovico Rella. "Machine Learning, Meaning Making: On Reading Computer Science Texts." *Big Data and Society* 10, no. 1 (January 2023). https://doi.org/10.1177/20539517231166887.

Amoore, Louise, and Volha Piotukh. "Interview with N. Katherine Hayles." *Theory, Culture & Society* 36, no. 2 (2019): 145–55.

Anderson, Chris. "The End of Theory: The Data Deluge Makes the Scientific Method Obsolete." *Wired Magazine*, June 23, 2008. https://www.wired.com/2008/06/pb-theory.

Angwin, Julia, Jeff Larson, Surya Mattu, and Lauren Kirchner. "Machine Bias There's Software Used Across the Country to Predict Future Criminals. And It's Biased Against Blacks." *ProPublica*, May 23, 2016. https://www.propublica.org/article/machine-bias-risk-assessments-in-criminal-sentencing.

Atanasoski, Neda, and Kalindi Vora. *Surrogate Humanity: Race, Robots, and the Politics of Technological Futures*. Durham: Duke University Press, 2019.

Apprich, Clemens. "The Corrupt State of Artificial Intelligence." *Texte zur Kunst* 109 (March 2018): 136–41.

Apprich, Clemens. "The Never-Ending Network: A Repetitive and (thus) Differentiating Concept of Our Time." In *The Eternal Network: The Ends and Becomings of Network Culture*. Edited by Kristoffer Gansing and Inga Luchs, 24–32. Amsterdam: Institute of Network Cultures, 2020.

Apprich, Clemens, Florian Cramer, Wendy Hui Kyong Chun, and Hito Steyerl. *Pattern Discrimination*. Lüneburg: meson press, 2018.

Aristotle. *Physics*. Edited by David Bostock. Translated by Robin Waterfield. Oxford: Oxford University Press, 1996.

Ashby, W. Ross. *Design for a Brain: The Origin of Adaptive Behavior*. New York: John Wiley & Sons, 1960.

Ashby, W. Ross. *Introduction to Cybernetics*. New York: John Wiley & Sons, 1957.

Ashby, W. Ross. "The Mode of Action of Electro-Convulsive Therapy." *Journal of Mental Science* 99, no. 415 (April 1953): 202–15.

Banet-Weiser, Sarah. *Authentic™: The Politics of Ambivalence in a Brand Culture*. New York: New York University Press, 2012.

Barad, Karen. *Meeting the Universe Halfway: Quantum Physics and the Entanglement of Matter and Meaning*. Durham: Duke University Press, 2007.

Bates, David W. *An Artificial History of Natural Intelligence: Thinking with Machines from Descartes to the Digital Age*. Chicago: University of Chicago Press, 2024.

Bates, David W., and Nima Bassiri. *Plasticity and Pathology: On the Formation of the Neural Subject*. New York: Fordham University Press, 2015.

Bateson, Gregory, Don D. Jackson, Jay Haley, and John Weakland. "Toward a Theory of Schizophrenia." *Behavioral Science* 1, no. 4 (1956): 251–64.

Baudrillard, Jean. *Simulacra and Simulation*. Ann Arbor: University of Michigan Press, 1994.

Bechmann, Anja, and Geoffrey C. Bowker. "Unsupervised by Any Other Name: Hidden Layers of Knowledge Production in Artificial Intelligence on Social Media." *Big Data & Society* 6, no. 1 (2019): 1–11.

Bengio, Yoshua. "Deep Learning of Representations: Looking Forward." In *International Conference on Statistical Language and Speech Processing*, 1–37. Berlin: Springer, 2013.

Benjamin, Walter. "On the Mimetic Faculty." In *Selected Writings: Volume 2, Part 2. 1931–1934*. Edited by Michael W. Jennings. Translated by Edmund Jephcott, 720–22. Cambridge, MA: Belknap Press, 1999. Originally written in 1933.

Bennett, Jane. *Vibrant Matter: A Political Ecology of Things*. Durham: Duke University Press, 2010.

Bergermann, Ulrike. "biodrag: Turing-Test, KI-Kino und Testosteron." In *Machine Learning: Medien, Infrastrukturen und Technologien der Künstlichen Intelligenz*. Edited by Christoph Engemann and Andreas Sudmann, 339–64. Bielefeld: transcript, 2018.

Berry, David M. "Prolegomenon to a Media Theory of Machine Learning: Compute-Computing and Compute-Computed." *Media Theory* 1, no. 1 (2017): 74–87.

Bertman, Stephen. "The Role of the Golem in the Making of *Frankenstein*." *Keats-Shelley Review* 29, no. 1 (2015): 42–50.

"'Bilateral AI': Austrian Science Fund 'Cluster of Excellence' Funding for a JKU-Led Project." Johannes Kepler University Linz. https://www.jku.at/en/news-events/news/detail/news/bilaterale-ki-projekt-unter-leitung-der-jku-erhaelt-fwf-cluster-of-excellence.

Bilski, Emily D. "Artificial Intelligence *Avant La Lettre*: The Golem of Jewish Mysticism, Legend and Art." In *AI: More Than Human*. Edited by Chloe Wood, Suzanne Livingston, and Maholo Uchida, 25–31. London: Barbican International, 2019.

Bitsch, Annette. *Diskrete Gespenster: Die Genealogie des Unbewussten aus der Medientheorie und Philosophie der Zeit*. Bielefeld: transcript, 2009.

Black, Emily, Manish Raghavan, and Solon Barocas. "Model Multiplicity: Opportunities, Concerns, and Solutions." *SSRN Electronic Journal* (2022). http://dx.doi.org/10.2139/ssrn.4142472.

Boden, Margaret. *Mind as Machine: A History of Cognitive Science*. Oxford: Oxford University Press, 2006.

Bogost, Ian. *Alien Phenomenology, or What It's Like to Be a Thing*. Minneapolis: University of Minnesota Press, 2012.

Bolter, Jay David, and Richard Grusin. *Remediation: Understanding New Media*. Cambridge, MA: MIT Press, 2000.

Bostrom, Nick. *Superintelligence*. Oxford: Oxford University Press, 2014.

Boysen, Benjamin. "The Embarrassment of Being Human: A Critique of New Materialism and Object-Oriented Ontology." *Orbis Litterarum* 73, no. 3 (2018): 225–42.

Boysen, Benjamin, and Jesper Lundsfryd Rasmussen, eds. *Against New Materialisms*. London: Bloomsbury, 2025.

Braidotti, Rosi. "The Contested Posthumanities." In *Conflicting Humanities*. Edited by Rosi Braidotti and Paul Gilroy, 9–45. New York: Bloomsbury, 2016.

Brassier, Ray. "Deleveling: Against 'Flat Ontologies'." In *Under Influence — Philosophical Festival Drift*. Edited by Channa van Dijk, Eva van der Graaf, Michiel den Haan, Rosa de Jong, Christiaan Roodenburg, Dyane Til, and Deva Waal, 64–80. Amsterdam: Omnia, 2015.

Broussard, Meredith. *Artificial Unintelligence: How Computers Misunderstand the World*. Cambridge, MA: MIT Press, 2018.

Brown, Bill. "Materiality." In *Critical Terms for Media Studies*. Edited by W. J. T. Mitchell and Mark B. N. Hansen, 49–63. Chicago: University of Chicago Press, 2010.

Brown, Bill. "Reification, Reanimation, and the American Uncanny." *Critical Inquiry* 32 (Winter 2006): 175–207.

Bruder, Johannes. *Cognitive Code: Post-Anthropocentric Intelligence and the Infrastructure of the Brain*. Montréal: McGill-Queen's University Press, 2020.

Bruder, Johannes. "Infrastructural Intelligence: Contemporary Entanglements between Neuroscience and AI." *Progress in Brain Research* 233 (2017): 101–28.

Bryant, Levi R. *x Objects*. Ann Arbor: Open Humanities Press, 2011.

Bryant, Levi R., Nick Srnicek, and Graham Harman. "Towards a Speculative Philosophy." In *The Speculative Turn: Continental Materialism and Realism*. Edited by Levi Bryant, Nick Srnicek, and Graham Harman, 1–18. Melbourne: re.press, 2011.

Buck-Morss, Susan. *Hegel, Haiti and Universal History*. Pittsburgh: Pittsburgh University Press, 2009.

Burks, Arthur W. "Editor's Introduction." In *Theory of Self-Reproducing Automata*, by John von Neumann. Edited by Arthur W. Burks, 3–64. Urbana: University of Illinois Press, 1966.

Burks, Arthur W., Herman H. Goldstine, and John von Neumann. "Preliminary Discussion of the Logical Design of an Electronic Computing Instrument." In *The Origins of Digital Computers: Selected Papers*. Edited by Brian Randell, 399–413. Berlin: Springer Verlag, 1982.

Caliskan, Aylin, Joanna J. Bryson, and Arvind Narayanan. "Semantics Derived Automatically From Language Corpora Contain Human-Like Biases." *Science* 356, no. 6334 (2017): 183–86.

Carr, Nicholas. *The Shallows: What the Internet Is Doing to Our Brain*. New York: W. W. Norton, 2011.

Cerf, Vincent. "PARRY Encounters the DOCTOR." *Network Working Group* 21 (January 1973). https://tools.ietf.org/html/rfc439.

Chaitin, Gregory J. "A Century of Controversy Over the Foundations of Mathematics." Lecture in *Conversations with a Mathematician: Math, Art, Science and the Limits of Reason*, 5–40. London: Springer, 2002.

Chaitin, Gregory J. "The Limits of Reason." *Scientific American* 294, no. 3 (March 2006): 74–81.

Cheney-Lippold, John. "A New Algorithmic Identity: Soft Biopolitics and the Modulation of Control." *Theory Culture & Society* 28, no. 6 (2011): 164–81.

Cheney-Lippold, John. *We are Data: Algorithms and the Making of Our Digital Selves*. New York: New York University Press, 2018.

Christian, Brian. *The Alignment Problem: Machine Learning and Human Values*. New York: W. W. Norton, 2021.

Christiano, Paul, Jan Leike, Tom B. Brown, Miljan Martic, Shane Legg, and Dario Amodei. "Deep Reinforcement Learning From Human Preferences." *arXiv*, February 17, 2023. https://doi.org/10.48550/arXiv.1706.03741.

Chude-Sokei, Louis. "Race and Technology: A Creole History." *Technosphere Magazine*, April 15, 2017. https://technosphere-magazine.hkw.de/p/Race-and-Technology-A-Creole-History-fTkwqWGX4M24K2MixKVrUk.

Chude-Sokei, Louis. *The Sound of Culture: Diaspora and Black Technopoetics*. Middletown: Wesleyan University Press, 2016.

Chun, Wendy Hui Kyong. *Discriminating Data: Correlation, Neighborhoods, and the New Politics of Recognition*. Cambridge, MA: MIT Press, 2021.

Chun, Wendy Hui Kyong. *Programmed Visions: Software and Memory*. Cambridge, MA: MIT Press, 2011.

Chun, Wendy Hui Kyong. "Queerying Homophily." In *Pattern Discrimination*. Edited by Clemens Apprich, Florian Cramer, Wendy Hui Kyong Chun, and Hito Steyerl, 59–98. Lüneburg: meson press, 2018.

Chun, Wendy Hui Kyong. "The Enduring Ephemeral, or the Future Is a Memory." *Critical Inquiry* 35, no. 1 (Autumn 2008): 148–71.

Cixous, Hélène. "Fictions and Its Phantoms: A Reading of Freud's *Das Unheimliche* (The 'Uncanny')." *New Literary History* 7, no. 3 (Spring 1976): 525–48.

Colby, Kenneth M. *Artificial Paranoia: A Computer Simulation of Paranoid Processes*. New York: Pergamon Press, 1975.

Colby, Kenneth M., James B. Watt, and John P. Gilbert. "A Computer Method of Psychotherapy: Preliminary Communication." *Journal of Nervous and Mental Disease* 142, no. 2 (1966): 148–52.

Colby, Kenneth M., Sylvia Weber, and Franklin D. Hilf. "Artificial Paranoia." *Artificial Intelligence* 2 (1971): 1–25.

Copeland, B. Jack. "Artificial Intelligence." In *The Essential Turing: Seminal Writings in Computing, Logic, Philosophy, Artificial Intelligence, and Artificial Life Plus the Secrets of Enigma*. Edited by B. Jack Copeland, 353–61. Oxford: Clarendon Press, 2013.

Cramer, Florian. "What is 'Post-Digital'?" *APRJA* 3, no. 1 (2014): 10–24. https://lab404.com/142/cramer.pdf.

Crawford, Kate. *Atlas of AI: Power, Politics, and the Planetary Costs of Artificial Intelligence*. New Haven: Yale University Press, 2021.

Crawford, Kate, and Vladan Joler. "Anatomy of an AI System: The Amazon Echo as an Anatomical Map of Human Labour, Data and Planetary Resources." AI Now Institute and Share Lab website, September 7, 2018. https://anatomyof.ai.

Davis, Martin. *Engines of Logic: Mathematics and the Origin of the Computer*. New York: W. W. Norton, 2001.

Davis, Martin. *The Universal Computer: The Road from Leibniz to Turing*. Boca Raton: CRC Press, 2018.

de Beauvoir, Simone. *The Second Sex*. Translated by H. M. Parshley. London: Jonathan Cape, 1953.

DeLanda, Manuel. *Intensive Science and Virtual Philosophy*. London: Bloomsbury, 2022.

DeLanda, Manuel. *Intensive Science and Virtual Philosophy*. New York: Continuum, 2002.

Deleuze, Gilles. *Difference and Repetition*. Translated by Paul Patton. New York: Columbia University Press, 1994.

Deleuze, Gilles. *The Fold: Leibniz and the Baroque*. Minneapolis: University of Minnesota Press, 1992.

Deleuze, Gilles, and Félix Guattari. *Anti-Oedipus: Capitalism and Schizophrenia*. Translated by Robert Hurley, Mark Seem, and Helen R. Lane. Minneapolis. University of Minnesota Press, 1983.

Deleuze, Gilles, and Félix Guattari. "Body Without Organs." In *Anti-Oedipus: Capitalism and Schizophrenia*. Translated by Robert Hurley, Mark Seem, and Helen R. Lane, 149–66. Minneapolis: University of Minnesota Press, 1983.

Dhaliwal, Ranjodh Singh, Théo Lepage-Richer, and Lucy Suchman. *Neural Networks*. Lüneburg: meson press, 2024.

Dick, Stephanie. "Artificial Intelligence." *Harvard Data Science Review* 1, no. 1 (Summer 2019). https://hdsr.mitpress.mit.edu/pub/0aytgrau/release/3.

Dolar, Mladen. "Automatismen der Wiederholung: Aristoteles, Kierkegaard und Lacan." In *Automatismen*. Edited by Hannelore Bublitz, Roman Marek, Christina L. Steinmann, and Hartmut Winkler, 129–52. Munich: Wilhelm Fink, 2010.

Dolar, Mladen. "Comedy and Its Double." In *Stop That Comedy! On the Subtle Hegemony of the Tragic in Our Culture*. Edited by Robert Pfaller. Vienna: Sonderzahl, 2005.

Dolar, Mladen. "What's the Matter? On Matter and Related Matters." In *Subject Lessons: Hegel, Lacan, and the Future of Materialism*. Edited by Russell Sbriglia and Slavoj Žižek, 39–43. Evanston: Northwestern University Press, 2020.

Domasio, Antonio. *The Feeling of What Happens: Body and Emotion in the Making of Consciousness*. New York: Mariner Books, 2000.

Domingos, Pedro. "A Few Useful Things to Know about Machine Learning." *Communications of the ACM* 55, no. 10 (2012): 78–87.

Douven, Igor. *The Art of Abduction*. Cambridge, MA: MIT Press, 2022.

Dreyfus, Hubert L. *What Computers Still Can't Do: A Critique of Artificial Reason*. Cambridge, MA: MIT Press, 1992.

Dyer-Witheford, Nick, and Svitlana Matviyenko. *Cyberwar and Revolution: Digital Subterfuge in Global Capitalism*. Minneapolis: University of Minnesota Press, 2019.

Eagleman, David. *Incognito: The Secret Lives of the Brain.* New York: Random House, 2012.

Eubanks, Virginia. *Automating Inequality: How High-Tech Tools Profile, Police, and Punish the Poor.* New York: Picador, 2018.

Evens, Aden. *Logic of the Digital.* London: Bloomsbury, 2017.

Fann, K. T. *Peirce's Theory of Abduction.* The Hague: Martinus Nijhoff, 1970.

Fazi, M. Beatrice. "Beyond Human: Deep Learning, Explainability and Representation." *Theory, Culture & Society* 38, no. 7–8 (2021): 55–77.

Fazi, M. Beatrice. "Can a Machine Think (Anything New)? Automation Beyond Simulation." *AI & Society* 34 (2019): 813–24.

Fazi, M. Beatrice. *Contingent Computing: Abstraction, Experience, and Indeterminacy in Computational Aesthetics.* London: Rowman & Littlefield, 2018.

Fazi, M. Beatrice. "Digital Aesthetics: The Discrete and the Continuous." *Theory, Culture & Society* 36, no. 1 (2019): 3–26.

Fazi, M. Beatrice. "Incomputable Aesthetics: Open Axioms of Contingency." *Computational Culture* 5 (January 2016). http://computationalculture.net/incomputable-aesthetics-open-axioms-of-contingency.

Feigelfeld, Paul. "Chinese Whispers — Die epistolarische Epistemologie des Gottfried Wilhelm Leibniz." In *Vision als Aufgabe: das Leibniz-Universum im 21. Jahrhundert.* Edited by Martin Grötschel, 265–75. Berlin: Berlin-Brandenburgische Akademie der Wissenschaften, 2016.

Fink, Bruce. "The Nature of Unconscious Thought." In *Reading Seminars I and II: Lacan's Return to Freud.* Edited by Richard Feldstein, Bruce Fink, and Maire Jaanus, 170–92. Albany: State University of New York, 1996.

Fink, Bruce. "The Nature of Unconscious Thought, or How the Other Half 'Thinks'." In *The Lacanian Subject: Between Language and Jouissance.* Edited by Bruce Fink, 14–24. Princeton: Princeton University Press, 1997.

Fisher, Mark. *The Weird and the Eerie.* London: Repeater Books, 2016.

"Flat Ontology." Larval Subjects website, February 24, 2010. https://larvalsubjects.wordpress.com/2010/02/24/flat-ontology-2/.

Fong, Ruth C., Walter J. Scheirer, and David D. Cox, "Using Human Brain Activity to Guide Machine Learning." *Scientific Reports* 8 (2018). https://doi.org/10.1038/s41598-018-23618-6.

Forbes, Nancy. *Imitation of Life: How Biology Is Inspiring Computing.* Cambridge, MA: MIT Press, 2004.

Freud, Sigmund. "A Note Upon the 'Mystic Writing-Pad'." In *Sigmund Freud, The Ego and the Id and Other Works.* Translated by James Strachey, 227–34. London: Vintage, 1961.

Freud, Sigmund. *An Outline of Psychoanalysis.* Edited and translated by James Strachey. New York: W. W. Norton, 1969.

Freud, Sigmund. *Beyond the Pleasure Principle.* Translated by James Strachey. New York: W. W. Norton, 1990.

Freud, Sigmund. "Project for a Scientific Psychology (unfinished manuscript)." In *The Origins of Psychoanalysis: Letters to Wilhelm Fliess, Drafts, and Notes, 1887–1902.* Edited by Anna Freud and Ernst Kris, 345–44. New York: Basic Books, 1960.

Freud, Sigmund. "Project for a Scientific Psychology (1895)." In *Standard Edition of the Complete Psychological Works*, Vol. 1, 283–398. London: Hogarth Press, 1953–1974.

Freud, Sigmund. "Remembering, Repeating and Working-Through." In *The Standard Edition of the Complete Psychological Works of Sigmund Freud*, Vol. 6, 147–56. New York: Basic Books, 1914.

Freud, Sigmund. "The Dynamics of Transference." In *The Standard Edition of the Complete Psychological Works of Sigmund Freud,* Vol. 12, 97–108. London: Hogarth Press, [1912] 1953–1974.

Freud, Sigmund. *The Ego and the Id.* Translated by Joan Riviere. New York: W. W. Norton, [1923] 1960.

Freud, Sigmund. *The Interpretation of Dreams.* Edited and translated by James Strachey. New York: Basic Books, [1955] 2010.

Freud, Sigmund. *The Question of Lay Analysis.* Translated by James Strachey. New York: W. W. Norton, 1978.

Freud, Sigmund. "The Scientific Literature of Dreams." In *The Interpretation of Dreams,* Edited and translated by James Strachey, 1–50. New York: Basic Books, [1955] 2010.

Freud, Sigmund. "The Uncanny." In *The Standard Edition of the Complete Psychological Works of Sigmund Freud, Volume XVII: An Infantile Neurosis and Other Works.* Edited by James Strachey, 19–252. London: Hogarth Press, 1955.

Galloway, Alexander R. *Protocol: How Control Exists after Decentralization.* Cambridge, MA: MIT Press, 2006.

Galloway, Alexander R. "The Poverty of Philosophy: Realism and Post-Fordism." *Critical Inquiry* 39, no. 2 (2013): 347–66.

Galloway, Alexander R. *Uncomputable: Play and Politics in the Long Digital Age.* London: Verso, 2021.

Gast, Lilli. "Das Unheimliche der Ambivalenz." *Forum der Psychoanalyse* 27 (2011): 349–58.

Gates, Bill. *The Road Ahead.* London: Penguin, 1996.

Genova, Judith. "Turing's Sexual Guessing Game." *Social Epistemology* 8, no. 4 (1994): 313–26.

Géron, Aurélien. *Hands-On Machine Learning with Scikit-Learn, Keras, and TensorFlow: Concepts, Tools and Techniques to Build Intelligent Systems.* e-book. O'Reilly Media, 2019.

Giardina Papa, Elisa. "The Invisible Boyfriend." In *Computer Grrrls.* Edited by Inke Arns and Marie Lechner, 46–55. Dortmund: HMKV, 2021.

Ginzburg, Carlo, and Anna Davin. "Morelli, Freud and Sherlock Homes: Clues and Scientific Method." *History Workshop* 9, no. 1 (1980): 5–36.

Glissant, Édouard. *Poetics of Relation.* Translated by Betsy Wing. Ann Arbor: University of Michigan Press, 2010.

Gödel, Kurt. "Über formal unentscheidbare Sätze der Principia Mathematica und verwandter Systeme." *Monatshefte für Mathematik und Physik* 38 (1931): 173–98.

Goodfellow, Ian, Yoshua Bengio, and Aaron Courville. *Deep Learning.* Cambridge, MA: MIT Press, 2016.

Google. "Gemma Scope." Google AI for Developers. https://ai.google.dev/gemma/docs/gemma_scope.

Google. "The Google Assistant Can Help You Get Things Done Over the Phone." YouTube, June 27, 2018. https://www.youtube.com/watch?v=-qCanuYrR0g.

Google for Developers. Google's Machine Learning Crash Course, 2021. https://developers.google.com/machine-learning/crash-course.

Google for Developers. "Linear Regression: Loss." Crash Course. ML Concepts. Google Machine Learning Education. Google for Developers, 2020. https://developers.google.com/machine-learning/crash-course/descending-into-ml/training-and-loss.

Grace-Martin, Karen. "The Fundamental Difference Between Principal Component Analysis and Factor Analysis." *Analysis Factor*. https://www.theanalysisfactor.com/the-fundamental-difference-between-principal-component-analysis-and-factor-analysis/.

Guattari, Félix. *Chaosmosis: An Ethico-Aesthetic Paradigm*. Translated by Paul Bains and Julian Pefanis. Bloomington: Indiana University Press, 1995.

Guattari, Félix. "On Machines." *Journal of Philosophy and the Visual Arts*, issue on "Complexity: Architecture/Art/Philosophy." Edited by Andrew Benjamin, no. 6 (1995): 8–12.

Hall, Alfred Rupert. *Philosophers at War: The Quarrel Between Newton and Leibniz*. Cambridge: Cambridge University Press, 1980.

Hallinan, Blake, and Ted Striphas. "Recommended for You: The Netflix Prize and the Production of Algorithmic Culture." *New Media & Society* 18, no. 1 (2014): 117–37.

Halpern, Orit. *Beautiful Data: A History of Vision and Reason Since 1945*. Durham: Duke University Press, 2015.

Hanssen, Beatrice. "Language and Mimesis in Walter Benjamin's Work." In *The Cambridge Companion to Walter Benjamin*. Edited by David S. Ferris, 54–72. Cambridge: Cambridge University Press, 2004.

Hao, Karen. "Inside the Fight to Reclaim AI From Big Tech's Control." *MIT Technology Review* 124, no. 4 (2021): 48–52.

Haraway, Donna. "Situated Knowledges: The Science Question in Feminism and the Privilege of Partial Perspective." *Feminist Studies* 14, no. 3 (Autumn 1988): 575–99.

Harks, Tobias, and Sebastian Vehlken. *Neighborhood Technologies: Media and Mathematics of Dynamic Networks*. Brochure. diaphanes, 2015. https://www.diaphanes.net/titel/neighborhood-technologies-2515.

Harman, Graham. *Prince of Networks: Bruno Latour and Metaphysics*. Melbourne: re.press, 2009.

Hasbe, Sudhir, and Ryan Lippert. "The Democratization of Data and Insights: Expanding Machine Learning Access." Data Analytics. Google Cloud blog, November 16, 2020. https://cloud.google.com/blog/products/data-analytics/democratization-of-ml-and-ai-with-google-cloud.

Hassin, Ran R., James S. Uleman, and John A. Bargh, eds. *The New Unconscious*. New York: Oxford University Press, 2005. Online description. https://global.oup.com/academic/product/the-new-unconscious-9780195307696?cc=gb&lang=en&#.

Haugeland, John. *Artificial Intelligence: The Very Idea*. Cambridge, MA: MIT Press, 1985.

Hayles, N. Katherine. *How We Became Posthuman: Virtual Bodies in Cybernetics, Literature, and Informatics*. Chicago: University of Chicago Press, 1999.

Hayles, N. Katherine. *How We Think: Digital Media and Contemporary Technogenesis*. Chicago: University of Chicago Press, 2012.

Hayles, N. Katherine. "Hyper and Deep Attention: The Generational Divide in Cognitive Modes." *Profession* 1 (2007): 187–99.

Hayles, N. Katherine. "Speculative Aesthetics and Object-Oriented Inquiry (OOI)." *Speculations: A Journal of Speculative Realism* 5 (2014): 158–79.

Hayles, N. Katherine. *Unthought: The Power of the Cognitive Nonconscious*. Chicago: University of Chicago Press, 2017.

Hebb, Donald O. *The Organization of Behavior: A Neuropsychological Theory*. New York: John Wiley & Sons, 1949.

Hegel, Georg Wilhelm Friedrich. *The Phenomenology of Spirit*. Oxford: Clarendon Press, [1807] 1977.

Heikkilä, Melissa. "Dutch Scandal Serves as a Warning for Europe Over Risks of Using Algorithms." *Politico*, March 29, 2022. https://www.politico.eu/article/dutch-scandal-serves-as-a-warning-for-europe-over-risks-of-using-algorithms.

Heuer, Hendrik, Juliane Jarke, and Andreas Breiter. "Machine Learning in Tutorials — Universal Applicability, Underinformed Application, and Other Misconceptions." *Big Data & Society* 8, no. 1 (2021).

Hinton, Geoffrey E. "Geoffrey Hinton and Yann LeCun, 2018 ACM A. M. Turing Award Lecture 'The Deep Learning Revolution'." Association for Computing Machinery. YouTube, June 23, 2019. https://www.youtube.com/watch?v=VsnQf7exv5I.

Hinton, Geoffrey E., Simon Osindero, and Yee-Whye The. "A Fast Learning Algorithm for Deep Belief Nets." *Neural Computation* 18, no. 7 (2006): 1527–54.

Hochreiter, Sepp, and Jürgen Schmidhuber. "Long Short-Term Memory." *Neural Computation* 9, no. 8 (1997): 1735–80.

Hoffmann, Ernst T. A. "Automatons." In *The Serapion Brethren*. Translated by Alex Ewing, 352–82. London: George Bell and Sons, 1908.

Hoffmann, Ernst T. A. "The Sandman." In *Tales of E. T. A. Hoffmann*. Edited by Leonard J. Kent and Elizabeth C. Knight, 93–125. Chicago: University of Chicago Press, 1969.

Hofstadter, Douglas R. *Gödel, Escher, Bach: An Eternal Golden Braid*. New York: Basic Boks, 1999.

Hofstadter, Douglas R. "Foreword." In *Gödel's Proof*. Edited by Douglas R. Hofstadter, xvi–xv. New York: New York University Press, 2008.

Hornik, Kurt, Maxwell Stinchcombe, and Halbert White. "Multilayer Feedforward Networks are Universal Approximators." *Neural Networks* 2 (1989): 396–66.

Huyssen, Andreas. *After the Great Divide: Modernism, Mass Culture, Postmodernism*. Bloomington: Indiana University Press, 1986.

INTRA SPACE. "About." Accessed February 28, 2019. https://intraspace.akbild.ac.at/imprint.

Irani, Lilly, and M. Six Silberman. "Turkopticon: Interrupting Worker Invisibility in Amazon Mechanical Turk." In *Proceedings of the SIGCHI Conference on Human Factors in Computing Systems*, 611–20. New York: Association for Computing Machinery, 2013.

Jakobson, Roman, and Morris Halle. *Fundamentals of Language*. Berlin: Mouton de Gruyter, 1971.

Jaton, Florian. "Assessing Biases, Relaxing Moralism: On Ground-Truthing Practices in Machine Learning Design and Application." *Big Data & Society* 8, no. 1 (2021). https://journals.sagepub.com/doi/full/10.1177/20539517211013569.

Jentsch, Ernst. "On the Psychology of the Uncanny." In *Uncanny Modernity: Cultural Theories, Modern Anxieties*. Edited by Jo Collins and John Jervis. New York: Palgrave Macmillan, [1906] 2008.

Johnston, John. *The Allure of Machinic Life: Cybernetics, Artificial Life, and the New AI*. Cambridge, MA: MIT Press, 2008.

Joler, Vladan, and Matteo Pasquinelli. "The Nooscope Manifested: AI as Instrument of Knowledge Extractivism." *Fritz AI*, 2020. https://nooscope.ai.

Jones, Allan. "Five 1951 BBC Broadcasts on Automatic Calculating Machines." *IEEE Annals of the History of Computing* 26, no. 2 (April 2004): 3–15.

Joque, Justin. *Revolutionary Mathematics: Artificial Intelligence, Statistics and the Logic of Capitalism*. London: Verso, 2022.

Jung, Carl. *Aion: Researches into the Phenomenology of the Self*. London: Routledge, 1991.

Kamper, Dietmar. "Mimesis und Simulation: Von den Körpern zu den Maschinen." *Kunstforum International* 114 (1991): 86–105. https://www.kunstforum.de/artikel/mimesis-und-simulation.

Kelly, Kevin. *Out of Control: The New Biology of Machines, Social Systems, and the Economic World.* New York: Basic Books, 1994.

Kendler, K. S., and Assen Jablensky. "Kraepelin's Concept of Psychiatric Illness." *Psychological Medicine* 41, no. 6 (2011): 1119–26.

Kitchin, Rob. "Thinking Critically About and Researching Algorithms." *The Programmable City Working Paper* 5 (2014). https://papers.ssrn.com/sol3/papers.cfm?abstract_id=2515786.

Kittler, Friedrich. *Discourse Networks 1800/1900.* Translated by Michael Metteer. Stanford: Stanford University Press, 1990.

Kittler, Friedrich. *Grammophone, Film, Typewriter.* Stanford: Stanford University Press, 1999.

Kittler, Friedrich. "There is no Software." In *Software Studies.* Edited by Matthew Fuller, 79–100. Cambridge, MA: MIT Press, 2008.

Kittler, Friedrich. "The World of the Symbolic — A World of the Machine." In *Literature, Media, Information Systems.* Edited by John Johnston, 130–46. New York: Routledge, 2012.

Kline, Morris. *Calculus: An Intuitive and Physical Approach.* New York: John Wiley & Sons, 1977.

Koch, Gertrud. "Animation of the Technical and the Quest for Beauty." In *Machine.* Edited by Thomas Pringle, Gertrud Koch, and Bernard Stiegler, 1–24. Lüneburg: meson press, 2019.

Kowalski, Robert. "Algorithm = Logic + Control." *Communication of the ACM* 22, no. 7 (1979): 424–36.

Kozma, Robert, Cesare Alippi, Yoonsuck Choe, and Francesco Carlo Morabito, eds. *Artificial Intelligence in the Age of Neural Networks and Brain Computing.* Cambridge, MA: Academic Press, 2018.

Krämer, Sybille. *Symbolische Maschinen: Die Idee der Formalisierung in geschichtlichem Abriß.* Darmstadt: Wissenschaftliche Buchgesellschaft, 1988.

Krizhevsky, Alex, Ilya Sutskever, and Geoffrey E. Hinton. "ImageNet Classification with Deep Convolutional Neural Networks." *Communications of the ACM* 60, no. 6 (2017): 84–90.

Kubie, Lawrence S. "Communication Between Sane and Insane: Hypnosis." In *Cybernetics: The Macy Conferences 1946–1953. The Complete Transactions.* Edited by Claus Pias, 416–45. Zürich: diaphanes, 2016.

Kurgan, Laura, Dare Brawley, Brian House, Jia Zhang, and Wendy Hui Kyong Chun. "Homophily: The Urban History of an Algorithm." *e-flux journal* (October 2019). https://www.e-flux.com/architecture/are-friends-electric/289193/homophily-the-urban-history-of-an-algorithm/.

Lacan, Jacques. "Aggressiveness in Psychoanalysis." In *Écrits: The First Complete Edition in English.* Translated by Bruce Fink, 82–101. New York: W. W. Norton, 2006.

Lacan, Jacques. *On Feminine Sexuality: The Limits of Love and Knowledge, Seminar XX.* Translated by Bruce Fink. New York: W. W. Norton, 1998.

Lacan, Jacques. "Psychoanalysis and Cybernetics, or on the Nature of Language." Lecture in Paris, France. June 22, 1955.

Lacan, Jacques. "Science and Truth." In *Écrits: The First Complete Edition in English.* Translated by Bruce Fink, 736–45. New York: Norton, [1965] 2006.

Lacan, Jacques. "Seminar on 'The Purloined Letter'." In *Écrits: The First Complete Edition in English*. Translated by Bruce Fink, 11–48. New York: W. W. Norton, 2006.

Lacan, Jacques. *The Ego in Freud's Theory and in the Technique of Psychoanalysis 1954–1955, Seminar II*. Translated by Sylvana Tomaselli. Cambridge: Cambridge University Press, 1988.

Lacan, Jacques. *The Ego in Freud's Theory and in the Techniques of Psychoanalysis 1954–1955, Seminar II*. Translated by Sylvana Tomaselli. New York: W. W. Norton, 1991.

Lacan, Jacques. *The Ethics of Psychoanalysis 1959–1960: The Seminar of Jacques Lacan: Seminar VII*. Edited by Jacques Alain Miller and Jacques Lacan. Abingdon: Routledge, 1992.

Lacan, Jacques. *The Four Fundamental Concepts of Psychoanalysis, Seminar XI*. Translated by Alan Sheridan. New York: W. W. Norton, 1998.

Lacan, Jacques. "The Function and Field of Speech and Language in Psychoanalysis." In *Écrits: The First Complete Edition in English*. Translated by Bruce Fink, 197–268. New York: W. W Norton, [1996] 2006.

Lacan, Jacques. "The Mirror Stage as Formative of the I Function as Revealed in Psychoanalytic Experience." In *Écrits: The First Complete Edition in English*. Translated by Bruce Fink, 75–81. New York: W. W. Norton, 2006.

Lacan, Jacques. "The Neurotic's Individual Myth." Translated by Martha Evans. In *Sigmund Freud: Critical Assessments, Vol. II: The Theory and Practice of Psychoanalysis*. Edited by Laurence Spurling, 386–404. London: Routledge, 1989. Originally published in *Psychoanalytic Quaterly* 48 (1979): 405–25.

Lacan, Jacques. *The Seminar of Jacques Lacan, Book III: The Psychoses*. Translated by Russell Grigg. New York: W. W. Norton, 1993.

Lacan, Jacques. *The Seminar of Jacques Lacan, Book XI: The Four Fundamental Concepts of Psychoanalysis*. New York: W. W. Norton, 1981.

Lacan, Jacques. "Tuché and Automaton." In *The Seminar of Jacques Lacan, Book XI: The Four Fundamental Concepts of Psychoanalysis*. Translated by Alan Sheridan, 53–67. New York: W. W. Norton, 1981.

Lake, Brendan M., Tomer D. Ullman, Joshua B. Tenenbaum, and Samual J. Gershman. "Building Machines That Learn and Think Like People." *ArXiv* (2016). https://arxiv.org/abs/1604.00289.

Lamarre, Thomas. *The Anime Machine: A Media Theory of Animation*. Minneapolis: University of Minnesota Press, 2009.

Lambert, Nathan, Louis Castricato, Leandro von Werra, and Alex Havrilla. "Illustrating Reinforcement Learning from Human Feedback (RLHF)." *Hugging Face*, December 9, 2022. https://huggingface.co/blog/rlhf.

Laplanche, Jean. "Psychoanalysis as Anti-Hermeneutics." *Radical Philosophy* 79 (September/October 1996): 7–13.

Latour, Bruno. *An Inquiry into Modes of Existence: An Anthropology of the Moderns*. Translated by Catherine Porter. Cambridge, MA: Harvard University Press, 2013.

Latour, Bruno. "From Realpolitik to Dingpolitik or How to Make Things Public." In *Making Things Public: Atmospheres of Democracy*. Edited by Bruno Latour and Peter Weibel, 14–41. Cambridge, MA: MIT Press, 2005.

Latour, Bruno. "Irreductions." In *The Pasteurization of France*. Translated by Alan Sheridan and John Law, 153–212. Cambridge, MA: Harvard University Press, [1984] 1988.

Latour, Bruno. *Reassembling the Social: An Introduction to Actor-Network-Theory*. Oxford: Oxford University Press, 2005.

Latour, Bruno. *We Have Never Been Modern.* Translated by Catherine Porter. Cambridge, MA: Harvard University Press, 1993.

Lave, Jean, and Etienne Wenger. *Situated Learning: Legitimate Peripheral Participation.* Cambridge: Cambridge University Press, 1991.

LeCun, Yann. *Modeles Connexionnistes de l'Apprentissage*. PhD thesis, Université Pierre et Marie Curie, 1987.

LeCun, Yann, Yoshua Bengio, and Geoffrey E. Hinton. "Deep Learning." *Nature* 521 (2015): 436–44.

Leviathan, Yaniv, and Yossi Matias. "Google Duplex: An AI System for Accomplishing Real-World Tasks Over the Phone." Google AI (blog), May 8, 2018. https://ai.googleblog.com/2018/05/duplex-ai-system-for-natural-conversation.html.

Lewicki, Pawel, Thomas Hill, and Maria Czyzewsk. "Nonconscious Acquisition of Information." *American Psychology* 47, no. 6 (1992): 796–801.

Lewis-Kraus, Gideon. "The Great A. I. Awakening." *New York Times*, December 14, 2016. https://www.nytimes.com/2016/12/14/magazine/the-great-ai-awakening.html.

Light, Ben, Jean Burgess, and Stephanie Duguay. "The Walkthrough Method: An Approach to the Study of Apps." *New Media & Society* 20 (2018): 881–900.

Lindley, Joseph, Haider Akmal, and Paul Coulton. "Design Research and Object-Oriented Ontology." *Open Philosophy* 3, no. 1 (2020): 11–41.

Liu, Lydia H. "After Turing: How Philosophy Migrated to the AI Lab." *Critical Inquiry* 50, no. 1 (2023): 2–30. https://doi.org/10.1086/726293.

Liu, Lydia H. "The Cybernetic Unconscious: Rethinking Lacan, Poe, and French Theory." *Critical Inquiry* 36, no. 2 (2010): 288–320.

Liu, Lydia H. *The Freudian Robot: Digital Media and the Future of the Unconscious.* Chicago: University of Chicago Press, 2010.

López, A. J. "Contesting the Material Turn; or, the Persistence of Agency." *Cambridge Journal of Postcolonial Literary Inquiry* 5, no. 3 (2018): 371–86.

Luchs, Inga. "AI for All? Challenging the Democratization of Machine Learning." *APRJA* 12, no. 1 (2023): 135–47.

Luchs, Inga, Clemens Apprich, and Marcel Broersma. "Learning Machine Learning: On the Political Economy of Big Tech's Online AI Courses." *Big Data & Society* 10, no. 1 (2023): 1–12.

Lüdicke, Martina. "Doppelgänger." In *GOLEM*, exhibition catalogue. Berlin: Jewish Museum Berlin, 2016.

Mackenzie, Adrian. *Machine Learners: Archaeology of a Data Practice.* Cambridge, MA: MIT Press, 2017.

Malabou, Catherine. *Morphing Intelligence: From IQ Measurement to Artificial Brains.* Translated by Carolyn Shread. New York: Columbia University Press, 2019.

Manning, Christopher. "Word Vector Representations: word2vec." Quoted in Brian Christian, *The Alignment Problem: Machine Learning and Human Values*, 3f. New York: W. W. Norton, 2020.

Männistö-Funk, Tiina, and Tanja Sihvonen. "Voices from the Uncanny Valley: How Robots and Artificial Intelligences Talk Back to Us." *Digital Culture & Society* 4, no. 1 (2018): 45–64.

Marchi, Scott de, and Scott E. Page. "Agent-Based Models." *Annual Review of Political Science* 17 (2014): 1–20.

Marcus, Gary. "Deep Learning Is Hitting a Wall." *Nautilus*, March 10, 2022. https://nautil.us/deep-learning-is-hitting-a-wall-238440.

Marx, Karl. *Capital: A Critique of Political Economy*, Vol. 1. London: Lawrence and Wishart, 1996.

Marx, Karl. "Fragment on Machines." In *Grundrisse: Foundations of the Critique of Political Economy*. Translated by Martin Nicolaus, 690–712. London: Penguin, 1993.

Marx, Karl. *Grundrisse: Foundations of the Critique of Political Economy*. Translated by Martin Nicolaus. London: Penguin, 1993.

Matviyenko, Svitlana, and Judith Roof, eds. *Lacan and the Posthuman*. London: Palgrave Macmillan, 2018.

McCarthy, John, Marvin Minsky, Nathaniel Rochester, and Claude E. Shannon. "A Proposal for the Dartmouth Summer Research Project on Artificial Intelligence." August 31, 1955. http://www-formal.stanford.edu/jmc/history/dartmouth/dartmouth.html.

McCulloch, Warren S. "Discussion of the General and Logical Theory of Automata by John von Neumann." In *Cerebral Mechanisms in Behavior: The Hixon Symposium*. Edited by Llyod A. Jeffress, 32–33. New York: John Wiley & Sons, 1951.

McCulloch, Warren S. "The Beginning of Cybernetics." In *Cybernetics: The Macy Conferences 1946–1953*. Edited by Claus Pias, 345–60. Zürich: diaphanes, 2016.

McCulloch, Warren S., and Walter H. Pitts. "A Logical Calculus of the Ideas Immanent in Nervous Activity." *Bulletin of Mathematical Biophysics* 5 (1943): 115–33.

McGuire, Michael T., Stephen Lorch, and Gardner C. Quarton, "Man-Machine Natural Language Exchanges Based on Selected Features of Unrestricted Input — II: The Use of the Time-Shared Computer as a Research Tool in Studying Dyadic Communication." *Journal of Psychiatric Research* 5, no. 2 (1967): 179–91.

Meillassoux, Quentin. *After Finitude: An Essay on the Necessity of Contingency*. Translated by Ray Brassier. London: Bloomsbury, 2009.

Mersch, Dieter. "Kreativität und Künstliche Intelligenz: Einige Bemerkungen zu einer Kritik algorithmischer Rationalität." *Zeitschrift für Medienwissenschaft* 11, no. 2 (2019): 65–74.

Meyrink, Gustav. *The Golem*. Translated by Mike Mitchell. Sawtry: Dedalus Books, 2017.

Mikolov, Tomas, Kai Chen, Greg Corrado, and Jeffrey Dean. "Efficient Estimation of Word Representations in Vector Space." *arXiv*, September 6, 2013. https://doi.org/10.48550/arXiv.1301.3781.

Millar, Isabel. *The Psychoanalysis of Artificial Intelligence*. e-book. London: Palgrave Macmillan, 2021.

Minsky, Marvin. *The Society of Mind*. New York: A Touchstone Book, 1985.

Minsky, Marvin, and Seymour A. Papert. *Perceptrons: An Introduction to Computational Geometry*. Cambridge, MA: MIT Press, 1969.

Möbius, Paul J. *Über den physiologischen Schwachsinn des Weibes*. Halle a. d. S.: Verlag von Carl Marhold, 1903.

Mordvintsev, Alexander, Christopher Olah, and Mike Tyka. "Inceptionism: Going Deeper into Neural Networks." Google Research. https://blog.research.google/2015/06/inceptionism-going-deeper-into-neural.html.

Mori, Masahiro. "The Uncanny Valley." *IEEE Spectrum*, June 12, 2012. https://spectrum.ieee.org/automaton/robotics/humanoids/the-uncanny-valley.

Mullachery, Vikram, Aniruddh Khera, and Amir Husain. "Bayesian Neural Networks." *arXiv*, January 30, 2018. https://arxiv.org/abs/1801.07710.

Munn, Luke. *Automation Is a Myth.* Stanford: Stanford University Press, 2022.

Nenda, Neel. "What is Gemma Scope?" Google for Developers. YouTube, November 14, 2024. https://www.youtube.com/watch?v=fQP8uE-g1vo.

Nilsson, Nils J. *The Quest for Artificial Intelligence: A History of Ideas and Achievements.* Cambridge: Cambridge University Press, 2009.

Noble, Safiya Umoja. *Algorithms of Oppression: How Search Engines Reinforce Racism.* New York: New York University Press, 2018.

Nolan, Jonathan, and Lisa Joy. "The Bicameral Mind." *Westworld,* season 1, episode 10, directed by Jonathan Nolan. Aired December 4, 2016, on HBO.

Norvig, Peter. "Introduction to Machine Learning." Google Machine Learning Crash Course (MLCC), 2021. Google for Developers. https://web.archive.org/web/20220108211342/https://developers.google.com/machine-learning/crash-course/ml-intro.

O'Neil, Cathy. *Weapons of Math Destruction: How Big Data Increases Inequality and Threatens Democracy.* London: Penguin Books, 2016.

Parks, Lisa, and Nicole Starosielski. "Introduction." In *Signal Traffic: Critical Studies of Media Infrastructures.* Edited by Lisa Parks and Nicole Starosielski, 1–27. Urbana, Chicago: University of Illinois Press, 2015.

Parisi, Luciana. *Contagious Architecture: Computation, Aesthetics, and Space.* Cambridge, MA: MIT Press, 2013.

Parisi, Luciana. "Critical Computation: Digital Automata and General Artificial Thinking." *Theory, Culture & Society* 36, no. 2 (2019): 89–121.

Parisi, Luciana. "Das Lernen lernen oder die algorithmische Entdeckung von Informationen." In *Machine Learning: Medien, Infrastrukturen und Technologien der Künstlichen Intelligenz.* Edited by Christoph Engemann and Andreas Sudmann, 93–114. Bielefeld: transcript, 2018.

Parisi, Luciana. "Instrumental Reason, Algorithmic Capitalism, and the Incomputable." In *Alleys of Your Mind: Augmented Intelligence and Its Traumas.* Edited by Matteo Pasquinelli, 125–37. Lüneburg: meson press, 2015.

Pasquinelli, Matteo. "Introduction." In *Alleys of Your Mind: Augmented Intelligence and Its Traumas.* Edited by Matteo Pasquinelli, 7–18. Lüneburg: meson press, 2015.

Pasquinelli, Matteo. "Machines that Morph Logic: Neural Networks and the Distorted Automation of Intelligence as Statistical Inference." *Glass Bead Journal* Site 1 (2017). http://www.glass-bead.org/wp-content/uploads/GB_Site-1_Matteo-Pasquinelli_Eng.pdf.

Pasquinelli, Matteo. "On the Origins of Marx's General Intellect." *Radical Philosophy* 2, no. 6 (Winter 2019): 43–56.

Pasquinelli, Matteo, and Vladan Joler. "The Nooscope Manifested: AI as Instrument of Knowledge Extractivism." *AI & Society* 36 (2021): 1263–80.

Peirce, Charles Sanders. "Pragmatism as the Logic of Abduction." In *The Essential Peirce, Volume 2: Selected Philosophical Writings (1893–1913).* Edited by Peirce Edition Project, 226–41. Bloomington: Indiana University Press, 1998.

Peirce, Charles Sanders. "The Law of Mind." In *The Essential Peirce, Volume 1.* Edited by Peirce Edition Project, 312–33. Bloomington: Indiana University Press, 1998.

Peters, Benjamin. "The Computer Never Was a Brain, or the Curious Death and Designs of John von Neumann." In *Verhaltensdesign: Technologische und ästhetische Programme der 1960er und 1970er Jahre.* Edited by Jeannie Moser and Christina Vagt, 113–23. Bielefeld: transcript Verlag, 2018.

Peters, John Durham. *The Marvelous Clouds: Toward a Philosophy of Elemental Media.* Chicago: University of Chicago Press, 2015.

Pias, Claus, ed. *Cybernetics: The Macy Conferences 1946–1953.* Zürich: diaphanes, 2016.

Pias, Claus. "Störung als Normalfall." *Zeitschrift für Kulturwissenschaften* 5, no. 2 (2011): 27–43.

Pias, Claus. "The Age of Cybernetics." In *Cybernetics: The Macy Conferences 1946–1953.* Edited by Claus Pias, 11–26. Zurich: diaphanes, 2016.

Pickering, Andrew. *The Cybernetic Brain: Sketches of Another Future.* Chicago: University of Chicago Press, 2010.

Pötzsch, Holger, and N. Katherine Hayles. "Posthumanism, Technogenesis, and Digital Technologies: A Conversation with N. Katherine Hayles." *Fibreculture Journal* 23 (2014): 96–107.

Pringle, Thomas, Gertrud Koch, and Bernard Stiegler. *Machine*. Lüneburg: meson press, 2019.

Reigeluth, Tyler, and Michael Castelle. "What Kind of Learning Is Machine Learning?" In *The Cultural Life of Machine Learning: An Incursion into Critical AI Studies.* Edited by Jonathan Roberge and Michael Castelle, 79–115. Cham: Palgrave Macmillan, 2021.

Rieder, Bernhard. *Engines of Order: A Mechanology of Algorithmic Techniques.* Amsterdam: Amsterdam University Press, 2020.

Rosenblatt, Frank. "The Perceptron: A Probabilistic Model for Information Storage and Organization in the Brain." *Psychological Review* 65, no. 6 (1958): 386–408.

Rumelhart, David E., Geoffrey E. Hinton, and Ronald J. Williams. "Learning Internal Representations by Error Propagation." In *Parallel Distributed Processing: Explorations in the Microstructure of Cognition*, Vol. 1. Edited by David E. Rumelhart, James L. McClelland, and the PDP Research Group, 318–62. Cambridge, MA: MIT Press, 1986.

Rumelhart, David E., Geoffrey E. Hinton, and Ronald J. Williams. "Learning Representations by Back-Propagation Errors." *Nature* 323, no. 6088 (1986): 533–36.

Rumelhart, David E., James L. McClelland, and PDP Research Group. *Parallel Distributed Processing: Explorations in the Microstructure of Cognition. Volume 1: Foundations.* Cambridge, MA: MIT Press, 1986.

Russell, Stuart J., and Peter Norvig. *Artificial Intelligence: A Modern Approach.* New Jersey: Prentice Hall, 2003.

Samuel, Arthur L. "Some Studies in Machine Learning Using the Game of Checkers." *IBM Journal of Research and Development* 3, no. 2 (1959): 210–29.

Sanzo, Kameron. "New Materialism(s)." Genealogy of the Posthuman. *Critical Posthumanism*, April 25, 2018. https://criticalposthumanism.net/new-materialisms.

Sartre, Jean-Paul. *Being and Nothingness: A Phenomenological Essay on Ontology.* Translated by Hazel E. Barnes. New York: Washington Square Press, 1992.

Saussure, Ferdinand de. *Course in General Linguistics.* Translated by Roy Harris. London: Duckworth, 1983.

Sbriglia, Russell, and Slavoj Zizek, "Introduction: Subject Matters." In *Subject Lessons: Hegel, Lacan, and the Future of Materialism.* Edited by Russell Sbriglia and Slavoj Žižek, 1–15. Evanston: Northwestern University Press, 2020.

Schmidgen, Henning. *Das Unbewußte der Maschine: Konzeptionen des Psychischen bei Guattari, Deleuze und Lacan.* Munich: Wilhelm Fink Verlag, 1997.

Scholem, Gershom. *On the Kabbalah and Its Symbolism.* New York: Schocken Books, 1965.

Scholem, Gershom. "The Golem of Prague & the Golem of Rehovot." *Commentary Magazine,* January 1966. https://www.commentarymagazine.com/articles/gershom-scholem/the-golem-of-prague-the-golem-of-rehovoth.

Schrage, Michael. *Recommendation Engines.* Cambridge, MA: MIT Press, 2020.

Schröter, Jens. "The Internet and 'Frictionless Capitalism'." *tripleC* 10, no. 2 (2012): 302–12.

"Science: The Thinking Machine." *Times Magazine*, January 24, 1949. https://time.com/archive/6602078/science-the-thinking-machine.

Scott, Geoffrey. "What Is a Vector Space?" Department of Mathematics, University of Toronto. https://www.math.toronto.edu/gscott/WhatVS.pdf.

Shannon, Claude E. "A Mathematical Theory of Communication." *Bell System Technical Journal* 27, no. 3 (July 1948): 379–423; 623–56.

Shannon, Claude E. "A Symbolic Analysis of Relay and Switching Circuits." *Transactions American Institute of Electrical Engineers* 57, no. 12 (1938): 713–23.

Shannon, Claude E., and Warren Weaver. *The Mathematical Theory of Communication.* Urbana: University of Illinois Press, 1949.

Shapiro, Steven. *Discognition.* eBook. London: Repeater Books, 2016.

Shirer, Michael. "IDC Forecasts Improved Growth for Global AI Market in 2021." IDC blog, February 23, 2021. https://www.idc.com/getdoc.jsp?containerId=prUS47482321.

Simon, Herbert A. *The Sciences of the Artificial.* Cambridge, MA: MIT Press, 1996.

Simondon, Gilbert. *L'Individuation à la lumière des notions de forme et d'information.* Paris: Jérôme Millon, 2005.

Simondon, Gilbert. *On the Mode of Existence of Technical Objects*. Translated by Cecile Malaspina and John Rogove. Minneapolis: Univocal, 2017.

Slater, Avery. "The Golem and the Game of Automation." Lecture at the IEEE conference on Norbert Wiener in the 21st Century, October 26, 2021. https://c4ejournal.net/2021/10/27/avery-slater-the-golem-and-the-game-of-automation-2021-c4ej-44.

Stark, Luke. "Animation and Artificial Intelligence." In *Proceedings of the 2024 ACM Conference on Fairness, Accountability, and Transparency*, 1663–71. New York: Association for Computing Machinery, 2024. https://doi.org/10.1145/3630106.3658995.

Stark, Luke. "Artificial Intelligence and the Conjectural Sciences." *BJHS Themes* 8 (2023): 35–49.

Steinhoff, James. *Automation and Autonomy: Labour, Capital and Machines in Artificial Intelligence Industry.* Cham: Palgrave Macmillan, 2021.

Stiegler, Bernard. "Anamnesis and Hypomnesis." *Ars Industrialis*, 2006. https://arsindustrialis.org/anamnesis-and-hypomnesis#_ftnref4.

Stiegler, Bernard. "Relational Ecology and the Digital Pharmakon." *Culture Machine* 13 (2012). https://culturemachine.net/wp-content/uploads/2019/01/464-1026-1-PB.pdf.

Stiegler, Bernard. *What Makes Life Worth Living: On Pharmacology.* Cambridge: Polity, 2013.

Taussig, Michael. *Mimesis and Alterity: A Particular History of the Senses.* New York: Routledge, 1993.

TensorFlow Playground. TensorFlow website. https://playground.tensorflow.org/.

Terranova, Tiziana. "Free Labor: Producing Culture for the Digital Economy." *Social Text* 18, no. 2 (2000): 33–58.

Terranova, Tiziana. "Pirate Modernity and Hypersocial Networks." Lecture at the conference "Recursive Colonialism, Artificial Intelligence & Speculative Computation," December 10, 2020. https://recursivecolonialism.com/topics/pirate.

"The Thinking Machine: W. Ross Ashby and the Homestat." Science blog. British Library, April 20, 2016. https://britishlibrary.typepad.co.uk/science/2016/04/the-thinking-machine.html.

"Things." Special issue. *Critical Inquiry* 28, no. 1 (Autumn 2001).

Tomšič, Samo. *The Capitalist Unconscious: Marx and Lacan*. London: Verso, 2015.

Turing, Alan M. "Computing Machinery and Intelligence." *Mind: A Quarterly Review of Psychology and Philosophy* 59, no. 236 (1950): 433–60.

Turing, Alan M. "Intelligent Machinery." In *The Essential Turing: Seminal Writings in Computing, Logic, Philosophy, Artificial Intelligence, and Artificial Life plus the Secrets of Enigma*. Edited by B. Jack Copeland. Oxford: Clarendon Press, [1948] 2013.

Turing, Alan M. "Letter to W. Ross Ashby." *The Turing Archive*, November 19, 1946. https://www.alanturing.net/turing_archive/archive/l/l23/L23-001.html.

Turing, Alan M. "On Computable Numbers, with an Application to the Entscheidungsproblem." *Proceedings of the London Mathematical Society* 42, no. 1 (1936): 230–65.

Turing, Alan M. "On Computable Numbers, with an Application to the Entscheidungsproblem." In *The Essential Turing*. Edited by B. Jack Copeland, 58–90. Oxford: Oxford University Press, [1936] 2004.

Turing, Alan M. "Proposal for Development in the Mathematics Division of an Automatic Computing Engine (ACE)." In *A. M. Turing's ACE Report of 1946 and Other Papers*. Edited by B. E. Carpenter and R. W. Doran, 20–105. Cambridge, MA: MIT Press.

Turkle, Sherry. *Life on the Screen: Identity in the Age of the Internet*. New York: Simon & Schuster, 1995.

Uleman, James S. "Introduction: Becoming Aware of the New Unconscious." In *The New Unconscious*. Edited by Ran R. Hassin, James S. Uleman, and John A. Bargh, 1–15. Oxford: Oxford University Press, 2006.

Vickers, John. "The Problem of Induction." *Stanford Encyclopedia of Philosophy* website, November 15, 2006; substantive revision March 14, 2014, Fall 2017 Edition, https://plato.stanford.edu/archives/fall2017/entries/induction-problem.

Virno, Paolo. *A Grammar of the Multitude: For an Analysis of Contemporary Forms of Life*. Los Angeles: Semiotext(e), 2004.

Vogl, Joseph. "Formationen des Wissens: Zur Einführung." In *Kursbuch Medienkultur: Die maßgeblichen Theorien von Brecht bis Baudrillard*. Edited by Claus Pias, Joseph Vogl, Lorenz Engel, Oliver Fahle, and Britta Neitzel, 485–88. Stuttgart: DVA, 2004.

Vogl, Joseph. "Technologie des Unbewußten: Zur Einführung." In *Kursbuch Medienkultur: Die maßgeblichen Theorien von Brecht bis Baudrillard*. Edited by Claus Pias, Joseph Vogl, Lorenz Engel, Oliver Fahle, and Britta Neitzel, 373–76. Stuttgart: DVA, 2004.

Von Neumann, John. "Probabilistic Logics and the Synthesis of Reliable Organisms from Unreliable Components." In *Automata Studies*. Edited by Claude E. Shannon and J. McCarthy, 43–98. Princeton: Princeton University Press, 1956.

Von Neumann, John. *The Computer and the Brain*. New Haven: Yale University Press, 1958.

Von Neumann, John. "The General and Logical Theory of Automata." In *John von Neumann: Collected Works*. Edited by A. H. Taub, 288–326. Oxford: Pergamon Press, 1961.

Von Neumann, John. "The General and Logical Theory of Automata." In *Theory of Self-Reproducing Automata*. Edited by Arthur W. Burks, 288–328. Urbana: University of Illinois Press, 1966.

Von Neumann, John. *Theory of Self-Reproducing Automata.* Edited by Arthur W. Burks. Urbana: University of Illinois Press, 1966.

Vygotsky, Lev S. *Mind in Society: The Development of Higher Psychological Processes.* Edited by Michael Cole, Vera John-Steiner, Sylvia Scribner, and Ellen Souberman. Cambridge, MA: Harvard University Press, 1978.

Vygotsky, Lev S. *The Collected Works of L. S. Vygotsky: The History of the Development of Higher Mental Functions.* Edited by Robert W. Rieber. Translated by Marie J. Hall. New York: Plenum, 1997.

Walter, W. Grey. *The Living Brain.* New York: W. W. Norton, 1963.

Weatherby, Leif, and Brian Justie. "Indexical AI." *Critical Inquiry* 48, no. 2 (Winter 2022): 381–415.

Wegener, Mai. *Neuronen und Neurosen: Der psychische Apparat bei Freud und Lacan: Ein historisch-theoretischer Versuch zu Freuds Entwurf von 1895.* Munich: Wilhelm Fink Verlag, 2004.

Wegenstein, Bernadette. "Body." In *Critical Terms for Media Studies.* Edited by W. J. T. Mitchell and Mark B. N. Hansen, 19–34. Chicago: University of Chicago Press, 2010.

Weizenbaum, Joseph. *Computer Power and Human Reason: From Judgment to Calculation.* New York: W. H. Freeman, 1976.

Weizenbaum, Joseph. "ELIZA — A Computer Program for the Study of Natural Language Communication Between Man and Machine." *Communications of the ACM* 9, no. 1 (1966): 36–45.

Wiener, Norbert. *Cybernetics: Or Control and Communication in the Animal and the Machine.* Cambridge, MA: MIT Press, [1948] 1965.

Wiener, Norbert. *God & Golem, Inc.: A Comment on Certain Points Where Cybernetics Impinges on Religion.* Cambridge, MA: MIT Press, 1966.

Wiener, Norbert. "Some Moral and Technical Consequences of Automation." *Science* 131 (1969): 1355–58.

Wilden, Anthony. *System and Structure: Essays in Communication and Exchange.* London: Tavistock, 1972.

Wisniewski, David. *Golem.* New York: Clarion Books, 2007.

Wolfendale, Peter. *Object-Oriented Philosophy: The Noumenon's New Clothes.* Falmouth: Urbanomic, 2014.

Wolfram, Stephen. *A New Kind of Science.* Champaign: Wolfram Media, 2002.

Wynter, Sylvia. "Unsettling the Coloniality of Being/Power/Truth/Freedom: Towards the Human, After Man, Its Overrepresentation — An Argument" *New Centennial Review* 3, no. 3 (2003): 257–337.

Žižek, Slavoj. "Desire: Drive = Truth: Knowledge." *Umbr(a)* (1997). https://www.lacan.com/zizek-desire.htm.

Žižek, Slavoj. "Philosophy, the 'Unknown Knowns', and the Public Use of Reason." *Topoi* 25, no. 1–2 (2006): 137–42.

Zupančič, Alenka. *Ethics of the Real: Kant and Lacan.* London: Verso, 2000.

Zupančič, Alenka. *What* IS *Sex?* Cambridge, MA: MIT Press, 2017.

INDEX

Note: Page numbers followed by 'n' denotes note numbers

For Product Safety Concerns and Information please contact our EU representative GPSR@taylorandfrancis.com Taylor & Francis Verlag GmbH, Kaufingerstraße 24, 80331 München, Germany

Batch number: 10249327

Printed by Printforce, the Netherlands